U2

The Ultimate Compendium
of Interviews, Articles, Facts
and Opinions
from the Files of Rolling Stone

BY

THE EDITORS

OF

Rolling Stone

FOREWORD BY ELYSA GARDNER

HYPERION

NEW YORK

Library of Congress Cataloging-in-Publication Data
U2—the Rolling stone files : the ultimate compendium of interviews, articles, facts & opinions from
    the files of Rolling stone / by the editors of Rolling stone ; foreword by Elysa Gardner. — 1st ed.
        p.   cm.
        Articles reprinted from Rolling stone.
        Includes discography and videography.
        ISBN 0-7868-8001-5
        1. U2 (Musical group) 2. Rock music—History and criticism.
    I. Rolling stone (New York, N.Y.)
    ML421.U2U16 1994
    782.42166′092′2—dc20   93-44466
                                                                    CIP
                                                                    MN

First Edition
10 9 8 7 6 5 4 3 2 1

CONTENTS

FOREWORD

"*ALL THE NEWS THAT FITS.*" ROLLING STONE's classic slogan was our guideline when choosing the material for *U2: The ROLLING STONE Files*. Since U2's early days, the band has appeared regularly in the pages of ROLLING STONE. We've gone back to the very first news piece in February 1981, pulled out every U2 album and concert review, and selected a variety of "Random Notes." Also featured here are the classic interviews with Bono and the Edge, as well as in-depth profiles of the band from each phase of its career. In addition, we've compiled U2's numerous wins in the annual ROLLING STONE readers and critics polls and included the Edge's and Bono's lists of favorite albums, too.

Together in one volume, ROLLING STONE's coverage of U2 shows the the group practically growing up before our very eyes. What an evolution—from Bono Vox's youthful, arrogant braggadocio and wide-eyed fervor to the Fly's world-weary voice of experience and indulgence in rock & roll decadence. Within these pages is a compelling document of those dozen-plus tumultuous years.

A number of people helped to make *U2: The ROLLING STONE Files* possible. Many thanks to Shawn Dahl, Anthony DeCurtis, Dulcy Israel, Fred Woodward, Jann S. Wenner, Kent Brownridge and John Lagana at ROLLING STONE, and Mary Ann Naples, Bob Miller, Victor Weaver, and Laura Chittenden at Hyperion. Much appreciation also goes to Sarah Lazin, Laura Nolan, Lora Corrado, James Henke, Bill Flanagan, Caren Gerszberg, Anton Corbijn, Alan Light, Adam J. Raider, Zev Barrow, Jeff Jackson, Vic Garbarini, Principle Management, and the Wasserman Group Public Relations. *Muchas gracias* to twelve years' worth of "Random Notes" scribes: Christopher Connelly, Merle Ginsberg, Sheila Rogers, Chris Mundy and Jancee Dunn. Most of all, kudos to Elysa Gardner and all the writers whose work appears here.

U2 is the first in a series of *ROLLING STONE Files* books. Look for future volumes on artists such as Neil Young and the Grateful Dead.

Holly George-Warren, Editor
Rolling Stone Press
October 1993

ELYSA GARDNER

INTRODUCTION

U2 MADE ITS FIRST APPEARANCE on the cover of ROLLING STONE just before spring in 1985. The photo, like many pictures of the band taken around that time, was almost Spartan in its simplicity: It featured the four musicians in plain dress, staring directly and rather solemnly into the camera. In contrast, the caption accompanying the photo seemed a bit flashy. "Our Choice: Band of the Eighties," it proclaimed. That this assertion seemed to suggest an epitaph for a decade that was just settling into middle age wasn't its nerviest aspect. No, the true chutzpah here lay in the choice itself, this sober-looking group of fellows whose faces, as Christopher Connelly pointed out in his story, were not even familiar to all of their fans. "They have yet to notch a Top Ten album or single," Connelly wrote. "Only now are they beginning to tour arena-sized venues. But for a growing number of rock & roll fans, U2 . . . has become the band that matters most, maybe even the *only* band that matters."

I was a seventeen-year-old high school student when this article ran, and therefore in a better position than any professional journalist to speculate on which rock bands mattered and why. My first exposure to U2's music had been a few years earlier, while riding in an older, hipper friend's car. The friend was entertaining me with a compilation tape featuring artists considered edgy and progressive at the time, artists favored among certain peers of mine who dressed primarily in black and took every opportunity to voice their disdain for Top Forty radio, shopping malls and other suburban afflictions. I listened attentively to electronic dirge after electronic dirge, depressed by my inability to appreciate the subversive splendor of it all, until a song called "Gloria" came on. It was a single from U2's second album, 1981's *October;* and while it was certainly noisy and left-of-center enough to qualify as a respectable alternative-rock track, it was also everything the other songs on the cassette were ashamed to be—tender, urgent, vulnerable, resolute. "They're from Ireland," my friend responded, when I asked who the band was. "They're, like, religious freaks, I think. But it's a great song, isn't it? Really powerful."

This, perhaps, was one of the main reasons that U2 did matter, and has continued to matter, to such a large and disparate group of music fans: Regardless of how you interpret, or misinterpret, the sentiments in its songs, it's difficult to deny the compelling intensity the group has shown in voicing them, or the exalted beauty and strength with which that intensity is relayed in U2's music. "We don't take ourselves seriously," lead singer Bono once told *Musician* magazine editor Bill Flanagan, author of the U2 chapter in *The* ROLLING STONE *Illustrated History of Rock & Roll,* "but we take our music very seriously." And as Bono and his band mates have pointed out in numerous interviews—proudly at certain points in the band's career, a bit defensively at others—this sort of seriousness has been shared by all those artists who have mattered in rock & roll, especially as the genre has matured beyond its original image as adolescent escapism.

In preparation for this book, I thumbed through many back issues of ROLLING STONE, and among the articles I came across was another band profile by Christopher Connelly. The subject was the readers' choice for the 1983 Band of the Year and, coincidentally, the other group whose career I followed as avidly as U2's while in high school: the Police. In trying to describe the niche then occupied by this British trio, Connelly wrote:

> Such is [the Police's] power that they—along with Bruce Springsteen—stand at the center of what could be called postalienationist rock & roll. From its beginning, rock & roll has sought to address its audience's essential difference and separation from the rest of the culture, and to issue a call to like-minded youth: we gotta all get together against them. That sort of defiant, nervy alienation, from the Who to the Sex Pistols, has characterized much of rock & roll as long as it has existed.
>
> Postalienationist rock & roll takes as a given the alienation that young people feel—from their jobs, their families, their lovers. Rather than accentuating that difference or acclaiming it proudly, it instead tries to forge connections back to a larger community without ever losing sight of the differences that created the split in the first place.

U2 is clearly, in some way, heir to each of the bands mentioned in this excerpt. Like the Sex Pistols, the Irish musicians first came together as musically inexperienced teenagers (at Dublin's Mount Temple school, in 1978), united more by their desire to shake up the world—or at least the world of rock & roll—than by some concise artistic vision. Like the Police, U2 latched onto what Flanagan described in his *Illustrated History* essay as a "conception of the rock trio as a single musical personality, with the bass and voice carrying the central line of the song, the drums kicking along and accenting the bass, and the guitar providing color and atmosphere rather than leads." And I think that Bono has proven somewhat akin to Sting as a lyricist, in that while both men have been accused of pedantry and bombast—at times justifiably so—both have achieved some of their best work by using beautifully simple metaphors, images of immediate, universal significance: Sting's lonely message in a bottle, for example, or the sad eyes and crooked crosses in U2's "In God's Country," from *The Joshua Tree* (1987).

Like the Who and Springsteen, U2 has parlayed this ability to communicate with the listener on a basic, almost visceral level into an extraordinary rapport with its fans, a relationship in which the audience's devotion to the band transcends mere musical appreciation. In 1987, ROLLING STONE ran a story about a California-based U2 fan club named A Celebration (after one of the group's early British singles), whose members donated their dues to charities they thought were in line with the philanthropic ideals promoted by the band. "U2 fans are a special group, there's a special link between us," one teenaged member commented in the article. "It's more than the music. It's the meaning behind the music. What U2 says is what we want to be."

Such adulation might seem a little daunting, but then U2 had never really aspired to anything less. The band was introduced to ROLLING STONE readers in February 1981, in a profile by the magazine's former music editor, James Henke. Like Flanagan, Henke was among U2's earliest supporters in the U.S. press; his article in ROLLING STONE was, in fact, one of the first nods the band received from an American journalist. Even at this stage in its career, U2 was harboring some heavy ambitions, as its twenty-year-old front man revealed rather guilelessly in the interview. (At that point, the former Paul Hewson was still going by his full stage name, Bono Vox; a Dublin schoolmate had christened him thus after a local hearing-aid store. U2 guitarist Dave Evans was in turn dubbed the Edge by Bono.) "I don't mean to sound arrogant," Bono told Henke, "but . . . I do feel that we are meant to be one of the great groups. There's a certain spark, a certain chemistry, that was special about the Stones, the Who, and the Beatles, and I think it's also special about U2."

Twelve years later, Henke still remembers that remark as "pretty outrageous, coming from a guy that age." The writer was impressed by his subject's drive, though, and by what he saw and heard at the first show he attended by this band whose progress he would watch and document over the next decade. "It was in a school gymnasium or auditorium, in Coventry, England," Henke recalled, when I phoned him to discuss the story. "I rode up with them from London in a small van. The place wasn't sold out; a hundred people may have shown up. But there was definitely a certain charisma in their performance; you could see that they really had something on stage. And Bono was clearly connecting with the audience; however many people were there, he was captivating all of them."

During that time, Bono also revealed to Henke, in addition to a preco-
cious confidence, a reluctance to be identified with the musical movement
that had kicked doors open for U2 and other young bands more note-
worthy for their energy than their technical prowess. If U2's members
joined forces in punk's typical do-it-yourself fashion, and if they admired
such punk role models as Patti Smith and the Ramones, they were still
keenly aware of the dichotomy between the values that punk was founded
on and the values that it ultimately came to represent. The singer explained
it like this:

> The idea of punk at first was, "Look, you're an individual, express yourself
> how you want to, do what you want to do." But that's not the way it came
> out in the end. The Sex Pistols were a con, a box of tricks sold by Malcolm
> McLaren. Kids were sold the imagery of violence, which turned into the
> reality of violence, and it's that negative side that I worry about. People like
> Bruce Springsteen carry hope. Like the Who—"Won't Get Fooled Again."
> I mean, there is a song of endurance, and that's the attitude of the great bands.
> We want our audience to think about their actions and where they are going,
> to realize the pressures that are on them, but at the same time, not to give
> up.

From the start, U2's postalienationist rock has stressed communion over
segregation, compassion over blame, hope over despair. If punk basically
went for the groin, and the "new wave" of pop it helped engender aimed
toward the head, U2's music appealed to that emotional center located
directly between them. Essentially, U2 took what it saw as punk's positive
aspects—the unabashed candor and lean, direct musical approach that Bono
would refer to years later, with a gaudy majesty at which any self-respecting
punk would sneer, as "three chords and the truth"—and adapted them to
a larger, softer compass, one that would accommodate the romantic idealism of Bono's lyrics, the plangent sensuality of his voice and the radiant
lyricism of the Edge's guitar work. In doing so, the band revitalized arena
rock, proving, as the Who and Springsteen had before them, that popular
music could be openly, grandly passionate without being bloated or banal.
That U2 rejected punk's nihilism so instantly and with such fervor may
have owed something to the fact that all but one of its members, bassist
Adam Clayton, were practicing Christians—hardly "religious freaks," as my
high school friend had suggested, but young men who were struggling to
come to terms with their faith and its ramifications. In fact, the band came
close to breaking up after recording its second album, 1981's *October,*
because their growing spiritual convictions were leading Bono, the Edge,

and drummer Larry Mullen Jr. to question whether rock stardom was a worthwhile pursuit. Bono and Mullen had both turned to Christianity after the untimely deaths of their mothers; but in fact it was the Edge who took the longest time to resolve his religious dilemma, nearly leaving the band in 1982 to devote himself to serving God.

"We were getting involved in reading books, the Big Book," Bono later told ROLLING STONE senior features editor Anthony DeCurtis of that period. "Meeting people who were more interested in things spiritual, superspiritual characters that I can see now were possibly far too removed from reality. But we were *wrapped up* in that." The child of a Catholic father and a Protestant mother, Bono has openly expressed mixed feelings about religion, especially as it's been manifested in Irish politics—which haven't exactly seen Catholics and Protestants getting along famously—and American evangelism. "I am a Christian, but at times I feel very removed from Christianity," he told contributing editor David Breskin in a 1987 ROLLING STONE interview. "To me, we are living in the most un-Christian times. When I see these racketeers, the snake-oil salesmen on these right-wing television stations, asking for not your $20 or your $50 but your $100 in the name of Jesus Christ, I just want to throw up." In Ireland, he added, "they force-feed you religion. . . . It's about control: birth control, control over marriage. This has nothing to do with liberation."

In any case, *War,* the 1983 follow-up to *October,* suggests that the spiritual crises U2's members had endured also profoundly impacted the band's songwriting. In his ROLLING STONE review of *War,* J.D. Considine wrote:

> *Boy* [U2's 1981 debut album] waxed poetic on the mysteries of childhood without really illuminating any of them; *October,* its successor, wrapped itself in romance and religion but didn't seem to understand either. Without a viewpoint that could conform to the stirring rhythms and sweeping crescendos of their music, U2 often ended up sounding dangerously glib. With their third album, *War,* U2 have found just such a perspective, and with it, have generated their most fulfilling work yet.

Indeed, *War* was the album that established U2's reputation in the Eighties as a band inclined toward, and worthy of, Big Important Statements. And if it didn't shoot the group into the pop stratosphere—that feat wouldn't be accomplished until four years later, with *The Joshua Tree*—it did give credence to Bono's boast that U2 was destined for rock & roll greatness. ROLLING STONE writers, at least, were convinced: They voted U2 Band of the Year in the magazine's critics' poll for 1983, over such esteemed competitors as the Police and R.E.M. And in the readers' poll that year, U2 was edged out only by the Police.

Ultimately, ROLLING STONE cited *War* among the best recordings of the Eighties, when the magazine chose the decade's Top 100 albums in late 1989. The album entered in fortieth place (*The Joshua Tree* rated at Number Three). *"War* is a powerful fusion of politics and militant rock & roll," ROLLING STONE editors explained, "an album that anticipated the political awareness that would come back into vogue as the decade progressed." Actually, it's a bit ironic that *War* was the album that turned many Americans onto U2's music, since in terms of its political subject matter, it's the most Irish work the band has released to date. Though *War*'s overriding theme is the general need for spiritual awareness and social reform, its central metaphor is the religious and political strife that has racked Ireland for years, what the country's natives refer to as "the troubles." The first track, "Sunday Bloody Sunday," concerns the bitter history behind and legacy of a 1972 event in which thirteen Irish Catholic civilians were killed by British paratroopers during a civil rights demonstration in Northern Ireland. The last track, "40," ends the album with a plea for deliverance (incorporating lyrics from the Bible's Fortieth Psalm) that alludes to the opener's refrain of "How long must we sing this song?" and thus, also, to the ongoing violence that Bloody Sunday has come to symbolize.

However ardently U2 addressed the troubles, the band insisted on not taking sides in the matter. To support the radical Irish Republican Army, and the terrorist tactics it has employed in the name of liberating Northern Ireland and its Catholic constituency, made as little sense to the young men as endorsing the Unionists, that faction of the region's Protestant majority that has been equally militant in seeking to retain ties with Britain. An original lyric, later deleted, to "Sunday Bloody Sunday" demanded: "Don't talk to me about the rights of the IRA." The point was, U2 stressed, there should be no sides—a peaceful resolution, putting an end to the bloodshed, was needed. To emphasize this point, Bono introduced the song at a Belfast concert with what would become a signature disclaimer: "This is not a rebel song." So began U2's image problem with the IRA and, more significantly, its public dedication to what Christopher Connelly described in 1985 as "a pacifism ready to wage moral battle with its enemies."

While the band had always given riveting live performances, the fire in its new material made for a show that was truly unforgettable. "Bono solidified the success of *War*," Connelly wrote, "by crystallizing its messages onstage in bold physical images. His most memorable gesture was brandishing a white flag—what he termed as 'a flag drained of all color'— during 'Sunday Bloody Sunday,' as if to say that in war, surrender was the bravest course." The flag, like the singer's opening comment about the song, quickly became the stuff of U2 legend. "New Year's Day," another powerful (and powerfully catchy) pacifist's anthem on *War,* about the Soviet domination of Poland, began getting radio airplay in the States, elevating the group above the status of college-dorm favorites. U2 had arrived in America.

As if to commemorate this achievement, U2 rang out 1983 by releasing in November *Under a Blood Red Sky,* recorded live during the *War* tour at Colorado's Red Rocks Amphitheater. (The title refers to a lyric from "New Year's Day.") Musically confident and relentless in its energy, the album captures the band at an early peak, when its members—all still in their early twenties—were perhaps realizing that their aspirations to the ranks of rock royalty had become the expectations of fans and critics everywhere, and were relishing each performance as an opportunity to seize the crown. But as its next studio effort would prove, U2's evolution had just begun.

The Unforgettable Fire, released in October 1984, was greeted by the press with something less than the wild praise that had been lavished on its predecessor. In a lukewarm ROLLING STONE review of the album, then senior editor Kurt Loder wrote: "With *The Unforgettable Fire,* U2 flickers and nearly fades, its fire banked by a misconceived production strategy and occasional interludes of soggy, songless self-indulgence. This is not a 'bad' album, but neither is it the irrefutable beauty the band's fans anticipated. What happened?"

Well, one of the things that had happened was that U2 replaced Steve Lillywhite, the producer of its three previous studio albums, with a team consisting of former Roxy Music keyboardist Brian Eno and Canadian producer Daniel Lanois. The choice of Eno, a quirky conceptualist who had collaborated with many famous artists (including a U2 hero, David Bowie) but was recognized in his own right for having pioneered a cerebral, rather mellow branch of avant-garde pop known as "ambient music," might have seemed a boldly experimental stroke on the part of a relatively established guitar rock band. But for Loder, and others, the experiment hadn't been entirely successful. "As a producer," Loder observed, "Eno is most valuable as a conceptual organizer and sonic strategist, a master of atmospheres. But with guitarist Dave 'the Edge' Evans churning out squalls of postpsychedelic ambience, U2 already had more atmosphere than it knew what to do with."

Loder's critique invoked a paradox that was touched on years earlier by Jon Pareles, in his ROLLING STONE review of *October.* "U2's contribution to the progress of rock," Pareles wrote, "is that they've divorced guitar heroics from the idea of a dazzling guitar hero." While the Edge has certainly honed his technique and expanded his repertoire over the years, Pareles's assessment is as valid today as it was in 1981. Clearly, as U2 has refined and diversified its sound, no single element has been more funda- mental to that sound than the epic minimalism of Edge's playing, with its inspired incorporation of echo and reverb, its bursts of color and light where mile-a-minute leads might otherwise be. Production-wise, *The Unforgettable Fire* is distinguished by nothing so much as an attempt to get even further beyond the sort of trite guitar dominance that Pareles dryly referred to as "thrust(ing) of the crotch." As Loder again noted, however, *Fire*'s sonic adventurousness, whether it works for you or doesn't, couldn't obscure what many pointed to as the album's primary problem. "What all [Eno's] masterful marshaling of tribal-style chants, ethnoramic percussion and lush electronic sounds often serves to reveal here, dismayingly enough, is a creative vacuum where the band should be." The album, Loder wrote, simply "lacks consistently strong, well-defined material."

As a whole, *The Unforgettable Fire* didn't exactly knock me over on first listen, either. There was no denying the lead-off single, "Pride (In the Name of Love)," a soaring tribute to Martin Luther King Jr. that remains one of U2's greatest accomplishments. (In fact, the song—U2's first U.S. Top Forty hit—was chosen in 1988 by ROLLING STONE editors as Number 46 in their list of the Top 100 Singles of the last 25 years.) While hearing the single on the radio for the first time, I decided that the band must have outdone itself—that the impossible, an album superior to *War,* was immi- nent. Of course, with its instant hook, blow-the-roof-off vocal and promi- nent guitar line, "Pride" would not have seemed out of place on *War*. The same could not be said for most of the other songs on this delicately melodic, rather ethereal album, of which I've since grown extremely fond—even though I still believe a couple of tracks would have been better off left in the studio bin. (My cousin, a big fan of the band, insists that the incomprehensible "Elvis Presley and America" must have been recorded underwater.)

In retrospect, *The Unforgettable Fire* seems very much a spiritual ancestor to 1991's stronger, more consistent *Achtung Baby:* Both albums were re- corded at points in U2's career when a good deal of hype was certain to attend whatever new product the group would deliver, and both demon- strate the band's response to such pressure by radically defying what popular logic predicted its approach would be—musically as well as thematically. Like its direct predecessor, *Fire* uses a unifying symbol attesting to the band's social conscience: here, Martin Luther King Jr., saluted in the single "Pride" and in "MLK," the gentle paean that closes the album. But the imagery on

Fire is more lyrical and often more elusive than it had been on *War;* this time the band seemed more focused on stirring the imagination than on stirring outrage.

Perhaps most strikingly, U2's fourth studio album reveals, through lyrics that wistfully evoke cultural icons ranging from the civil rights leader to Coca-Cola, a fascination with the country that had recently embraced the band. If America's love affair with U2 began with *War,* the band's love affair with America began with *The Unforgettable Fire*. This mutual infatuation would intensify and bear fruit in two Number One albums before the decade ended; although as the material on and reception of these albums would prove, neither party in this relationship would be entirely uncritical of the other.

For now, though, even an album that everyone didn't love couldn't tarnish U2's image as rock's coolest and yet most socially responsible new heroes. Only months after printing Loder's mixed review of *The Unforgettable Fire,* ROLLING STONE ran its "Band of the Eighties" cover story, gushing, "The group has become one of the handful of artists in rock & roll history . . . that people are eager to identify themselves with." Readers concurred, choosing U2 as their favorite band in the 1985 poll. And "Pride" was everywhere—on MTV, on college radio stations, in shopping malls.

Above all, this was the period in which U2 confirmed, for anyone who may have had a lingering doubt, that its live show was as sonically and emotionally gripping as that of any band that had come before it. At Live Aid, while performing a stunning rendition of "Bad," a song from *Fire* that remains a U2 concert staple, Bono dived into the crowd and, as a security guard looked on helplessly, hugged a female fan. A fellow journalist, whom I'd expect to have a wry take on such sentimental stuff, recalls that the moment nearly reduced him to tears. In the following year, 1986, U2 gave a series of dazzling performances on behalf of another good cause, Amnesty International, headlining a roster that included Sting, Peter Gabriel, Lou Reed, Jackson Browne and Joan Baez on an American tour that billed itself as a "Conspiracy of Hope."

In 1985 U2 released another kind of tour memento, a mini-album called *Wide Awake in America*. In addition to live versions of "Bad" and "A Sort of Homecoming," another track from *The Unforgettable Fire,* the EP includes two songs that were recorded during sessions for that album but didn't made the final cut. Graceful and atmospheric, "Three Sunrises" and "Love Comes Tumbling" certainly would not have been out of place on *Fire*. It continued to be the case, however, that U2 was generally getting more attention and praise for its performing skills, and for the passionate idealism embodied in its music, than for its recorded output. In fact, U2 was at that time selling more T-shirts and merchandise than groups that sold twice as many records.

To my own teenaged ears—and I'd still maintain this—the albums the band released in the early Eighties were, at their peaks, as enjoyable listening as virtually any pop music that was selling like hotcakes back then, from Michael Jackson to Duran Duran. U2 was facing something of a dilemma in its recording career by mid-decade, however. *The Unforgettable Fire* had been an important step forward, a provocative and often enchanting testament to the group's musical progress and its refusal to be stereotyped as just another above-average guitar band. But *Fire* was uneven and, for all its lovely imagery, lacked thematic coherence. What U2 now needed to do was release an album as ambitious and sophisticated as *Fire,* but with the emotional impact and clear sense of purpose that had distinguished *War.* To make the leap from heroes to superstars, U2 had to find a way to merge its strengths and make them accessible to a mass audience of record-buyers— hopefully without compromising anything in the process.

The band realized this goal with *The Joshua Tree.* Released in March 1987, U2's fifth studio album was another Eno-Lanois collaboration (with old producer Steve Lillywhite mixing a few of the tracks), but this time, though the production was stellar, the band and its new material were the stars. As Steve Pond wrote in his glowing ROLLING STONE review, "U2 . . . weds the diverse textures of *The Unforgettable Fire* to fully formed songs, many of them as aggressive as the hits on *War.*" Pond conceded that U2's new album didn't boast any "sure-fire smash hits," but predicted nonetheless that it would prove the group's most successful album to date. "For a band that's always specialized in inspirational, larger-than-life gestures," he wrote, *"The Joshua Tree* could be the big one, and that's precisely what it sounds like."

And that's precisely what *The Joshua Tree* was, shooting to Number One on the album charts, spawning two Number One singles—the haunting bolero "With or Without You" and the oddly anthemic "I Still Haven't Found What I'm Looking For"—and landing the band on the cover of *Time* magazine, all within months of its release. Where ROLLING STONE readers were concerned, U2 *was* rock & roll in 1987: In the readers' poll for that year, the band placed first in the categories Artist of the Year, Best Band, Best Album, Best Single ("With or Without You" won, while "Where the Streets Have No Name," the album's third hit track, and "I Still Haven't Found What I'm Looking For" placed second and third, respectively), Best Male Singer, Best Songwriter (Bono), Best Guitarist,

Best Bass Player, Best Drummer, Best Live Performance, Best Video, Best Album Cover, and even Sexiest Male Artist. (Bono edged out George Michael and Jon Bon Jovi—no mean feat in 1987.) The magazine's critics were a bit more conservative, but did grant U2 a couple of big titles, Artist of the Year and Best Band, as well as Best Guitarist and second place, to Bruce Springsteen's *Tunnel of Love,* in the Best Album category.

ROLLING STONE's coverage of U2 that year included, as well as an on-the-road piece and more "Random Notes" than you could shake a stick at, another cover story on the band, in May. During that interview, Anthony DeCurtis encountered a Bono who still wasn't sure that he'd found what he was looking for. "I must say, I don't feel very qualified to be a pop star," Bono told DeCurtis. "I feel very awkward at times in the role. I think there are other people far better suited than me." The singer spoke with typical frankness about his writing on *The Joshua Tree,* which seemed to portray a very different America than the land of Elvis and egalitarian dreams depicted on *The Unforgettable Fire.* "You know, America's the promised land to a lot of Irish people," Bono mused. "I'm one in a long line of Irishmen who made the trip to the U.S., and I feel a part of that. That's why I embraced America early on, when a lot of European bands were throwing their noses up. And America, indeed, seemed to embrace us. Of course, my opinions have changed from utter stars in the eyes."

Ridden with struggling workers, desperate lovers and assorted symbols of political corruption and moral decay—gamblers, heroin, the Ku Klux Klan—the songs on *The Joshua Tree* are quite dramatic in their ambivalence. The American landscape painted on the album combines a bittersweet romanticism with a dark sense of foreboding. DeCurtis's story revealed that Bono had visited Central America before recording "Bullet the Blue Sky," whose lyrics include a stinging indictment of U.S. foreign policy. When Edge was about to lay down his apocalyptic guitar solo for the track, the singer advised him, "Put El Salvador through your amplifier."

"The underbelly of America has come open to us," Bono told DeCurtis. "America seems to be everything that's great about the world and everything that's terrible about the world all rolled into one. . . . For us, it's the contradictions of the place, the paradoxes, the strangeness—that's what 'Bullet the Blue Sky' is all about." As DeCurtis observed, "Bono sometimes seems overwhelmed by the task of confronting the monumental problems in America and the world." Quoting a line from the deceptively buoyant "In God's Country"—"We need new dreams tonight"—the singer admitted to his interviewer that he was finding it harder to summon forth the idealism that fans had come to expect of U2:

I'm looking around—there's elections coming up all over the place, in England, in the U.S. I'm sick and tired of party politics. You know, the left, the right—I'm sick of the left, I'm sick of the right. Even the *liberals* are giving me a pain in the ass. We need new solutions to new problems. . . . I nearly feel like going, "Tutti frutti," at the moment, "be-bop-a-lula." I'm starting to think that actually says *more,* because words are failing me at the moment, they're really failing me.

In December 1987, ROLLING STONE welcomed Bono into the ranks of pop culture's elite by granting him the prestigious "Rolling Stone Interview"—sort of the magazine's equivalent of a star on the Walk of Fame, or a Friars Roast. Speaking to David Breskin, Bono adopted a somewhat lighter tone than he had used with DeCurtis, but touched on many of the same themes: his discomfort with his rock star status ("At the moment, actually, I'm going for bastard lessons"), his growing interest in and concern about America, his dismay over the general state of affairs in the world. In DeCurtis's article, Bono had insisted, "One of the reasons I'm attracted to people like Martin Luther King, Gandhi, Christ, to pacifism, is because naturally I'm *not* a pacifist. Naturally, I'm the guy that would not turn the other cheek." Bono repeated this assertion almost verbatim to Breskin, adding that he had been a difficult, aggressive child and teenager, who fought with his father, brother and schoolmates. "They used to call me the Antichrist," the singer laughed. The point seemed to be that, for all his pontificating, Bono was a reluctant role model, who realized the limitations of what he could do as a pop star and a human being. As he told DeCurtis, "I'm a very real person, good and bad."

But in light of the music U2 was producing, and the way the band was presenting it on tour, some began to suspect that Bono was protesting too much. As I've said, one of U2's best qualities has been its ability to use grand gestures in an honest, purposeful manner. For me, and for millions of others, *The Joshua Tree* is a masterwork of hyperbole in service of the plain truth. But it's also the album that marked the beginning of a wave of backlash against U2, and its singer in particular. There had been some, of course, for whom the social and spiritual consciousness in the band's songs had always bordered on self-consciousness, or even self-righteousness, and for whom its over-the-top delivery had been a bit rich to the taste. But now that U2 and its music seemed to be everywhere—indeed, the same ROLLING STONE readers' poll that awarded the group so many superlatives also placed U2 second in the "Hype of the Year" category, right behind Michael Jackson—its image, and whatever messages it was sending out, took on an added dimension of grandiosity. Not helping matters was what many saw as Bono's messianic posturing during concerts, the fact that he'd taken to assessing, sometimes bitterly and often at length, the same world problems he had claimed left him speechless.

Anti-U2 sentiment came to a head toward the end of the Eighties, in the wake of *Rattle and Hum* (1988). Conceived as another tour memento, albeit one on a much larger scale than *Wide Awake in America* or *Under a Blood Red Sky,* this double-album-length recording and movie project wound up being the culmination of the Irish band's stormy romance with America. Produced by Jimmy Iovine (who also manned the boards for *Under a Blood Red Sky*), the album offsets live recordings from U2's *Joshua Tree* tour with new studio tracks that convey, both texturally and in their lyrics, a feverish preoccupation with tracing rock & roll's roots in American music and culture. As Bono told Breskin, the frustration evident on *The Joshua Tree* had not dampened the affection and respect fueling *The Unforgettable Fire*. "I think the only reason we get away with our criticism of America is because people know that we love to *be* in America," the singer said. "America has given me much more than I could ever give it."

Critical reaction to *Rattle and Hum* tended to agree with, to say the least, this last comment. DeCurtis gave the album a generally favorable (but less than wildly enthusiastic) review in ROLLING STONE, but admitted, "For all its excitement, *Rattle and Hum* seems a tad calculated in its supposed spontaneity." Other critiques were less, well, charitable. "By almost any rock & roll fan's standards, U2's *Rattle and Hum* is an awful record," Tom Carson declared in the *Village Voice*. "But the chasm between what it thinks it is and the half-baked, overweening reality doesn't sound attributable to pretension so much as to monumental know-nothingism."

There can be little doubt that this was not U2's finest hour. Three years later, while reviewing *Achtung Baby* for ROLLING STONE, I described *Rattle and Hum* as "misguided and bombastic." When considering certain tracks and the companion film, that judgment seems fairly accurate. For Bono to record a duet with Bob Dylan ("Love Rescue Me," which Dylan co-wrote), when the singers' voices mix like oil and water, still strikes me as misguided; and for U2's singer to interrupt a live version of "Silver and Gold," a song he wrote for Little Steven Van Zandt's 1985 protest album *Sun City: Artists United Against Apartheid,* with a discourse about the plight of South Africa's Bishop Desmond Tutu, still strikes me as bombastic.

The album as a whole is marked less by a sense of self-importance, however, than by the band's overzealous impulse to get across the fact that rock stars can also be rock fans. It would be ridiculous to assume that when Bono sang with Dylan, or with B.B. King (on the song "When Love Comes to Town"), that he was deeming himself worthy of their venerability. Instead, there's a sense on those tracks, however goofy, of, "Hey, mom, look at me!" And for those who can get past all the name-dropping and hero worship, *Rattle and Hum* does offer some lovely moments. The shimmering "Heartland," a testament to Bono's enduring belief in what's good about America, and the achingly melodic "All I Want Is You" are two of the most beautiful ballads U2 has ever released. And enlisting Harlem's New Voices of Freedom choir to join the band for a rousing rock-gospel rendition of "I Still Haven't Found What I'm Looking For" was an inspired touch.

As a group, ROLLING STONE readers certainly had no problem finding something to like in *Rattle and Hum:* In 1988, the band once again swept the magazine's readers' poll, taking virtually all of the same categories it had claimed the previous year, including Best Album and Best Single (the chugging, Bo Diddleyesque "Desire"). Yet another cover story accompanied the publication of the poll's results, in early 1989. Making note of all the flak attending U2's most recent project—there was the quote from Carson's *Voice* review, in all its glory—Steve Pond at once defended the band and interrogated its members. Plainly, there was no avoiding certain basic questions, such as how did the guys feel about all the negative press they had gotten, and where do they go from here?

The musicians were less than eager to discuss the *Rattle and Hum* film, hemming and hawing about, as the writer relayed it, "compromises they had to make for the cameras." (Luckily, director Phil Joanou was available for comment, and only too willing to take the blame for what he himself described as "an overly serious, pretentious look at U2.") Of the press, the Edge admitted, "I'm sick to death of reading about U2." As usual, Bono had the most to say: "There is . . . a sense of feeling misunderstood, and a sense of antagonism toward us. You know, *Rattle and Hum* was the end of something," the singer announced.

Indeed, while the Eighties had indisputably been an amazing decade for U2, the band had reached another crucial turning point, and needed a new direction to remain relevant into the Nineties. And for those looking for some indication of what that direction might be, a clue existed in a comment Bono would make near the end of Pond's interview:

Wherever I look, words have been used up. Gone. They don't mean anything. *God. Light. Sex.* And the most powerful word has got to be *love.* . . . That's the key for U2 as well. With all these big ideals, we've got to bring things down to two people, really. One is good, two is better. And that's where I see us going.

Ironically, the breakup of a marriage would be instrumental in bringing Bono's plan to fruition. The Edge's separation from Aislinn O'Sullivan, his wife since 1984 and the mother of his three children, actually occurred *during* the making of U2's *Achtung Baby* album, rather than before it. In an interview for *Musician,* Flanagan asked Bono how much of an impact his band mate's ordeal had had on the singer's writing. "I was going down that road anyway," Bono replied. "I don't know which came first, to be honest. The words or what Edge went through. They're all bound up in each other. But there are a lot of other experiences that went on around the same time." The Edge had offered a similar explanation when Flanagan had spoken to him a few months earlier. "There's a lot of stories in there," Edge said, "and it's not just my story." But as the guitarist later told ROLLING STONE music editor David Fricke, all of *Achtung Baby*—"the whole album"—was to at least some extent influenced by his marital problems.

After a long series of recording sessions in Dublin and Berlin (a process that was disrupted when demo tapes from the former city were stolen in the latter one, and quickly bootlegged), *Achtung Baby* was finally released in November 1991. It was the first album U2 had released in three years—the first of all-new material in nearly four—and so eager were fans for its arrival that ROLLING STONE decided to put U2 on the cover of the issue coinciding with the album's release. The cover story was an essay about the making of *Achtung Baby* by Brian Eno, who had assisted the album's principal producer, Daniel Lanois. Lanois was by now a recognized name in his own right, having worked with Bob Dylan and Peter Gabriel. (Steve Lillywhite had also been on board for a few tracks.)

Eno's essay focused primarily on the musical and technical aspects of recording the album, stressing how much the band had experimented and evolved sonically; so readers would have to wait to hear the new songs to truly realize what a bold departure *Achtung Baby* represented in terms of its lyrics. ROLLING STONE's cover, however, featuring Bono in black leather and shades—and a photograph accompanying the article, of the singer hamming it up with a couple of transvestites—might have tipped off a few more attentive folks to the fact that U2 wasn't up to its usual bag of tricks. The hints were provided courtesy of photographer Anton Corbijn, who previously had portrayed the band in its then-familiar guise as earnest, reflective young men, most notably for the covers of *The Unforgettable Fire* and *The Joshua Tree*.

Corbijn's *Achtung Baby* cover contrasted even more sharply with U2's Eighties persona. For it, the photographer had assembled a colorful, rather garish photo montage, featuring images ranging from a psychedelic car to a hand-held snake. There was a shot of Bono in front of a topless woman and a photo of Adam Clayton completely nude, facing the camera unflinchingly. (Not surprisingly, less than all of Clayton was shown in most countries.) More pictures were included in the lyric sheets, one of them featuring the band in drag. If such images hinted that our boys had some good, dirty fun on their minds, the truth was even more shocking. Because on *Achtung Baby,* the band that had fearlessly tackled social, political, and spiritual dilemmas embarked on its most intrepid adventure yet—into the human heart, and the human libido. And what U2 found there was rarely funny, at least not in the glib, giddy sense suggested by a bunch of would-be drag queens.

The band had explored romantic, and even carnal, love on its previous efforts, but never before with the sense of intimacy, or anguish, that distinguishes the material on *Baby.* That the songs had been influenced by the Edge's personal heartbreak is obvious; but as the guitarist and Bono told *Musician,* the whole truth was more complicated—and clearly had much to do with the lyricist himself. In my ROLLING STONE review, I wrote, "Squarely acknowledging his own potential for hypocrisy and inadequacy, and addressing basic human weaknesses rather than the failings of society at large, Bono sounds humbler and more vulnerable than in the past." Certainly not since U2's pre-*War* work had the singer seemed to communicate his thoughts and feelings in such a delicate, personal manner; only now he was doing so with another decade of life experience under his belt. And while Bono had never been one to conceal his struggles with emotional or spiritual insecurity, his self-doubt had now taken on a weary, ironic edge that made it more poignant and more profound. "I'd join the movement/If there was one that I could believe in. . . . I'd break bread and wine/If there was a church I could receive in," he confesses, on a moody track called "Acrobat"; and on the chilling ballad "Love Is Blindness," Bono sings, "I don't want to see / Won't you wrap the night around me."

U2's detractors could have easily dismissed such lyrics as a self-conscious attempt to ditch the smug, prissy reputation the band held for some. Bono outsmarted them, though, by creating an alter ego: the Fly. It was the Fly, in fact, who had appeared on that ROLLING STONE cover, smirking behind dark sunglasses; and it was he, not Bono, who had been clowning with the transvestites in that picture inside the magazine. There's even a song named after him on *Achtung Baby,* a nasty, clamorous little ditty Bono described to David Fricke as "like a phone call from hell, but the guy liked it there." Explaining the Fly to Fricke, Bono said, "The character is just on the edge of lunacy. It's megalomania and paranoia." But as the writer observed, it was actually something more than that. "The Fly is very much an offshoot of Bono's own outspoken, proselytizing nature," Fricke noted, "and his willingness, ever since U2's earliest days, to go out on a long, thin limb to explain his and the band's socio-spiritual agenda. The difference is, he agrees, in the Fly's comic exaggeration."

Appropriately, the tour that the Fly and U2's other three members set up to promote *Achtung Baby* was an exercise in glorious, flagrant excess that contrasted sharply with the rugged straightforwardness the band's fans had come to expect. Designed by Eno and a team of British production artists, the Zoo TV extravaganza was all techno-gimmickry and show-biz flash, all the things to which U2 had served as an alternative in the Eighties. Of course, like the Fly, Zoo TV was based on certain fundamental characteristics and goals that U2 had always embodied; it just presented them with a fresh, perverse twist. As the musicians played, huge video screens behind them put forth words and phrases—many of them puzzling or outrageous—that touched on provocative issues without spelling out any specific messages. Images were projected as well, some serious, others scathingly satirical, others simply goofy. And, lest we forget, there were the Fly's onstage phone calls to the White House—or the United Nations, or anywhere else he could stir up mischief, situations in which Bono would have used the opportunity to try making a difference in the world. (It was just as well, because George Bush never took the Fly's phone calls.)

Yet the most conspicuous aspect of these shows may well have been the new music itself. Gone, or far less pronounced anyway, were the sort of folkie, earthy textures that had colored *The Joshua Tree* and *Rattle and Hum*. Instead, *Achtung Baby* combined the sonic ferocity of *War* with the quirky ambience of *The Unforgettable Fire,* and added a slew of neat, state-of-the-art surprises, like electronically derived hip-hop beats, and cacophonous bursts of guitar distortion that made most of the Edge's previous shenanigans sound tame in comparison. Overall, the album, like the tour that accompanied it, has a flashy feel, but a rock-solid emotional center—namely, the songs themselves, which rival any that U2 had produced in terms of both compositional strength and sheer emotional impact. "We had this idea that irony was the enemy of soul," Bono told Fricke of the band's early days, but it's the reconciliation of those elements that makes U2's first album of the Nineties so astonishing.

Predictably, the band once again cleaned up in ROLLING STONE's readers' poll, winning the 1992 titles for artist, band, album, single (the sublime ballad "One"), songwriter, producer (Lanois), male singer, drummer, tour and album cover. The group's critically and commercially successful return to the rock scene after a three-year sabbatical was heralded as "Comeback of the Year," and once again, Bono was named premier male sexpot—an interesting choice this time, given that he had spent the year hiding behind a pair of shades and a rather buffoonish persona. Former ROLLING STONE senior writer Alan Light raised this point when he interviewed the singer in early 1993 (for the third issue in less than a year and a half featuring Bono on the cover), and dared to ask if or when the Fly would be swatted out. "It's always the music that tells you," replied Bono, who fortunately conducted the interview out of character. "And so if I want to take the glasses off, I just gotta change my tune."

In fact, Bono dispensed with the Fly shortly after speaking to Light (or at least put the pest to rest for a while), but only to instantly reemerge in a pair of more insidious guises. The "mirror-ball man," a slimy cowboy-preacher inspired by those American televangelist types that had long been the object of Bono's scorn, materialized toward the end of Zoo TV's run in the States; he was replaced on the last leg of the band's European tour by a hideously tacky fellow known as MacPhisto, who Bono would later describe to DeCurtis as the Fly's "logical conclusion, which is when he's fat and playing Las Vegas." Brandishing an affected British accent, and the sort of engaging personality one would expect from a has-been actor who's had one too many vodka tonics, MacPhisto would appear onstage (during encores, usually) in a uniform that included a gold-lamé suit, platform shoes, and white face makeup—and bright red devil's horns.

"I just didn't feel like doing the mirror-ball man in Europe," Bono explained to Fricke in the summer of 1993. "Like, who is the mirror-ball man, anyway? Well, he is the devil. So I thought, great, put on a pair of horns. Might as well spell it out." Or as Bono had told Fricke the previous year, in discussing his struggle to come to terms with the decadent aspects of rock stardom, "Mock the devil, and he will flee from thee." Clearly, U2 had come a long way from the simple, starry-eyed spirituality of *October*.

A July 1993 article in ROLLING STONE announced the impending release of another U2 album. *Zooropa* had originally been planned as an EP, another of U2's post-tour mini-projects; but as the band concluded its Stateside journey, approaching the end of its world tour as well, what Bono described to David Fricke as "a kind of freak energy" infected the musicians. Produced by Eno, the Edge, and mixer du jour Flood, who had engineered *Achtung Baby,* the album was praised in DeCurtis's ROLLING STONE review as "a daring, imaginative coda to *Achtung Baby.*" Indeed, while *Zooropa* lacks the monumental presence characterizing U2's Big Albums—that is, *War, The Joshua Tree* and *Achtung Baby*—it's nonetheless an audacious and dazzling collection that picks up where *Baby* and Zoo TV left off, both texturally and thematically. Beginning with the title track, on which an eerily detached recitation of TV ad slogans gives way to an explosion of spiritual ambivalence, *Zooropa* reveals what DeCurtis called an "atmosphere . . . of grim, determined fun, a fever-dream last waltz on the deck of the *Titanic.*" On one song, "Babyface," a man seems to attempt making love to a video-generated image; on another, the haunting "Stay (Far Away, So Close!)," lovers failing to communicate with each other turn to their television set, trying to throw their arms around the world. Then there's "The Wanderer," a portrait of a God-less, morally bankrupt society sung by guest star Johnny Cash. (After some of the criticism he received for *Rattle and Hum,* perhaps Bono was a bit reluctant to duet with another roots-rock legend.)

However bleak, though, the songs on *Zooropa* never lapse into hopelessness; as on its previous albums, U2 imbues even its darkest sentiments with a sense of yearning that precludes cynicism. Similarly, the synthesizers, loops and electronic samples pervading the arrangements on U2's 1993 effort don't detract from the music's sense of humanity. While in the early Eighties U2's members had been as wary of such techno-pop staples as they were of the irony often associated with them, they had since realized that soulfulness—or lack of it—lies not in the means of presentation, but in the presentation itself. "The way we feel about it," Bono told *Musician* writer Joe Jackson, "is that rock & roll—whatever that is these days—is mutating and that it's always technology that spurs these mutations."

As U2's preeminent technophile, and *Zooropa*'s coproducer, the Edge was pushed yet further into the spotlight in 1993. When ROLLING STONE ran another U2 profile by Anthony DeCurtis in October, it was the guitarist alone whose mug graced the cover. (All previous U2 covers had featured either Bono or the whole band.) In the story, Edge reflected on how U2 had challenged itself, toying with its image in recent years, and on how some of its more conservative fans had reacted to this risky behavior. "People come to the shows who have seen U2 before," he mused, "and you're constantly having to deal with their expectations as opposed to what you're trying to do. I know there are a lot of people who come away disappointed . . . because we didn't play 'Sunday Bloody Sunday' or whatever other old song they wanted to hear."

Of the *Zooropa* album specifically, the Edge said, "We were starting to lose trust in the conventional sound of rock & roll . . . of guitar in particular—and, you know, those big reverb-laden drum sounds of the Eighties or those big, beautiful, pristine vocal sounds with all this lush ambience and reverb." As Bono had told Jackson, "If we're committed to the art of rock & roll at all we have to move forward to see what we can make of the beast by pushing everything to its limits." And that, Edge explained to DeCurtis, entailed "searching for other sounds that had more life and more freshness."

Considering the ground U2 has covered since ROLLING STONE declared it the band of the Eighties, it's anyone's guess where the band's search will take it before this decade is over, or in the years after that. And it's this uncertainty, ultimately, that will ensure the group's status among the great rock artists—all of whom have pushed limits and continually forced fans to redefine their expectations—to whose ranks U2's members once dreamily aspired. The quality that Bono referred to, in his first ROLLING STONE profile, as "a certain spark, a certain chemistry" is really less what distinguishes bands of this caliber over the years than the ability to keep that chemistry fresh by constantly shaking up and adding things to the mix, without ever losing sight of the basic elements that made it so special in the first place.

During a Dublin performance on *The Joshua Tree* tour (one that, thanks to a bootlegging street vendor, found its way into my tape collection), Bono paused in the middle of singing "I Still Haven't Found What I'm Looking For" to shout, with a curious sense of elation, "I hope I never find it!" I hope so, too.

JAMES HENKE

U2: HERE COMES THE "NEXT BIG THING"

ERE I AM, AN AMERICAN WRITER, dining with an Irish band in a Greek restaurant in the heart of England. Strange? Well, so is the scene that's unfolding in front of me. A few feet away, two musicians are seated on a platform. One is playing bouzouki, a stringed instrument similar to a mandolin, while the other, a heavy-set fellow in black suit and dark glasses who looks remarkably like the Godfather, is hammering away at a small electric keyboard with built-in rhythm machine. In front of them, approving patrons toss plate after ceramic plate to the floor, where they shatter at the feet of U2's Bono Vox, who is demonstrating that a rock singer from Ireland can be quite a lively dancer.

Though this seems like some sort of international celebration, it's only another preshow dinner for U2. The band, which has been touring Britain nonstop since the release of its debut album, *Boy,* in mid-October, has garnered more than the usual amount of attention—thanks in part to an overzealous English music press. Since early last year, the media have been touting U2—vocalist Vox, drummer Larry Mullen, guitarist "the Edge" and bassist Adam Clayton—as the Next Big Thing. If all the publicity weren't enough, Island Records President Chris Blackwell proclaimed the group the label's most important signing since King Crimson.

In concert, the loquacious Vox tries to play down all the hype—he regularly tells audiences to "forget all that stuff you may have read and make up your own minds"—but privately he concurs with the press. "I don't mean to sound arrogant," he tells me after the dancing has died down, "but even at this stage, I do feel that we are meant to be one of the great groups. There's a certain spark, a certain chemistry, that was special about the Stones, the Who and the Beatles, and I think it's also special about U2."

A mighty boast, to be sure. But *Boy,* scheduled for a late-January U.S. release, does indicate that U2 is a band to be reckoned with. Their highly original sound can perhaps best be described as pop music with brains. It's accessible and melodic, combining the dreamy, atmospheric qualities of a band like Television with a hard-rock edge not unlike the Who's. In particular, Edge's guitar playing and Bono's singing stand out; the lyrical guitar lines slice through every song, while the vocals are rugged, urgent and heartfelt.

The title *Boy* is appropriate and significant: not only are the band members young—Bono and Adam are twenty, Larry and Edge nineteen—but the bulk of their songs deal with the dreams and frustrations of childhood. "We're playing to an audience in Britain that ranges in age from seventeen to twenty-five," Bono explains. "There is massive unemployment, and there is real disillusionment. U2's music is about getting up and doing something about it."

But wasn't that also the aim of punk? "The idea of punk at first was, 'Look, you're an individual, express yourself how you want, do what you want to do,'" Bono says. "But that's not the way it came out in the end. The Sex Pistols were a con, a box of tricks sold by Malcolm McLaren. Kids were sold the imagery of violence, which turned into the reality of violence, and it's that negative side that I worry about. People like Bruce Springsteen carry hope. Like the Who—'Won't Get Fooled Again.' I mean, there is a song of endurance, and that's the attitude of the great bands. We want our audience to think about their actions and where they are going, to realize the pressures that are on them, but at the same time, not to give up."

Part of U2's attitude comes from the fact that they are, as Bono puts it, "appreciative of our background." The group formed in 1978 at an experimental school in Dublin. "It was multidenominational," he explains, "which, in terms of Dublin and Ireland, is quite unique. It was also coeducational, which was unusual too. We were given freedom, and when you're given freedom, you don't rebel by getting drunk."

That message comes across again when the group headlines a show at London's Marquee club a few days later. After a rousing forty-five-minute set, the band returns to the stage for an encore. But before launching into another song, Bono makes a short speech about the little boy pictured on the British version of U2's LP. "Some people have been asking about the boy on the cover of the album," he says. "Well, he happens to be a kid who lives across the street from me. We put him on the cover 'cause he's a pretty smart kid. And sometimes I wonder what his future will be like—and I wonder about ours."

At this point, U2's future looks bright. The band has managed to deal level-headedly with its sudden popularity in the U.K. In addition, they've shunned such traditional rock & roll pitfalls as booze and drugs. Finally, the band is willing to work. A three-month U.S. trek will begin in March, and Bono is, as usual, confident about the band's chances in the States. "Right now, the word is 'go!' for U2," he says. "It is my ambition to travel to America and give it what I consider it wants and needs."

DEBRA RAE COHEN

BOY ALBUM REVIEW

★ ★ ★ ½

"I WILL FOLLOW," THE KICKOFF cut from the debut album by Irish whiz kids U2, is a beguiling, challenging, perfect single. With its racing-pulse beat, tinkling percussion and mantra-simple chorus of dogged affection ("If you walkaway, walkaway / I walkaway, walkaway—I will follow"), it's already a dance-floor favorite.

Unfortunately, much of the rest of *Boy* doesn't quite equal that first vital piece of precocity. U2 plays smart, bass-heavy trance-pop, urged on by the earnest vocal emoting of Bono Vox and enlivened by the ringing accents of the versatile guitarist who calls himself the Edge. But their songs—mostly chronicles of psychic growing pains—are a diffuse and uneven lot. "Out of Control" boasts the same heady rumble as "I Will Follow," while "Stories for Boys" is carried by its B-movie guitar line and soaring youthful harmonies. Other tunes, however, are less successful. "An Cat Dubh" and the seemingly interminable "Shadows and Tall Trees" ramble without resolution, neither coalescing into identifiable hooks nor attaining the seductive atmospherics of, say, Echo and the Bunnymen.

Hopefully, U2 may yet justify Island's hyped-up optimism. With the help of creative producer Steve Lillywhite, they've already blended echoes of several of Britain's more adventurous bands into a sound that's rich, lively and comparatively commercial. And, unlike the real innovators, they'll have the tour support to back it up. U2 is talented, charming and potentially (they're all still under twenty-one) exceptional. But as a new Next Big Thing, they're only the next best thing to something *really* new.

JON PARELES

OCTOBER ALBUM REVIEW

★ ★ ★

IT'S IMPOSSIBLE TO TAKE U2 as seriously as they take themselves. When lead singer Bono emotes lines like "No one is blinder than he who will not see" or "Open the door, open the door," I want to usher him aside and wish him a speedy recovery from adolescence. Of course, he means every word. Certainly, he feels like an existential castaway. But until Bono outgrows the urge to reinvent every cliché from scratch ("He was my brother!" "There's a fire in me!") and shout it to the world, the way to enjoy U2 is to consider the vocals as sound effects and concentrate, as the band does, on the sound of the guitar.

U2's contribution to the progress of rock is that they've divorced guitar heroics from the idea of a dazzling guitar hero. Though they're downright worshipful of the Edge's heavy-on-the-reverb Stratocaster—side two of *October* opens with his tuning the thing up—he's about as much of a technical wizard as Neil Young. When a U2 song has more than two chords (one of them E minor, the people's key), it's a shock. Yet the sound the Edge gets, abetted by producer Steve Lillywhite, is as powerful as the lyrics are silly. His power chords create a terrifying aural abyss for Bono to plunge into, and his simple single-note riffs, drenched in echo and glory, point toward a way out. All this without a single thrust of the crotch.

Unlike U2's debut album, *Boy, October* generally keeps the guitar in the foreground, not breaking up the echoes with *Boy's* endless glockenspiels. Perhaps as a result of touring the DOR circuit, U2 try a little funk in "I Threw a Brick Through a Window" and use trumpet ("With a Shout") and timbales ("Is That All?") like British neofunkers A Certain Ratio. "October" signals its profundity by utilizing acoustic piano accompaniment. With experiments like these, U2 are obviously attempting to vary their sound, but none of the strategies works as well yet as their basic power-trio dynamics.

Also unlike *Boy, October* is barely coherent. *Boy* was an intriguing, one-time-only document—the inside story from children at the brink of manhood—and its compositions were sparked by the tension between the Edge's world-beating guitar playing and Bono's fearful pride. Thank goodness U2 don't have enough showbiz in their souls to repeat the concept on *October*. Unfortunately, when they try to tap other primal experiences ("I'm falling!"), they sound so sensitive it hurts. Sheer sonic grandeur can carry these guys through one record like *October,* though. And by their next LP, U2 may have figured out what to do with their *angst*.

J.D. CONSIDINE

WAR ALBUM REVIEW

★ ★ ★ ★

U2 get militant about peace

FROM THE START, IT WAS CLEAR that U2 could create impressive music. The jagged guitar riff and thundering drone that launched "I Will Follow" and the rest of their 1981 debut album, *Boy,* was eloquent and visceral. It was also musically uncomplicated; these four young Dubliners had an instinctive sense for making the most out of simple shifts in dynamics and elementary voicings, and it gave their sound a rough, exhilarating grandiloquence. The only problem was that once U2 caught a listener's attention, they had little to say. *Boy* waxed poetic on the mysteries of childhood without really illuminating any of them; *October,* its successor, wrapped itself in romance and religion but didn't seem to understand either. Without a viewpoint that could conform to the stirring rhythms and sweeping crescendos of their music, U2 often ended up sounding dangerously glib.

With their third album, *War,* U2 have found just such a perspective, and with it, have generated their most fulfilling work yet. *War* makes for impressive listening, but more important, it deals with a difficult subject in a sensible way. That subject is the sectarian strife in Northern Ireland, or what the Irish call "the troubles." U2 are not the first group to play soldiers with this topic; Belfast's Stiff Little Fingers have dealt with the problem explicitly, the Clash somewhat more obliquely. But no one has caught the paradox between stance and action so accurately.

"Sunday Bloody Sunday," which opens the album, apparently addresses Bloody Sunday, a 1972 incident in which British paratroopers killed thirteen civilians in an illegal civil-rights demonstration in Londonderry. As an acoustic guitar and a sizzling hi-hat build tension, vocalist Bono Vox sings, "I can't believe the news today. . . ." The band slips into some lush, sustained chords as he wonders, "How long? How long must we sing this song?" then jumps back into a militant, jagged dance beat.

It's great drama, and it lends a certain amount of credence to the song's wistful chorus, "Tonight, we can be as one. Tonight!" But Vox tips his hand when he sings the urgent disclaimer, "I won't heed the battle call / It puts my back up, puts my back up against the wall." What Vox and the band are saying, then, is that it's pointless to take irresponsible risks when confronting irresponsible authority—but one must still take some sort of stance.

Unlike the Clash, who wrestle with imperialist foreign policy, or the Gang of Four, who try to transfer a Marxist dialectic to the dance floor, U2 don't pretend to have the answers to the world's troubles. Instead, they devote their energies to letting us know that they are concerned and to creating an awareness about those problems. And not only is that refreshing, but it makes sense, because U2 understand that it's the gesture, not the message, that counts.

Complementing U2's lyrical growth is a newly developed dark sense of humor, which the band uses to striking effect throughout the album. "Seconds," for example, opens with a sleepy funk riff driven by a cheerful toy bass drum. It's a pleasant juxtaposition, but as the song's subject matter becomes clear—the insanity of nuclear blackmail, where, as Bono Vox puts it, "the puppets pull the strings"—you realize that this jolly noisemaker is no more an innocent plaything than is the one in Gunter Grass' *The Tin Drum*. Similarly, "New Year's Day" includes the wisecrack, "So we are told, this is a golden age / Gold is the reason for the wars we wage"—a remark far wiser than it at first seems.

Yet *War* isn't all jaded ideals and sour wit, for as Bono Vox makes his pronouncements, his vocalise reveals the full flower of U2's melodic abilities. In between the bitter humor of "Seconds," he breaks into joyous flights of wordless melody, his voice soaring in multi-tracked polyphony over the song's slippery rhythms. "Surrender" is lighter still, thanks to its airy melody and the Edge's coolly sustained guitar. In fact, this song is the one instance where the music says more than lyrics ever could, because hearing Vox's blissful tenor floating over the backing vocals (courtesy of Kid Creole's Coconuts) is a better definition of "Surrender" than anything in Webster's.

Generally, the album's musical strengths are largely the product of well-honed arrangements and carefully balanced dynamics. Even as the Edge spins increasingly sophisticated guitar lines, he maintains the minimalist bluntness that sparked *Boy*. And while bassist Adam Clayton and drummer Larry Mullen Jr. have swung to more dance-oriented rhythms, their songs hurtle along with the sort of brusque purposefulness more frequently associated with punk.

U2 may not be great intellectuals, and *War* may sound more profound than it really is. But the songs here stand up against anything on the Clash's *London Calling* in terms of sheer impact, and the fact that U2 can sweep the listener up in the same sort of enthusiastic romanticism that fuels the band's grand gestures is an impressive feat. For once, not having all the answers seems a bonus.

JAMES HENKE

BLESSED ARE THE PEACEMAKERS

With a battle hymn of rock & roll, Ireland's U2 preaches the politics of love

B ONO VOX LIKES TO THINK of himself as a revolutionary, a man with a mission. And when he gets fired up, which is practically all the time, he just loves to talk. If he's with a group of people, he dominates the conversation. And if it's just one-on-one, the other person is lucky to get a word in edgewise. It's like the boy can't help it; he's got to spread his message.

Right now, as he and the other members of U2 are airborne, flying from a show in London to one in Glasgow, Bono is on a real roll. The matter at hand is why he feels U2 is a special band, and why it is that they've developed such a strong following on both sides of the Atlantic. At a time when pop music is dominated by swishy, style-soaked synthesizer bands whose main concern seems to be their ability to make people dance and forget the problems of the world, U2 stands out as a real exception.

For one thing, they're a rock band in the more traditional sense of the word. Guitar, bass and drums—no electronic keyboards, no computerized drums. Granted, their sound is modern—dominated by Larry Mullen's boomy drumming and Dave "the Edge" Evans's droning, neopsychedelic guitar playing—but they're still a far cry from trendy technofunksters. And *War,* their third and latest album, doesn't shy away from weighty issues: its songs grapple with such topics as the strife in Northern Ireland, Polish Solidarity and nuclear terror.

Then there are the band members themselves. Fashion-conscious these guys are not. No pouf hairdos. No photo spreads in *Vogue* or the *Face*. Black jeans and a sleeveless black combat jacket will do just fine, thank you. And their lifestyle doesn't jibe with that of the usual rock & roller, either. Though they don't support any particular denomination, three of them— Bono, Mullen and Evans—are devoted Christians. Not rabid Bible thumpers, mind you, but if they get bored traveling between gigs, there's a good chance they'll pick up the Good Book and read a few verses.

And all those factors, Bono believes, make U2 truly revolutionary. "I think that, ultimately, the group is totally rebellious, because of our stance against what people accept as rebellion," he says. "The whole thing about rock stars driving cars into swimming pools—that's not rebellion. People would be very pleased if I did that, and our record company would be only too pleased to pay the bill, because we'd get in the news and sell more records. That's not rebellion.

"Revolution starts at home, in your heart, in your refusal to compromise your beliefs and your values. I'm not interested in politics like people fighting back with sticks and stones, but in the politics of love. I think there is nothing more radical than two people's loving each other, because it's so infrequent."

THERE ARE TWO EXPLANATIONS OF HOW Paul Hewson came to be called Bono Vox. One is that it's a somewhat skewed Latin translation of "good voice"—an appropriate moniker for a lead singer. The other is that it came from the brand name of a British hearing aid—a device one *didn't* need if Bono was around.

"I had the loudest mouth," he admits. "When we formed the group, I was the lead guitar player, singer and songwriter. Nobody talked back at first. But then they talked me out of being lead guitar player and into being a rhythm guitar player. And then they talked me out of being the rhythm guitar player and into just being the singer. And then they tried to talk me out of being the singer and into being the manager. But I held on to that. Arrogance may have been the reason."

U2 came together in 1978 at the Mount Temple Comprehensive School in Dublin. Larry Mullen was the only member with any musical experience, having played drums in a local marching band. When he was expelled from that outfit because of his long hair, he decided to form a rock group and put a note up on the school bulletin board. Bono, bassist Adam Clayton, guitarist Dave Evans (nicknamed "the Edge" apparently because of the shape of his head) and his brother, Dick, also a guitarist, all responded. (Dick soon dropped out to attend university but has since reemerged as a member of a frenzied postpunk act called the Virgin Prunes.)

All of the band members had solid middle- or lower-middle-class backgrounds: Clayton's father is a pilot for Aer Lingus, the Edge's father is an engineer who designs heating systems in the family garage, and Bono's and Mullen's fathers are civil servants. And all of the families tried to help the boys get their fledgling band off the ground.

Early practice sessions, for example, were held in a garden shed behind the Edge's house in the Dublin suburb of Malahide Village. "They were all quite serious about music," recalls Gwenda Evans, the Edge's mom. "They would come here every morning at about ten and really work very hard.

I used to make them lunch. I was amazed that they took it so seriously."

They may have taken their music seriously, but they found that their limited skills made it impossible for them to perform cover versions of songs by bands like Television, Talking Heads or the Patti Smith Group—the artists that they were fond of at the time. So they decided to write their own material.

Even at this early stage, the band began feeling that there was something special about its music. "When people came into our little rehearsals, they were touched by the music," says Bono. "The songs that we wrote really did have that spark, that ability to affect people."

But if they were really going to get the band off the ground, they needed a manager, and the only man they knew of who might be capable of the job was Paul McGuinness. Though his background was essentially in movies—he worked on such feature films as *Zandoz* and *The Great Train Robbery* and directed commercials in Dublin—he had also managed a group called Spud. In fact, he even had landed them a recording contract in Sweden, something of a major accomplishment considering the group's reportedly limited talent.

At first, McGuinness resisted U2's come-ons. They were so persistent, however, that he finally agreed to go see them—so he could tell them once and for all he wasn't interested. But the unexpected happened. "Edge's playing was quite unique," McGuinness recalls. "And Bono, he just looked the audience in the eyes as if to say, 'I dare you to look back.' And all I had ever seen before were performers who looked out over the audience at some imaginary spot. There was something special about them."

So McGuinness was hooked, and he and U2—the band settled on the name after trying out such titles as Feedback and the Hype—set out to get a recording contract. They got favorable write-ups in British music papers like *Sounds* and *New Musical Express*, a result of Bono's canny tactic of personally delivering demo tapes to journalists he felt would be sympathetic to the band's sound. But they had a rough time convincing record-company A&R personnel. After several showcase gigs in London failed to do the trick, the group decided to put together its own tour of Ireland, climaxing with a show in a 2000-seat stadium in Dublin—something no unsigned act had tried before. Bill Stewart, an A&R man for Chris Blackwell's Island Records, caught the show and signed the group.

But it was not the end of the band's rejections. Shortly before U2's first album, *Boy,* was to be released, McGuinness received a letter from the A&R department at Warner Bros. Records, the company that distributed their label, island, in the U.S. "I had sent Warner Bros. a demo tape several months earlier, before we had been signed by Island," McGuinness explains, "and they returned it to me with a curt letter saying they weren't interested in us." So he quickly fired back a response. "I thought they might like to know that they were releasing our album in a few weeks."

"**I FEEL THAT WE ARE MEANT** to be one of the great groups," Bono Vox proclaimed when *Boy* was released in America in early 1981. "There's a certain chemistry that was special about the Stones, the Who and the Beatles, and I think it's also special about U2."

It was certainly a mighty boast, especially coming from the mouth of a twenty-year-old. But the exuberant sound of *Boy* offered a fresh alternative to both the tired, assembly-line rock of bands like Journey and the mindless, head-banging music of some of Britain's second-generation punks. As a result, the album was a big hit with critics, and when U2 came to America for a three-month tour, their energetic stage show solidified their following.

The LP sold nearly 200,000 copies, but U2 was still far from being a chart-topping act in America. So when *October,* the followup to *Boy,* was released early the following year, McGuinness came up with an idea for a promotional gimmick—get the band a float in New York's massive St. Patrick's Day parade. An Irish band. An Irish parade. Hundreds of thousands of people would see them. Genius, right?

Well, not exactly. After McGuinness had made all the arrangements to land the band a spot in the parade, he found out that there was a possibility that the honorary marshal was to be Bobby Sands, the Irish Republican Army (IRA) hunger striker who had starved to death the previous year. Both McGuinness and the members of U2 had grown disillusioned with the incessant fighting between Protestants and Catholics in Northern Ireland and felt the IRA's terror tactics were definitely not helping to bring about peace. Surely, the parade's organizers would understand if the group no longer wanted to take part in the festivities. . . .

So McGuinness called the friend who had helped the band get the float in the first place. The two got together in a bar in New York, but McGuinness soon got in a rather heated debate about the IRA. "He kept telling me to keep my voice down," McGuinness recalls. "The place was full of New York policemen—Irish cops—and he thought I was going to get us killed."

As it turned out, U2 didn't ride up Fifth Avenue on a float. Instead, they played a show at the Ritz, one of New York's rock halls, that St. Patrick's Day. But the whole experience was to have a profound effect on the direction of the band's music.

SEVERAL MONTHS AFTER THAT CONCERT at the Ritz, U2 was onstage in Belfast, the capital of Northern Ireland and the scene of much of that country's violence. Partway through the set, Bono took the mike to introduce a new song.

"Listen, this is called 'Sunday Bloody Sunday.' It's not a rebel song. It's a song of hope and a song of disgust," he told the audience, most of whom no doubt identified the title with the day in 1972 when British troops opened fire on a group of unarmed Catholic demonstrators, killing thirteen of them.

Then Bono read some of the song's lyrics—lines like "Broken bottles under children's feet / Bodies strewn across a dead-end street / But I won't heed the battle call / It puts my back up, my back up against the wall"—before continuing: "We're gonna play it for you here in Belfast. If you don't like it, you let us know." The band pounded into the song, a fierce, crushing rocker, and when they were done, the audience wildly cheered its approval.

"It was very emotional," Larry Mullen says of that first live performance of "Sunday Bloody Sunday," a track on the *War* album. "It's a very special song, because it's the first time that we ever really made a statement."

Indeed, U2's first albums hardly dealt with the kind of subject matter tackled by the songs on *War*. *Boy* was a look at the growing pains of adolescence, while *October*'s compositions had lyrics of a more spiritual nature. It had been the band's experience with IRA supporters in New York that prompted them to write "Sunday Bloody Sunday." (In fact, the original lyrics to the song began, "Don't talk to me about the rights of the IRA.")

"Americans don't understand it," says Mullen, sitting in a hotel restaurant in Glasgow a few hours before the band's show. Normally the most reserved member of the group, the blond-haired drummer takes on an almost Bono-like fervor when discussing the troubles in Northern Ireland. "They call it a 'religious war,' but it has nothing to do with religion. It's like the Dylan song 'With God on Our Side.' During the hunger strikes, the IRA would say, 'God is with me. I went to Mass every Sunday.' And the Unionists [the Protestant majority that favors retaining ties with Britain] said virtually the same thing. And then they'd go out and murder each other. It's very hypocritical."

In fact, the key lines in "Sunday Bloody Sunday"—lines that critics who have viewed the song as purely political have missed—are those at the end: "The real battle just begun / To claim the victory Jesus won / On a Sunday, bloody Sunday."

As the Edge, who initially came up with the idea for the composition, points out, "Sunday Bloody Sunday" is not a song in which U2 takes sides with either faction in Northern Ireland. Instead, it's about the futility of war: "There's many lost," sings Bono. "But tell me who has won?" Though U2's members haven't personally experienced the violence between Catholics and Protestants in the North, they have witnessed the segregation that exists between the two religious groups in their homeland. Indeed, a mixed marriage like that of Bono's parents—his father is Catholic and his mother was Protestant—is still scorned by many Irishmen.

"In their relationship, they were proof that the bitterness between those two communities is ridiculous," Bono says of his parents. "I see in both of their churches aspects of things I don't fully like. But I like to think that I'd be able to go to a Catholic church or a Protestant church."

BONO WAS THE FIRST MEMBER of U2 to embrace Christianity. "When I was very young, I experienced death, and that can wake you up to certain facts," he says, referring to his mother's death when he was fifteen. It was also a death in the family that turned Larry Mullen to God; his mother was killed a few years ago in a motor accident.

But the band members shy away from discussing their beliefs in public. "It's a personal thing," says Mullen. "If you talk to a person about it, you should be telling *him,* not the public at large. It shouldn't be an angle."

"People would love to sensationalize our beliefs until they meant nothing," adds Bono. "Three of us are committed Christians. We refute the belief that man is just a higher stage of animal, that he has no spirit. I think that when people start believing that, the real respect for humanity is gone. You are just a cog in a wheel, another collection of molecules. That's half the reason for a lot of the pessimism in the world."

And though the band members had religious upbringings—Mullen came from a Catholic family, while the Edge and Clayton had Protestant parents—they don't like to refer to their beliefs as a religion per se.

"All religion seems to do is divide," explains the Edge. "I'm really interested in and influenced by the spiritual side of Christianity, rather than the legislative side, the rules and regulations." So the members of U2 aren't regular churchgoers, preferring to meet together in private prayer sessions.

And the money-grabbing preachers who bandy about the name of God on American TV raise their ire. "I turn on the television and see some of those people, and I get really scared," Bono says. "I really want not only to turn the television off, but to throw it out the window. I believe it's tarnishing something that's really strong, really beautiful. And when I say to people that I believe in God, they are often bombarded with images of macho gentlemen in suits, asking for money. And I go, 'What am I up against?' This particular battle is very real."

Adam Clayton is the only non-Christian member of the band, and there was a time last year when the curly-haired bassist feared he might be booted out of the group because he was "the weakest member" and had succumbed to the temptations of rock stardom, becoming "a vicious drunk." But those fears were erased when Bono asked him to be best man at his wedding to school sweetheart Alison Stewart last August.

Clayton still enjoys partaking of some of the vices so common to rock & roll, but he says he has also become more stable and more confident about his reasons for being in U2. "I can remember being confused when I first started playing," he says. "I found it difficult to work out whether the motivation was that I wanted to be *like* somebody in a band or I actually wanted to do something for myself. It took a couple of years before I was big enough *not* to emulate someone else."

As U2 CROSSES AMERICA ON ITS current two-month tour, the real message the band hopes to convey is a musical one. "Music can be more," Bono says. "Its possibilities are great. Music has changed me. It has the ability to change a generation. Look at what happened with Vietnam; music changed a whole generation's attitude toward war." But lately, he feels, music has lost that power.

"I believe that more than any other record, *War* is right for its time," Bono says. "It is a slap in the face against the snap, crackle and pop. Everyone else is getting more and more style-oriented, more and more slick. John Lennon was right about that kind of music; he called it 'wallpaper music.' Very pretty. Very well designed. Music to eat your breakfast to.

"Punk was supposed to be a revolution, but it wasn't a real one," he continues. "It was contrived in many ways, manipulated into a fashion thing. But we believed it. Punk rock fired us into trying to get music back to its roots. And I'd like to see a lot of the garage bands in America revolt. There has to be a garage-band revolution."

Judging from the response to *War*—the album has already sold nearly 500,000 copies and is edging in on the Top Ten—Americans are starting to listen to U2. But along with providing the group a larger audience, success will also put new pressures on the band.

A group whose members are still quite young—Bono and Clayton are twenty-three; the Edge and Mullen are twenty-one—is bound to be impressionable. So far, they have managed to avoid much of the rock & roll circus by opting not to move to London, the center of the British music scene. With the exception of Bono, who lives with his wife in a cottage on a beach in Dublin, the musicians still reside with their families. However, that, too, may change in the near future. "By the end of this year, I finally will be able to tell them that they all have enough money to buy their own houses," says manager McGuinness.

But U2 is not fearful of facing the future. "I think the important thing to retain through life is optimism," says Clayton. "It doesn't have to be something that you necessarily get from Christianity. You just have to feel that way about life."

And they try to project that feeling through their music. "The hope that's in the music comes from the hope that's in the band," says Bono. "I believe it's time to fight back in your spirit—right down deep inside. There is a great faith in this group."

■ **RANDOM NOTES** "SPRINGSTEEN STILL IN STUDIO, CHECKS OUT U2" (July 7, 1983)

The good news is that Bruce Springsteen has finished his new album, according to one reliable report. The bad news is that he doesn't like it and has decided to write more songs for the record. Springsteen and the band are currently holed up in an East Coast studio, hammering out arrangements of the tunes for the much-delayed LP, which at one point was to have been called *Born in the U.S.A.*

Springsteen has found time to contribute two songs to saxman Clarence Clemons' solo LP, produced by Ralph Schuckett. One of the songs is an instrumental, the other a raveup titled "Save It Up." Springsteen also managed to check out U2, who've been putting on some of the best rock shows in recent memory during their U.S. tour. The Boss was in the audience for their Philadelphia gig, at which the Irish band puckishly dedicated their encore to Steel Mill, one of Springsteen's first Jersey bar bands.

■ **RANDOM NOTES** "U2 LIVE: A BIT TOO MUCH" (September 15, 1983)

Here's a switch: U2 lead singer Bono says that the American response to the band's live shows has been so intense that they're going to hold back on the histrionics a bit in dates to come. "Los Angeles brought it to a head," says Bono, whose real name is Paul Hewson. "I lost my senses completely. I was trying to get the crowd to trust us. I went into the crowd with a flag, but I ended up standing on the balcony of the Sports Center. I threatened to jump off if they didn't back off. And, in fact, I did jump. The crowd caught me—but what about the others who followed me? Somebody could have died at that concert, and it was a real sickener for me. It's meant a total reevaluation of what we are about live. We don't need to use a battering ram. It has to be down to the music."

■ **RANDOM NOTES** "BONO BOOSTS ALARM; SINGER TO SERVE IRELAND" (November 10, 1983)

U2 lead singer Bono—who tore the roof off an already incendiary New York show by the Alarm last month with a rendition of Bob Dylan's "Knockin' on Heaven's Door"—has been appointed to a governmental committee by Ireland's prime minister, Garret FitzGerald. "I have this feeling that he wants me there as a troublemaker," says the enthusiastic twenty-three-year-old. "I wrote him a cheeky letter accepting." The committee's task will be to reassess the Irish government's youth policy, especially in light of the country's soaring unemployment problem. Bono has known FitzGerald for a year and a half, ever since he accosted him (FitzGerald was then the leader of the opposition) at Heathrow Airport and tried to engage him in a discussion of Ireland's problems. "I looked like an Iranian terrorist," Bono says, laughing.

Meanwhile, Bono's been busy writing songs for a new album and mixing—with ace boardman Jimmy Iovine—a live LP that'll be issued before year's end.

CHRISTOPHER CONNELLY

UNDER A BLOOD RED SKY
ALBUM REVIEW

★ ★ ★ ★

THIS IRISH BAND'S INCANTATORY power is no more vividly demonstrated than in concert, and this eight-song mini-album, culled from their last tour, gives ample evidence why people have been calling U2 the best live band of 1983. Producer Jimmy Iovine and his chief engineer, Shelly Yakus, have toned down the distorted guitar-and-drums sound of the band's previous boardman; Steve Lillywhite, without sacrificing the sheer rock & roll energy and slashing attack that have already made U2 popular.

Iovine's approach uncovers U2's secret weapon: the versatile, elastic playing of bassist Adam Clayton. Clayton's steady bottom creates the space for guitarist the Edge's dazzling fretboard wails throughout the record. "Gloria," which in its studio version sank under the weight of its overwrought piety, here turns into a blazing rocker, while the Edge's lonesome keyboards bring forth a "New Year's Day" that outstrips its original. But the high point is "Sunday Bloody Sunday." It may not be a rebel song, but it is practically everything else: an anguished, thoughtful synthesis of religious and political beliefs, backed by the bone-crushing arena-rock riff of the decade. This is "Stairway to Heaven" for smart people—even if it is played a tad too fast—and it kicks *Under a Blood Red Sky* over the rainbow.

Through it all; Bono is his ineluctable self, whether he's getting carried away (the "Send in the Clowns" interlude in the otherwise admirable "The Electric Co.") or carrying us away, as on the sweetly elegiac "40." I once saw U2 play "I Will Follow" three times in one set, establishing a never-to-be-broken major-band record for repetition. If I can still enjoy the version on this album, imagine how much you'll like it.

It's definitely a departure," declares U2's guitarist, the Edge, describing the band's fifth album, *The Unforgettable Fire,* due out before the end of the month. "There's an emphasis away from the guitar without losing the aggression." But the Edge—born Dave Evans— notes that the album nevertheless has a weightier slant, which he terms "the politics of the individual. We're pulling at areas that we really have strong feelings about: ones we feel we *can* comment on, that relate to our own situation and the situation of our country." The album includes a few songs about Dr. Martin Luther King Jr.; one of them, "Pride in the Name of Love," will accompany the LP's first video. Edge is quick to credit coproducer Brian Eno with some of the album's aural surprises. One track, tentatively titled "Elvis Presley and America," features an improvised vocal from band frontman Bono Vox. "It was a piece of music that Bono had never heard before. He came into the studio, took a microphone into the control room and sang—and it was such an inspired performance that we decided to leave it as it is." After a couple of weeks of U.S. dates late this year, the group plans a major tour next spring.

KURT LODER

THE UNFORGETTABLE FIRE
ALBUM REVIEW

★ ★ ★

U2 tones down its guitar attack on new LP:
Alliance with Eno yields flawed album

THE TITLE OF U2'S FIFTH ALBUM is perversely suggestive. Over the course of three studio LPs and one live-in-concert item, this stormy Irish guitar band, borne aloft by its grand, anthemic roar and an earnest concern for social issues, had ascended to the verge of substantial rock stardom in this country. Unfortunately, with *The Unforgettable Fire,* U2 flickers and nearly fades, its fire banked by a misconceived production strategy and occasional interludes of soggy, songless self-indulgence. This is not a "bad" album, but neither is it the irrefutable beauty the band's fans anticipated. What happened?

Initially, U2's decision to abandon the pop-conscious ministrations of its previous producers, Steve Lillywhite and Jimmy Iovine, and to hire instead the veteran experimentalist Brian Eno and his current collaborator, Canadian producer Daniel Lanois, seemed not only interesting but also admirably consistent with the band's vaunted idealism. The four members felt artistically constricted by their chart-tested monster-guitar format; the right producer—somebody with serious art credentials—would understand their impasse, would be able to help them grow. It sounded like a brave gamble: art over gold.

But idealism is not art. As a producer—as opposed to a producer-songwriter, the role he played with Talking Heads—Eno is most valuable as a conceptual organizer and sonic strategist, a master of atmospheres. But with guitarist Dave "the Edge" Evans churning out squalls of postpsyche-delic ambience, U2 already had more atmosphere than it really knew what to do with. In that narrow regard, Eno was an unnecessary addition to the team.

A more serious problem was the band's conceptual shortcomings. Like the German producer Conny Plank, another post-Spectorian studio *auteur* (who was also considered for this project), Eno is able to express his own ideas through the artists he produces (or *processes*). But short of co-writing songs, he cannot supply the musicians' art. And what all his masterful marshaling of tribal-style chants, ethnoramic percussion and lush electronic sounds often serves to reveal here, dismayingly enough, is a creative vacuum where the band should be. The album sounds formless and uninhabited.

Actually, that's not entirely true. Singer Bono is certainly at home here—as well he should be, given that his vocals are way out in front in the mix. Lacking consistently strong, well-defined material, the producers attempt to create dynamic tension in the tracks by focusing on discrete musical elements: the rich tone of Adam Clayton's bass, the hypnotic possibilities of Larry Mullen's drum patterns, the subtle symphonic swell of Eno's own synthesizer. And in the process they chop Evans' roaring guitar style into inventive snippets, enriching the mix but draining the band of its fundamental source of power. Bono tries to make up for that loss. His stentorian bellow remains impressive—particularly on "A Sort of Home-coming" and "Pride (In the Name of Love)," the two most successful tracks—and he exhibits a new sense of control (primarily on the title song, in which his fragile, cracked grasp of the falsetto phrase "stay tonight" suggests an engaging vulnerability).

Unfortunately, though, Bono's lyrics are too often a spew of artsy blather, unredeemed even by their own best intentions. Such lines as "True colors fly in blue and black / Through silken sky and burning flak" (from the song "Bad") apparently are intended to convey an image, a poetic truth, about the ravages of war. But the attempted metaphor is hopelessly muddled: If the "blue and black" refers to the traumatized flesh of war's victims, what are they doing flying through the sky? Why a "silken" sky? And on the pointlessly titled "Elvis Presley & America," Bono indulges in that most ancient of artsy pretensions, the on-the-spot improvisation, and delivers himself of some one-take babbling that makes the onstage effusions of, say, Patti Smith seem, in retrospect, paragons of spontaneous clarity.

One would like to be able to summon praise for such well-intentioned tracks as "Pride (In the Name of Love)," which was inspired by Martin Luther King, and "MLK," which appropriates King's initials for its title. But "Pride" gets over only on the strength of its resounding beat (a U2 trade-mark) and big, droning bass line, not on the nobility of its lyrics, which are unremarkable. And "MLK," a pensively pretty studio concoction, consists of one verse, sung twice, which begins, "Sleep, sleep tonight / And may your dreams be realized." An admirable sentiment, of course, but Bono brings no artistic illumination to it.

The Unforgettable Fire seems to drone on and on, an endless flurry of chinkety guitar scratching, state-of-the-art sound processing and the most mundane sort of lyrical imagery (barbed wire is a big concept). U2's original power flickers through only intermittently. When it does, though, you can forgive them the uncharacteristic flounderings found here (among a few memorable tracks) and hope they won't forget where their real fire lies the next time out.

KURT LODER

YEAR-END REVIEW OF
THE UNFORGETTABLE FIRE

At the end of 1984, ROLLING STONE editors looked
back at the important releases of the past
12 months.

LOOKING FOR A WAY OUT OF its big-guitar-band box, Ireland's U2 brought in experimentalist producer Brian Eno to oversee the group's fifth LP. This was a bold move, but not a successful one. The result is not even particularly "experimental," only disjointed. "Pride (In the Name of Love)" and "A Sort of Homecoming" have a big, resounding sound—which is what one would normally expect of U2—and ultimately draw you in; but most of the rest of this record is a muddle. The problem is not the production, it's the concept: by chopping Dave "the Edge" Evans' roaring guitar into inventive snippets, U2 sliced the heart out of its sound without finding anything to replace it. Despite the mightiest rhythmic endeavors of bassist Adam Clayton and drummer Larry Mullen, these sonic gropings never quite cohere into songs. The lyrics, by Bono, the band's powerful singer, are self-indulgent and scattered—in particular the pretentiously titled "Elvis Presley & America," an on-the-spot vocal improvisation that should have been run past the erase heads. And while one understands that these lads love peace, their allusions to Martin Luther King on two tracks amount to little more than well-intentioned name-dropping. Ideals are not art. They're not ground-breaking music, either.

TOP 100 ALBUMS OF 1984

December 20, 1984

In ROLLING STONE's annual survey of the year's best-selling albums, U2 entered the chart for the first time—with not one, but three recordings. *(The following chart is based on a nationwide telephone survey of record stores.)*

1 PRINCE AND THE REVOLUTION
Purple Rain—WB

2 BRUCE SPRINGSTEEN
Born in the U.S.A.—Columbia

3 LIONEL RICHIE
Can't Slow Down—Motown

4 MICHAEL JACKSON
Thriller—Epic

5 FOOTLOOSE
Soundtrack—Columbia

6 CYNDI LAUPER
She's So Unusual—Portrait/CBS

7 HUEY LEWIS AND THE NEWS
Sports—Chrysalis

8 VAN HALEN
1984—WB

9 TINA TURNER
Private Dancer—Capitol

10 BILLY JOEL
An Innocent Man—Columbia

11 CULTURE CLUB
Colour by Numbers—Virgin/Epic

12 THE CARS
Heartbeat City—Elektra/Asylum

13 MADONNA
Madonna—Sire

14 THE PRETENDERS
Learning to Crawl—Sire

15 BILLY IDOL
Rebel Yell—Chrysalis

16 ZZ TOP
Terminator—WB

17 THE POINTER SISTERS
Break Out—Planet/RCA

18 EURYTHMICS
Touch—RCA

19 THOMPSON TWINS
Into the Gap—Arista

20 THE SCORPIONS
First Sting—Mercury

21 LINDA RONSTADT
What's New—Asylum

22 RATT
Out of the Cellar—Atlantic

23 THE BIG CHILL
Soundtrack—Motown

24 THE POLICE
Synchronicity—A&M

25 JOHN COUGAR MELLENCAMP
Uh-Huh—Riva

26 EDDIE AND THE CRUISERS
Soundtrack—Scotti Bros./Epic

27 GHOSTBUSTERS
Soundtrack—Arista

28 HALL AND OATES
Rock 'n Soul, Pt. 1—RCA

29 GENESIS
Genesis—Atlantic

30 MÖTLEY CRÜE
Shout at the Devil—Elektra

31 HERBIE HANCOCK
Future Shock—Columbia

32 TWISTED SISTER
Stay Hungry—Atlantic

33 STEVIE RAY VAUGHAN
Couldn't Stand the Weather—Epic

34 THE JACKSONS
Victory—Epic

35 R.E.M.
Reckoning—I.R.S.

36 NIGHT RANGER
Midnight Madness—MCA

37 JOE JACKSON
Body and Soul—A&M

38 QUIET RIOT
Metal Health—Pasha/CBS

39 JULIO IGLESIAS
1100 Bel Air Place—Columbia

40 CHICAGO
Chicago 17—Full Moon/WB

41 LOU REED
New Sensations—RCA

42 PRINCE AND THE REVOLUTION
1999—WB

43 TALKING HEADS
Speaking in Tongues—Sire

44 ELTON JOHN
Too Low for Zero—Geffen

45 JEFFREY OSBORNE
Stay With Me Tonight—A&M

46 GEORGE WINSTON
December—Windham Hill

STEVE POND

PERFORMANCE REVIEW

Though they've cut out some of the theatrics,
Bono and crew remain as compelling as ever

THE IRISH BAND U2 HAD QUITE an act to follow when it touched down in the Los Angeles area on December 16th. That act was U2—specifically, the memory of the astounding show the group put on when it last played L.A. eighteen months ago.

Back then, lead singer Bono made the mistake of tacitly encouraging fans who jumped onstage; when they got out of hand, he asked them to stay put, then realized he'd irritated some of the crowd. Finally, to regain their faith, he made his way through the L.A. Sports Arena's loge section and then dropped a good ten feet into the arms of a seething mass of fans waiting to catch him. It was a remarkable, foolhardy display on the part of a performer determined to batter his way into an all-encompassing fan-performer trust; he didn't kill himself, and it made for a piece of riveting theater, but it was the kind of thing one wouldn't want him to do again.

Apparently U2 felt the same way: when the group wrapped up the first leg of its American tour at the Long Beach Arena, Bono stayed on the stage, and the band delivered a set that was less dramatic than the one in 1983. It was a wise move, because if there's one thing U2 doesn't need to rely on, it's an exaggerated performing style. Much of the group's music possesses a rather larger-than-life quality to begin with: the Edge's echoing, bravura guitar lines and Bono's deep-voiced delivery turn a song like "I Will Follow" and the stunning "October"/"New Year's Day" medley into majestic battle cries that hardly require any flag-waving reinforcement.

At the same time, the Long Beach show was part of a tour designed to support a new album, *The Unforgettable Fire,* that is deliberately less rousing and more quietly insinuating than the band's previous works. U2 performed half a dozen songs from that LP in the ninety-minute concert, dropping old favorites like "Out of Control" and "Two Hearts Beat as One." Surprisingly, the new material didn't seem out of place. "Pride (In the Name of Love)" and "Bad" were stretched out into showpieces every bit as rousing as the group's earlier songs, while "MLK" and "A Sort of Homecoming" became deliciously full-bodied reveries.

The new U2 show is not as much of a musical departure for the band as is the new U2 album; after all, in a live setting, blunt force usually works better than subtlety, especially when you're dealing with the simple but right-minded politics of "Sunday Bloody Sunday" or, for that matter, Band Aid's "Do They Know It's Christmas," a chorus of which Bono slipped into the closing song, "40." In the end, this performance proved that U2 has retained the urgency and commitment that make its concerts the most honestly touching and gripping rock shows this side of Bruce Springsteen's. If there were an Idealistic Anthemic Rock Band Sweepstakes, Bono and crew could blow the doors off newcomers like Big Country. In fact, they didn't even do too badly when compared to their last trip through town.

CHRISTOPHER CONNELLY

KEEPING THE FAITH

Pop may be king, but U2 has attracted a fanatical
following by playing thunderous rock & roll and by
addressing such topics as God and politics

THE RAMADA INN OF DÜSSELDORF, WEST GERMANY, stands on the
outskirts of town amid a host of low-slung corporate buildings: a
tall, sleek, bloodless base for junior industrialists away from home.
It's hard to imagine a place farther removed from the gritty, red-brick bustle
of U2's hometown, Dublin. Consider, then, the surprise of drummer Larry
Mullen Jr. as he snacked on some biscuits and tea in the hotel's bar one
morning. There in front of him was Ronnie Drew, the craggy-faced singer
for one of Ireland's most popular groups, the Dubliners. The fiftyish Drew,
rather an *éminence grise* of traditional Irish folk music, could hardly be
mistaken for a rock & roll buff—yet as he pulled up a chair next to Mullen,
he was quick to express his regard for the work of U2.

"Oh, you're a great band," Ronnie told Larry. "My kids just think
you're the greatest, have all your records, listen to them all the time. Yeah,
the kids love ya." They chatted briefly before Ronnie got up to leave. "You
know," he said gravely, "it would be a great honor if I could tell them that
you bought me a drink."

IN AMERICA, THEIR NAMES ARE not household words, and their faces
are unfamiliar even to some of their fans. They have yet to notch a
Top Ten album or single. Only now are they beginning to tour arena-sized
venues. But for a growing number of rock & roll fans, U2—vocalist Paul
"Bono" Hewson, 24; guitarist Dave "the Edge" Evans, 22; bassist Adam
Clayton, 24; and drummer Larry Mullen Jr., 22—has become the band that
matters most, maybe even the *only* band that matters. It's no coincidence
that U2 sells more T-shirts and merchandise than groups that sell twice as
many records, or that four of U2's five albums are currently on *Billboard*'s
Top 200. The group has become one of the handful of artists in rock & roll
history (the Who, the Grateful Dead, Bruce Springsteen) that people are
eager to identify themselves with. And they've done it not just with their

music but with a larger message as well—by singing "Pride (In the Name of Love)" while most other groups sing about pride in the act of love.

On record, U2's thunderous sound (developed with help from producer Steve Lillywhite) turned heads from the beginning. Instead of copping the straight-ahead squall of the Ramones and the Sex Pistols, U2 cast the brash, heroic spirit of punk in a new image. Their sound was echoey and atmospheric, while their lyrics were more attuned to the grayer areas of human existence. In 1981, the band's first LP, *Boy,* established a U.S. beachhead thanks to "I Will Follow," a keening single that found a home on college radio. *Boy*'s successor, *October,* was written and recorded in a mad dash after Bono's book of lyrics was stolen; it sold poorly.

U2's American breakthrough came with 1983's *War,* which marshaled the sounds of militarism—rat-a-tat-tat drums, savage guitar work, defiant vocals—in the service of pacifism, albeit a pacifism ready to wage moral battle with its enemies. Such songs as "New Year's Day" (about the Soviet domination of Poland) and "Sunday Bloody Sunday" (about a massacre of civilians by the British in Northern Ireland) became album-radio staples, and the LP sold over a million copies. U2's live shows had always drawn fervent audiences, but now Bono solidified the success of *War* by crystallizing its messages onstage in bold physical images. His most memorable gesture was brandishing a white flag—what he termed "a flag drained of all color"—during "Sunday Bloody Sunday," as if to say that in war, surrender was the bravest course. It was no wonder that *War*'s follow-up, a live mini-LP entitled *Under a Blood Red Sky,* also earned the group a gold album.

The band's appeal doesn't seem to be sexual: no member of U2 appears to have seen the inside of a health club or a New Wave haberdashery, and only Mullen could pass for a Cute Guy. U2's strength, it seems, goes deeper. Like most rock & roll bands, U2 articulates, at top volume, the alienation that young people can feel from their country, their hometown, their family, their sexuality. Like some of the best rock & roll bands, U2 also shows how that alienation might be overcome. But unlike anyone else in rock & roll, U2 also addresses the most ignored—and most volatile—area of inquiry: alienation from religion.

"Sadomasochism is not taboo in rock & roll," notes Bono. "Spirituality is." Indeed, when religion in America seems sadly synonymous with political conservatism and with the electronic evangelism of Jimmy Swaggart and Jerry Falwell, U2 dares to proclaim its belief in Christianity—at top volume—while grappling with the ramifications of its faith. Each member is careful to avoid discussing the specifics of his beliefs (the perfectly amiable Mullen, in fact, customarily declines to give interviews), and the band's musical message is hardly a proselytizing one. But even to raise the issue, to suggest that a person who loves rock & roll can unashamedly find peace with God as well, is a powerful statement. This is a band that onstage and offstage seems guided by a philosophy not included in such yuppie maxims as "feeling good" and "go for it": not how *might* we live our lives (what we can get away with), but how *ought* we to live our lives.

Lofty goals—but while the promise of U2's records has always been great, it is a promise that remains largely unfulfilled. In the past year and a half, U2 has found itself faced with several critical decisions: artistic, financial, personal, even patriotic. Each choice represented a test of whether the band could continue to articulate its message and fulfill its promise without drowning in contradictions. And while the outcome isn't settled yet, U2 seems to have come through its crises in good shape—due in large part, perhaps, to the band members' willingness to acknowledge their own weaknesses.

"It interests me that I'm portrayed as some sort of strong man," says Bono with genuine perplexity. "I don't see myself in that way. I know my weaknesses. When I see the albums, I don't see them as anthemic. I think that's what's uplifting, that's what connects with people. I think people relate to U2 because they've seen us fall on our face so many times."

CLAD FROM HEAD TO FOOT IN his usual color—black—Bono sat in the downstairs bar at a London hotel last November, merrily bouncing Edge's five-month-old daughter, Hollie, on his lap. In a few hours, U2 would head to Düsseldorf, where the band had been booked to perform at Rock Pop, a concert festival in nearby Dortmund that would be filmed and shown to much of Western Europe. The one-show tour would allow the band to rest up while giving it one more shot at breaking in West Germany—a land where Bono had once told a less-than-delirious audience, "In my country, it's customary to clap."

As Hollie gurgled approvingly, Bono read aloud from "The Rime of the Ancient Marincr," U2 being the sort of band that takes *The Oxford Companion to English Literature* along on tour. His road-ravaged voice was clear and suitably melodramatic, but by the third stanza, Hollie was grabbing for something round and shiny on the table in front of them. "Money," explained Bono to the tot. "That's what all the trouble's about."

He knew. At the beginning of 1984, the band not only had to hire a producer for the album that became *The Unforgettable Fire,* but it also began negotiating a new record contract. It was the latter choice that provoked more dread. "The greatest threat to the career of this band, or any other band," Edge had declared, "is financial success."

But choosing a producer to replace Steve Lillywhite came first. U2 had enjoyed working with Jimmy Iovine, who had offered to produce *Under a Blood Red Sky* for next to nothing just for the chance to work with U2. Paul McGuinness, the group's savvy manager, liked Iovine's commercially proven skills, but the band members chose the duo of Brian Eno and Daniel Lanois.

"We decided that the music should decide," explained Bono. "And we made some music, and we could see that it was a more abstract—dare I say it, *ambient*—record that we were going to make. And who better?" Who indeed? But Eno and Lanois kept U2 from harnessing its talents into compact, concise rock & roll songs and instead encouraged the group to preserve its more inchoate creations just as they were. Some of *The Unforgettable Fire* has an unfinished, slapdash quality, while other tracks—"A Sort of Homecoming," for example—seem fussy and unfocused.

Few listeners, though, had anything bad to say about the LP's stirring paean to Martin Luther King, "Pride (In the Name of Love)." Reaching the Top Twenty, it became U2's most successful single ever and helped to boost *The Unforgettable Fire*—named for a series of harrowing paintings drawn by survivors of Hiroshima and Nagasaki—into the Top Fifteen. The LP was not the commercial smasheroo that some had hoped for, but that is quite all right with everyone in the U2 camp. They followed their muse, and they have no regrets.

Also in '84, McGuinness negotiated an extraordinarily lucrative extension of the group's pact with Island Records. Almost overnight, four lads from Dublin became wildly rich, certainly millionaires.

Bono chafed when he talked about it. "I don't know. I don't have a million dollars in my pocket or in my bank account. I don't want to say that money is not important to me, because it is disgusting for me to say that at a time when a lot of people don't have money. So I'm thankful that I don't have to worry about my next meal. It is a threat to the band, because I don't want anything to take away from our focus. But I just don't want to see it."

IT WAS ONE IN THE MORNING IN Düsseldorf when Bono—his busby of black hair tucked under a hat—rested his boot-clad feet on a chair in his hotel room, opened a beer and talked about how he'd gotten here.

"We grew up on a street where people got a job, got married, had children . . . and *died*. And went to the pub. We'd meet a guy, he'd say, 'Drinking? Oh yeah, drinking Thursday night, drinking Friday night, drinking Saturday night, drinking Sunday morning after Mass, drinking Sunday night. Back to the jar on Tuesday night.' We would *see* this. And we just said, 'We will not become a part of this.' "

He was christened Paul Hewson, the second son of a Protestant mother and a Catholic father. His nickname—originally Bono Vox, though he spurns the second name nowadays—was hung on him by Guggi, a guy in his gang (Guggi's younger brother appeared on the *War* cover). To this day, Bono isn't sure what "Bono Vox" referred to, though his gift for gab may have had something to do with it. The nickname was just a way to fit in, really, alongside Clive Whistling Fellow and Man-of-Strength Arran and Guck Pants Delaney and Little Biddy One-Way Street and all the rest of the restless Irish kids who hung out on the streets of Ballymun, a district within Dublin. "We were this gang of *nut cases,*" Bono recalled. "We'd get electric drills, a saw, a hose, a sweeping brush, and just go into the heart of the city, in the street, and put on a performance. Just make it up on the spot. We kind of had our own way. We were very extreme in our alternatives."

Bono's early days were trouble-free. "I never suffered under Roman Catholicism," he said. "I never suffered under Protestantism. I never suffered under anything. I just grew up." His family even sent him to a nondenominational public school. His placid domestic life changed at age fifteen, though, when his mother died. "It was no longer a home; it was just a house," he recalled. "There were these three men: my father, my older brother and myself. And I was *such* a bastard. I used to fight a lot with my brother. In fact, I think there's still blood on the kitchen wall. I threw a knife at him once, actually. I missed.

"But my father had some incredible strength—and when his wife died, he didn't give in. He fought against it, he kept the house, he wouldn't let it go down. You can imagine three guys living in a house. It could go over. He wasn't letting it go. But I was."

The rage spilled over in school. But instead of making Bono cynical, the death of his mother fostered religious faith in him. He started seeing the finest cutups of his generation piddling away their wit and abilities, just as they had vowed not to. "Some really talented people started getting into drugs and dying. When you see somebody who has so much end up with so little, that can really upset you." The performance art of his early adolescence had hardened into an elitism. "I felt we were laughing at the same jokes as the years went by, and I backed off."

He remembered his promise to find a life outside what he saw around him, and he discovered rock & roll. He left some of his friends behind. "They still live on those extremes," Bono said. "Still go into pubs in order to get thrown out. But that's the kind of background of the group. That's where we come from."

"WE COULDN'T REALLY SAY we were an indigenous part of Bono's upbringing," declared Adam Clayton, as he and Edge sipped brandies in their hotel room one night later, the night before their concert. "We were accepted but we weren't the innovators."

Within the context of U2, the pair seem polar opposites. The English-born Clayton has blond, curly hair and a body that tends toward the mildly rotund, and is given to easy laughter, bon mots and even—gasp!—the occasional rock & roll indulgence. Edge has the wise, slightly sad face of an Irish shopkeeper, keeps his shirts buttoned to the neck, is soft-spoken but musically daring and seems possessed of an infinite store of dignity—a most unusual trait in a rock performer. The two have been close friends since their earliest days.

"The reason for being in a band initially was purely satisfaction," continued Edge, an acknowledged whiz kid academically. "Having started for that reason, we started writing songs, we started doing things. And our academic careers just went out the window. Because we suddenly realized that this was important to us."

"We would spend weekends watching telly and not mixing with people," recalled Adam, "because we weren't interested in girls and we weren't interested in getting drunk. So when somebody said, 'Let's form a band,' we thought of it as something to do with people we wanted to be with."

"I think it was an actual passion for playing music," said Edge. What galvanized the band musically was, of course, punk: Television, the Stranglers, Patti Smith. From the start, though, the band saw themselves as tied neither to American rock & roll nor to a cooler, European sound. They saw their rootlessness as both a strength and a weakness. But what truly made the band special—what would attract the attention of their manager-to-be, Paul McGuinness—was the lead singer.

"I think he did something which not many others did," recalled Edge, "and that was confront a crowd. Around that era, most bands were basically as good as their material. Bono was different. He went out there and he *assumed* this importance and this character and eyed the audience and was totally impressive—even though nothing behind him backed him up."

The group cut its teeth by playing opening gigs for a host of Irish bands whose names are largely lost to history. After winning a rock-band contest, U2 was signed to an Ireland-only deal by CBS, which issued the group's first record, a three-song EP called *U23*. CBS, though, declined to ink the band to a worldwide deal, and so the ever-energetic Bono took to passing out tapes of U2's performances to sympathetic journalists. The resultant buzz made its way to Island Records, which signed the group in 1980.

The years since have brought many changes for Adam and Edge—personal as well as professional. "We started working at the age of sixteen, roughly, up until now, when I'm twenty-four," said Adam, "and in that period we've seen an awful lot of the world, relatively little of our families, and have had absolutely no private life. I think there is a point where you sort of react against that. Now we're getting to a stage where we're defining our own personalities much more strongly. Edge is married, he has a child. Bono is married. You know, it's a different situation than what we were like eight years ago, just starting out. You have to face facts, but not see it as a threat to the band.''

Adam's private life—he is the one member of the band who is not avowedly religious—did cause some controversy. "In fact, I wasn't being really bad, I was being normal. But in the context of the story, the rock star with these clean-living people.''

"I would say there was an effort on your part to establish your own identity," Edge responded. "You're not a man who takes things to excess." Whatever Adam's past reputation, times have changed. "In fact, if the truth be known," said Edge, with a gleam in his eye, "Adam is such a boring old fart at this stage, it's myself and Bono that are hauled out of the nightclubs at two in the morning while Adam is home sleeping with his feet on a hot-water bottle. He's prematurely aged.''

Edge was kidding about himself, though. "Drugs, and the whole idea of smoking dope and getting absolutely drunk, seemed to me like an unjustifiable activity. The whole drug culture is a criminal thing; the same guys who deal the marijuana are the guys who deal heroin, who break people's legs, who get thirteen-year-olds hooked. I felt no attraction to that side of it." He paused. "Now, Adam, having no particularly strong moral standpoint . . .''

You could barely hear Edge talking over Clayton's laughter. "I mean, that story about Adam and the *corpse* in that Holiday Inn . . .''

D ESPITE THE BAND'S DEMOCRATIC structure, Bono has remained the group's primary lightning rod, the focal point for much of the criticism leveled at the band. And as he was pointing out over breakfast the next morning, he can get into some pretty hot water at times—like when he appeared onstage near Dublin with Bob Dylan. "He took me to the side of the stage and said, 'You know the words to "Leopardskin Pill-Box Hat"?' And I said yes. I was lying.

"So I came onstage and just sang. And I think a lot of people were very unimpressed by my performance." He howled with laughter for a moment. "I left the stage, and I said, 'Oh, God, what have I done?' And then Dylan's son came over and said, 'Listen, Bob would like you to close the show. He'd like you to sing "Blowin' in the Wind." ' He obviously figured I knew the words to 'Blowin' in the Wind.'

"I went out there, and Dylan sang all the verses I knew, so it was either go back and begin the song again or go forward—and I decided to forget it, and I just wrote this other verse. In the middle of this, Dylan turned round and said to his bass player, 'What key are we in?' 'Cause I'd changed the tune as well as the words.

"Well, the papers hung me from a tree the next day. And while I was driving through Dublin, I was stopped at the lights, and these two guys came up to me. And I rolled down the window, and one of them stuck his head in the car and started looking around, as Irishmen are given to do. He says, 'How are you, Bono?' And I say, 'How are you?' He says, 'I saw you up on the park with Dylan.' And I say, 'Oh, yeah?' He says, 'What were you *playin'* up there? *Jay-sus,* you were *way* off the mark.' "

That remark notwithstanding, U2 is generally respected for being one of the first Irish groups to remain in the Emerald Isle after hitting it big—and has come to be associated with Ireland by many. The band has taken great pains to avoid getting politically pigeonholed, especially with regard to the troubles in Northern Ireland. But last year, Bono was forced to "put my body where my mouth was" when Irish prime minister Garret FitzGerald, with whom Bono had had a running correspondence, asked the singer to serve on a government committee on unemployment.

Bono accepted—but the experience was ultimately disillusioning . . . and revealing. "There were good people there, you know," he said, "but there was another language I had to come up with, which is committee-speak.

"I realized that"—he exhaled deeply—"there *is* a battle, as I see it, between good and evil, and I think you've got to find your place in that. It may be on a factory floor, or it may be writing songs. When you're there—when you're where you should be and you know it in your heart—*that* is when you're involved. It may be trite looking back on it; you know, 'I can't change the world, but I can change a world in me.'

"But for me, that's what it comes down to: finding your place. I could go off and do all these things and right wrongs and go into a committee, but that's not where I am. I'm realizing I've got to find where I am. I'm the type of person who will get involved in anything. And I'm learning how to say no now."

For Bono, that occasionally meant saying no to his public as well. In the band's early days, he avidly sought out members of the audience after a show: to swap stories, have a beer or two, even go back to their houses. "I used to think that was because they were waiting around for two hours and I ought to do it. I realize now it's because *I* needed it."

The band's increasing fame has altered U2's unusually close personal relationship with its public, Bono said. "Now, when I go out, people aren't relating to *me,* they're relating to me as some sort of pop star. And so I go back to this place, and a hotel room can be a real prison cell at times. I can understand how a lot of people get into drugs. But I'm lucky because I have a lot more in my life than just that to hold me up."

What keeps him going? His family, his faith—and his belief in the importance of his art. "So much in rock & roll is instinct and gut," he said, after the band boarded a plane bound for Dublin. "I talk about it, and we talk about it, and we try to define the indefinable. God, it all gets down to one thing. I know it does. We feel that there's a rare spirit to the band, and we've spent the last five years trying to develop it and protect it at the same time. It's the *songs* we serve. That is our complete goal. If your ambition is for fame and fortune and you achieve that, you are then ambition*less* and you've come to the end. But that's not what we are.

"We have this light in the distance. I don't know what it is, a musical goal or what. But we're certain that we're going toward it. We're always arguing with each other and pushing people out of the way so we can get there. But it's for the *music,* it's not for the other things."

O N A WIND-WHIPPED DUBLIN EVENING, Bono sat sipping beers at the Docker, a riverfront pub just a block away from Windmill Lane, where U2's business office is located. Around him was an assortment of Eire's finest: the country's top television-commercial director, a couple of chatty colleens and about four barkeeps (all named Joe), plus a visitor from America. They were tucked into a little alcove just off the front door, and the visitor didn't *think* they were making a lot of noise until he found out later that two burglars had pried open the locked cellar door while they were talking. Eventually, Bono looked up from his pint and decided to show his U.S. guest a bit of the neighborhood.

He drove his visitor past the boarded-up docks along the river Liffey, docks once used by the Guinness brewery until the company moved its operation eastward fifteen years ago. Times have been lean since, he said. They pulled up at the Grand Canal; the G was missing from its large sign: WELCOME TO THE RAND CANAL.

It was dusk, and the wind was blowing with such authority that it was hard to hear Bono talking after they climbed out of his car. As the occasional young boy or stray dog trotted past, Bono started pointing out some of the sights, silhouetted against the darkening November sky. Look, he said, there's the bakery where the 1916 Easter Rebellion began; there's a factory that won an architectural prize in the 1940s but lies dormant today. He once joked to his wife, Ali, that they could move in there, and he still dreams of turning it into a museum.

He led the American across some of the tiny footbridges that cross the canal, then pointed out a row of three-story apartment buildings in the Irishtown district. He said he'd just finished writing a song called "I Don't Live in Irishtown." "It's about a man who isn't Protestant or Catholic, English or Irish."

He kept talking as the pair crossed another bridge. "During 'Pride,' I came out here with Chris," he said, referring to Chrissie Hynde, who sang backup vocals on the song. "We looked down into the water, and we saw this fish, and we saw this great big eel [going after it]. We wondered: Should we interfere with the course of nature?"

And?

"We threw a rock at the eel, and it swam away."

The American asked him about a brightly lit bridge in the distance, with cars and trucks whizzing across it. "It's brand-new," he said. "They call it the East Link. It's never been there before."

He walked around and thought for a moment. "People are interested in bridges," he sighed. "I guess I've always been more interested in what goes on underneath bridges."

JAMES HENKE

WIDE AWAKE IN AMERICA
ALBUM REVIEW★

LIKE *UNDER A BLOOD RED SKY*, this four-cut mini-LP is intended as a sort of U2 tour memento. It contains two live tracks and two outtakes from *The Unforgettable Fire*, and it carries a list price of only $4.98. But while *Under a Blood Red Sky* served a slightly deeper purpose—it was the group's first live record, and it capped a stage in U2's evolution as a band—*Wide Awake in America* is more a curio that will be of interest primarily to die-hard fans.

U2 has always been the kind of group that reinvents its songs onstage—tearing them apart, stretching them out, giving them an entirely different feel—and never was that tendency more apparent than on the *Unforgettable Fire* tour. Even the harshest critics of that atmospheric, out-of-focus LP had to admit that, onstage, the songs suddenly made sense. "Bad," one of the live cuts here, seemed to benefit the most from that album-to-stage transformation. On *The Unforgettable Fire,* the song is a one-dimensional mood piece; in concert, though, it became a showstopper, gradually building from its swirling keyboard intro to a droning, two-chord throb punctuated by the urgent screams of the group's lead singer, Bono. (In this case, the change may have been due to Bono's realization, after he'd written the song, that it was about heroin; during the tour, he frequently dedicated it to a friend from Dublin who had died of an overdose.) "A Sort of Homecoming" also has a harder edge in this live version, which was produced by Tony Visconti. Both Adam Clayton's bass and the Edge's guitar are more predominant in this mix, which is considerably cleaner than the studio LP's murky mess.

It's fairly obvious why the remaining two tracks didn't make it onto *The Unforgettable Fire*. With its prayerlike opening verse and its occasional bursts of Jimi Hendrix-style guitar pyrotechnics from the Edge, "Three Sunrises" sounds like it would have been more at home on *War,* while "Love Comes Tumbling," a beautiful, lilting ballad, is of relatively minor significance.

★Note: ROLLING STONE eliminated its star rating system for record reviews from April 25, 1985, to January 28, 1988.

Perhaps my greatest misgiving about *Wide Awake in America,* though, concerns its title. The reference is to a line from "Bad," but the implication—that the songs were recorded during the U.S. portion of the group's tour—is misleading. Both "Bad" and "A Sort of Homecoming" were recorded in England, not America.

DAVID FRICKE

U2 TO HELP AMNESTY INTERNATIONAL CELEBRATE BIRTHDAY

AMNESTY INTERNATIONAL, the nonprofit human-rights organization, will celebrate its twenty-fifth anniversary next year with a series of benefit concerts in the U.S., starring U2. The shows, tentatively scheduled for next summer, will also feature Simple Minds. Amnesty International officials are now meeting with top music-industry figures, including promoter Bill Graham and A&M Records president Gil Friesen, to recruit more acts for the shows and to secure concert sites. They also hope to meet with Band Aid's Bob Geldof and USA for Africa's Ken Kragen to discuss their benefit experiences.

"U2 has agreed to put themselves at our disposal for a week," said Mary Daly, communications director for Amnesty International USA, the organization's American chapter. "We approached them about doing one concert for the anniversary. But they responded with an enormous amount of enthusiasm." Last December, U2 donated proceeds from a concert at New York's Radio City Music Hall to Amnesty.

Daly said the organization hopes to raise $1 million from the concerts.

■ RANDOM NOTES (November 21, 1985)

U2's Bono contributed his vox to the next album by the Irish folk band Clannad.

■ RANDOM NOTES (December 5, 1985)

U2's management says that someone pretending to be U2 drummer Larry Mullen Jr. has been doing radio interviews.

■ YEAR-END RANDOM NOTES (December 19, 1985–January 2, 1986)

A major contender for the Band of the Eighties crown, U2 made a lot of money and a lot of friends throughout its 1985 sellout tour of North American arenas. Inspired by Bono's heroic, soaring tenor and the orchestral ring of the Edge's stabbing guitar, the band gave uplifting performances, highlighted by lengthy meditations on the bleak, relentless "Bad," during which Bono often quoted, with electric fervor, from the Rolling Stones' songs "Ruby Tuesday" and "Sympathy for the Devil."

"I think U2 are interesting because they are one of the few bands who seem to be able to hold a large stadium crowd. Bono wears his heart on his sleeve, and he creates inspiration and uplift through that. But when you've got the energy to touch all those people, you should make that your first priority and leave social work to people who are my age. I wouldn't like to see U2 burn out because they take too many of the world's problems on their shoulders. They're very compassionate. I think what Bono has to realize pretty soon is that no one man can do it all." **—Pete Townshend**

TOP 100 ALBUMS OF 1985

December 19, 1985–January 2, 1986

In ROLLING STONE's survey of 1985's best-selling albums, U2 entered the chart twice, with *The Unforgettable Fire* making an appearance for the second year in a row.

1 BRUCE SPRINGSTEEN
Born in the U.S.A.—Columbia

2 MADONNA
Like a Virgin—Sire

3 PHIL COLLINS
No Jacket Required—Atlantic

4 WHAM!
Make It Big—Columbia

5 USA FOR AFRICA
We Are the World—Columbia

6 TINA TURNER
Private Dancer—Capitol

7 DIRE STRAITS
Brothers in Arms—WB

8 TEARS FOR FEARS
Songs from the Big Chair—Mercury/Polygram

9 WHITNEY HOUSTON
Whitney Houston—Arista

10 PRINCE AND THE REVOLUTION
Around the World in a Day—Paisley Park/WB

11 BEVERLY HILLS COP
Soundtrack—MCA

12 BILLY OCEAN
Suddenly—Jive/Arista

13 SADE
Diamond Life—Portrait/CBS

14 JOHN FOGERTY
Centerfield—WB

15 STING
The Dream of the Blue Turtles—A&M

16 BRYAN ADAMS
Reckless—A&M

17 DON HENLEY
Building the Perfect Beast—Geffen

18 KOOL AND THE GANG
Emergency—De-Lite/Polygram

19 FREDDIE JACKSON
Rock Me Tonight—Capitol

20 MÖTLEY CRÜE
Theatre of Pain—Elektra

21 EURYTHMICS
Be Yourself Tonight—RCA

22 LUTHER VANDROSS
The Night I Fell in Love—Epic

23 JOHN COUGAR MELLENCAMP
Scarecrow—Riva/Polygram

24 TALKING HEADS
Little Creatures—Sire

25 HOWARD JONES
Dream into Action—Elektra

26 ARETHA FRANKLIN
Who's Zoomin' Who?—Arista

27 PRINCE AND THE REVOLUTION
Purple Rain—WB

28 HUEY LEWIS AND THE NEWS
Sports—Chrysalis

29 TALKING HEADS
Stop Making Sense—Sire

30 THE POWER STATION
The Power Station—Capitol

31 TEENA MARIE
Starchild—Epic

32 DAVID LEE ROTH
Crazy from the Heat—WB

33 'TIL TUESDAY
Voices Carry—Epic

34 MICK JAGGER
She's the Boss—Columbia

35 REO SPEEDWAGON
Wheels Are Turnin'—Epic

36 JULIAN LENNON
Valotte—Atlantic

37 THE POINTER SISTERS
Break Out—Planet/RCA

38 STEVIE WONDER
In Square Circle—Tamla

39 MIAMI VICE
Music from the Television Series—MCA

40 BILLY JOEL
Greatest Hits Volumes I and II—Columbia

41 R.E.M.
Fables of the Reconstruction—I.R.S.

42 BOB DYLAN
Empire Burlesque—Columbia

43 ERIC CLAPTON
Behind the Sun—WB

44 GEORGE THOROGOOD AND THE DESTROYERS
Maverick—EMI America

45 PAUL YOUNG
The Secret of Association—Columbia

46 THE TIME
Ice Cream Castle—WB

47 LOS LOBOS
How Will the Wolf Survive?—Slash/WB

48 MADONNA
Madonna—Sire

49 CYNDI LAUPER
She's So Unusual—Portrait/CBS

50 STANLEY JORDAN
Magic Touch—Blue Note

51 THE HONEYDRIPPERS
Volume One—Es Paranza

52 HEART
Heart—Capitol

53 CHICAGO
Chicago 17—Full Moon/WB

54 **U2**
The Unforgettable Fire—Island

55 JESSE JOHNSON'S REVUE
Jesse Johnson's Revue—A&M

56 GEORGE BENSON
20/20—WB

57 RATT
Invasion of Your Privacy—Atlantic

58 DEBARGE
Rhythm of the Night—Gordy

59 **U2**
Wide Awake in America—Island

60 LIONEL RICHIE
Can't Slow Down—Motown

61 BACK TO THE FUTURE
Soundtrack—MCA

62 SURVIVOR
Vital Signs—Epic

63 FOREIGNER
Agent Provocateur—Atlantic

64 A-HA
Hunting High and Low—WB

65 ALEXANDER O'NEAL
Alexander O'Neal—Tabu/Epic

66 TOM PETTY AND THE HEARTBREAKERS
Southern Accents—MCA

67 MAZE
Can't Stop the Love—Capitol

68 DEPECHE MODE
Some Great Reward—Sire

69 PHILIP BAILEY
Chinese Wall—Columbia

70 THE BIG CHILL
Soundtrack—Motown

71 THE BREAKFAST CLUB
Soundtrack—A&M

72 CAMEO
Single Life—Atlanta Artists/Polygram

73 THE FIRM
The Firm—Atlantic

74 THE HOOTERS
Nervous Night—Columbia

75 COMMODORES
Nightshift—Motown

76 CHAKA KHAN
I Feel for You—WB

77 RICKIE LEE JONES
The Magazine—WB

78 MANHATTAN TRANSFER
Vocalese—Atlantic

79 DAVID SANBORN
Straight to the Heart—WB

80 KATRINA AND THE WAVES
Katrina and the Waves—Capitol

81 AL JARREAU
High Crime—WB

82 FAT BOYS
Fat Boys—Sutra

83 SUZANNE VEGA
Suzanne Vega—A&M

84 KATE BUSH
Hounds of Love—EMI America

85 JOAN ARMATRADING
Secret Secrets—A&M

86 NEW EDITION
New Edition—MCA

87 THE MARY JANE GIRLS
Only Four You—Motown

88 PHIL COLLINS
Face Value—Atlantic

89 KLYMAXX
Meeting in the Ladies Room—MCA

90 EARL KLUGH
Soda Fountain Shuffle—WB

91 GENERAL PUBLIC
. . . All the Rage—I.R.S.

92 MARVIN GAYE
Dream of a Lifetime—Columbia

93 RICK SPRINGFIELD
Tao—RCA

94 CON FUNK SHUN
Electric Lady—Mercury/Polygram

95 BRYAN FERRY
Boys and Girls—EG/WB

96 THE CURE
The Head on the Door—Elektra

97 UB40
Little Baggariddim—Virgin/A&M

98 JOHN CAFFERTY AND THE BEAVER BROWN BAND
Tough All Over—Scotti Bros/Epic

99 VISION QUEST
Soundtrack—Geffen

100 SQUEEZE
Cosi Fan Tutti Frutti—A&M

1985 MUSIC AWARDS

February 27, 1986

In ROLLING STONE's annual readers and critics poll, U2 swept the awards for the first time in 1986, a result of the bands impact in 1985.

READERS PICKS:

BAND OF THE YEAR
U2
Dire Straits
The E Street Band
Tears for Fears
Talking Heads

SONGWRITER
Bruce Springsteen
Sting
Phil Collins
Mark Knopfler
Bono

BEST PERFORMANCE/LIVE AID
U2
Mick Jagger and Tina Turner
Led Zeppelin
The Who
David Bowie

BEST LIVE PERFORMANCE
Bruce Springsteen and the E Street Band
U2
Tina Turner
Prince and the Revolution
Sting

MALE SINGER
Bruce Springsteen
Sting
Phil Collins
Bono
Paul Young

BASS PLAYER
John Taylor
Sting
Adam Clayton
Garry Tallent (the E Street Band)
Geddy Lee (Rush)

GUITARIST
Mark Knopfler
The Edge
Eddie Van Halen
Jeff Beck
Eric Clapton

DRUMMER
Phil Collins
Tony Thompson (the Power Station)
Max Weinberg (the E Street Band)
Larry Mullen Jr.
Neil Peart (Rush)

CRITICS PICKS:
BAND OF THE YEAR
U2

1985 ARTISTS' PICKS

February 27, 1986

Bono listed the following in ROLLING STONE's survey of artists' favorite music of 1985.

BONO, U2

Macalla, Clannad, RCA

Ordinary Man, Christy Moore, Green Linnet

"The Bridge," Cactus World News, Mother: "A biased opinion, because I produced them."

Anthem, De Danann, Dara

The Storm, Moving Hearts, Tara

Full Moon, Paul Brady, Demon

Gunpowders, Light a Big Fire, Hotwire

Four Green Fields, Makem and Clancy, Blackbird: "This goes in my dusted-off category."

Rain Dogs, Tom O'Waits, Island: "He-should-have-been-an-Irishman category."

"The Banks of the Royal Canal," Bob Dylan (song written by Brendan Behan): "Bob-Dylan-recited-the-words-to-me-backstage-at-Slane-Castle category."

DAVID FRICKE

CARAVAN FOR HUMAN RIGHTS

The Making of the Amnesty International
Anniversary Concert

A S JACK HEALEY REMEMBERS IT, the meeting didn't take much longer than ten minutes.

Healey, the executive director of Amnesty International USA, was on his way to an Amnesty powwow in Finland late last August when he made a brief detour to Dublin to meet with Paul McGuinness, manager of the Irish band U2. He had never met McGuinness before, and he'd only seen U2 once, at the group's December 1984 New York show, a benefit for the world human-rights organization.

In fact, Healey wasn't exactly sure what he wanted from McGuinness and U2 other than advice and, he hoped, some participation in Amnesty's upcoming twenty-fifth anniversary in 1986. But when he walked out of U2's office in Dublin's Windmill Lane studios that August day, Healey had the beginnings of a very special birthday party.

"They asked me, 'What do you need?' " Healey recalls, referring to McGuinness and U2 vocalist Bono, who happened to be at the studio that day. "I told them Amnesty was celebrating its twenty-fifth anniversary and that we have to get our message across to the American people. I said, 'We want to do it in an incredible, respectful, classy way, and you guys can help us break out into the open.' "

Healey made a vague proposal about a series of rock concerts to raise American awareness of Amnesty International's human-rights work. McGuinness asked, "How much time do you need?" and Healey said a week or two. McGuinness then scribbled out a very simple letter: "We're writing this letter to confirm that U2 will be at your disposal in the USA for a week at least during the twenty-fifth . . . year of Amnesty International. . . . Please show this letter to anyone you wish as an indication of our total support for and commitment to this event. See you there!"

"I don't think we regarded it as quite a momentous occasion," McGuinness says, laughing in retrospect. But for Jack Healey, that letter was a major contribution to Amnesty's world-freedom effort, a potential ticket out of hell for torture victims and prisoners of conscience everywhere. The unconditional commitments by U2 and Sting, who signed up soon after, set in motion the biggest and certainly the most unique rock & roll benefit event since Live Aid—six major concerts staged across the U.S. and intended not just to raise money, but to raise the consciousness of young Americans about the basic human rights they take for granted.

Formally dubbed "A Conspiracy of Hope: Concerts for Amnesty International," the two-week tour is like a Rolling Thunder-meets-ARMS convoy of socially aware rock stars. Joining U2 and Sting, who will be performing with his current road band, are Peter Gabriel, Bryan Adams, Lou Reed (all with their respective bands), top New Orleans R&B outfit the Neville Brothers and veteran folk activist Joan Baez. The tour opens June 4th at the Cow Palace in San Francisco and takes in Los Angeles (the Forum, June 6th), Denver (McNichols Sports Arena, June 8th), Atlanta (the Omni, June 11th) and Chicago (Rosemont Horizon, June 13th) before climaxing with a six- to eight-hour Live Aid-style blowout June 15th at Giants Stadium in East Rutherford, New Jersey. That show will be broadcast live by MTV and the Westwood One radio networks, and there will be a special 800 phone number for call-in donations.

Other acts have agreed to show up and play at selective tour stops along the way. Jackson Browne will join the lineup in San Francisco, Los Angeles and New Jersey; Peter Townshend, Carlos Santana and Rubén Blades, the Springsteen of salsa, are all on the New Jersey bill. Madonna and hubby Sean Penn, as well as Meryl Streep, Anjelica Huston and Mia Farrow are all confirmed as emcees at the Giants Stadium bash. And concert promoter Bill Graham, who is producing the entire tour, was negotiating with artists to join the final concert right up until May 14th, when press conferences announcing the tour were to have been held simultaneously in cities along the route.

"This is a birthday party," insists Bono, a fervent Amnesty supporter and a key figure in organizing the tour. "People like us who are, as the joke goes, undernourished and overpaid don't have time for our families or our friends or doing good work. But we have a chance to congratulate people who do. That's where my respect goes—to the people who do this work.

"What's important about this event is, it's not a charity ball. And at the same time, it's not a lecture tour. It's a very prestigious thing to be asked to celebrate the twenty-fifth anniversary of this apolitical, very respected organization. Rock & roll must not be left out of that picture. And it isn't."

HUGO DE LEÓN PALACIOS IS A Guatemalan schoolteacher who was abducted in 1984 right in front of his students. Nguyen Chi Thien, a prominent Vietnamese poet currently being held in a Hanoi prison, has spent nearly half of his fifty-three years behind bars. He was arrested in 1961 for trying to "discredit the regime by writing romantic poetry" and sentenced to two years' hard labor. Lee Kwang-ung, a South Korean teacher, was arrested, tortured and then sentenced to seven years in prison for giving friends copies of a book by a poet living in North Korea.

Thozamile Gqweta is a black South African union leader who was arrested in February 1985 and charged with high treason. He had been arrested and detained by South African authorities seven times before. Riad al-Turk is a Syrian lawyer and a member of the Syrian Communist Party who was abducted in 1980 by, according to reports, 200 members of the security police. Al-Turk is still being held without charge and has not been permitted to see his family since his arrest. Tatyana Semyonova Osipova is currently serving a twelve-year sentence in a Russian labor camp. She was, according to Amnesty International, convicted for her work in documenting Soviet human-rights violations.

These are just a few of the thousands of people Amnesty International believes have been tortured or imprisoned because of their beliefs. (Frequently, governments deny either the existence of cases like these, or the particulars cited.) Jack Healey, the head of Amnesty's American branch since 1981, is hoping that the rock & roll crowds who come to the concerts will literally set these six prisoners free.

Money certainly will help; Healey hopes to raise as much as $3 million from the shows. But more than dollars, what Healey really wants from this tour are bodies—at least 25,000 new members who would actively participate in the letter-writing campaigns Amnesty uses as leverage against dictators, secret-police chiefs and others in target countries. These "freedom writers," as Healey calls them, "commit to writing twelve letters a year, one a month. Every time we send out information on a selected prisoner of conscience, hopefully that government will get 25,000 letters from those people. We think that might get them out."

To get the freedom writers rolling, Amnesty will provide information on these six special prisoners of conscience to fans at the shows. The concert programs will also include a freedom-writer's kit with preaddressed post cards for easy mailing.

"What I would like to see," says Bono, "is maybe the names of a few of these political prisoners, or their faces, at the end of the tour and hear of their release. It would be nice to see these people set free, to have people from schools in the area, after each concert, get together and say, 'Yeah, let's start writing letters.' "

"**T**HE ONE THING WE WERE TOLD once we had U2 and Sting was 'Don't worry about the talent,' " Jack Healey recalls. "People kept saying, 'The rest will move right in. You'll have your choice of so many acts you won't believe it.' "

As it turned out, that wasn't true. Paul McGuinness had an inkling of just how tough it might be to recruit acts for a two-week benefit tour when he wrote that letter for Healey last August. "I was telling him, 'You're going to need this letter, Jack. It's no good just telling people we're in. This is the kind of thing you're going to need to put under people's noses.' "

Waving U2 stationery in other managers' faces just wasn't enough in this situation. As Bill Graham explains, part of the problem was that this was not like Live Aid; he was asking acts to make a real commitment—two weeks for charity, at the height of the summer touring season—that some of them simply couldn't afford to make.

"June is a premium month," explains the veteran promoter. "There are tours going out that were set in January. Live Aid was truly a phenomenon that people felt they had to do. People were saying, 'No matter where I am, I'll leave Mozambique for one day to do this.' We're not asking you to leave Mozambique for one day. We're asking you to leave the road for two weeks. And with some acts, we came so close."

One of them, Bono says, was Van Morrison. "It would have been wonderful to have him there, because he's a soul singer of the highest caliber. His music has an ability to awaken, and just having one singer with that much soul could say more than any words could say. And he was prepared to do it. Ultimately, there were problems with logistics. But it was a great honor that he even *wanted* to do it."

Other acts, like Peter Gabriel, came through, though not without considerable hassle. "He had to blow out so many things to get involved," Bono explains. "There were tangles with his record label. They had arranged a trip to Japan for him. And when Amnesty asked him to do it, he rang me up and said, 'I'm not sure I can do this. But I have to.' "

Jack Healey and Amnesty International USA's communications director, Mary Daly, drew the short straw when it came to making phone calls. "We went after the superstars—Stevie Wonder, Dylan, Bruce Springsteen, Huey Lewis, Barbra Streisand, the unreachables," Healey says. "This is the hardest job I've ever had in my life. The rock & roll industry is a schmooze community. They like talking to each other a lot with very little paperwork. We're the opposite. We like a lot of paper and little talking."

Healey and Daly got a truckload of the usual excuses—"I don't have a band at the moment." "We're recording right now." They were also disappointed to find out how many top U.S. artists were unaware of Amnesty International altogether. But they didn't come away from all of their meetings empty-handed. Mick Jagger, Keith Richards, Bob Geldof, Paul Simon, Joan Armatrading, Pet Shop Boys, Mr. Mister, John Taylor of Duran Duran and Carly Simon all consented to do prerecorded video messages for Amnesty.

In addition to sorting out the lineup, the tour's organizers faced other problems. For example, a June 9th show at the Reunion Hall in Dallas was originally announced as the third stop on the itinerary, but that was canceled when the hall's management subsequently booked another show for that date. The makeup concert June 8th at McNichols Sports Arena in Denver was also up in the air until the Denver Nuggets were eliminated from the National Basketball Association playoffs.

Scheduling difficulties also caused Bill Graham to push the simultaneous press conferences back a week from their original date of May 7th. That delay left only three weeks between the announcement of the tour and the first concerts. Graham had to scramble to make his mail-order ticket plan work, and for a while it looked as if he'd have to abandon selling tickets through the mail for the Giants Stadium show.

No one expected to have any trouble getting an 800 phone number from AT&T for the June 15th telethon—until the phone company pointed out that June 15th was also Father's Day, the fifth-busiest calling day of the year. AT&T feared that the high volume of calls coming into Amnesty and to dads all across America would choke the company's lines, and for a time it hesitated to assign Amnesty an 800 number. Finally, though not without subtle coercion from some highly placed Amnesty board members, AT&T agreed to open an 800 line.

A lot has also gone right with this tour. The Hyatt Corporation is donating hotel rooms across the country. Amnesty is getting the Los Angeles Forum rent-free for the June 6th concert. Even in those venues charging rent, attempts have been made to whittle down costs as much as possible. John Scher, the local promoter working with Graham on the June 15th New Jersey show, says management officials at Giants Stadium "are prepared to work with us to make it less expensive. I'm going to sit down with the various union people that are represented there and see if we can get some breaks from them. Once all is said and done, everybody from a manpower and facility point of view will have tightened their belts and made it as financially attractive as possible."

Paul McGuinness does not know yet what this tour will cost U2. "The basic principle of funding this production is that anyone who incurs an extra expense as a result of doing these shows should have it covered. If we have to fly to America to do these shows, I have no embarrassment at charging these tickets to the show. But our crew is on salary anyway, so I wouldn't charge those costs to the show."

"We said early on that if we had to pay costs we would," Healey concedes. "We're not going to demand that same donation of services and things, as was done at Live Aid."

Still, Jack Healey and Mary Daly find it hard to disguise their disappointment at the superstars who, for one good reason or another, have not donated their time or talent. "I don't want it to sound like we're disappointed in them fundamentally," Daly insists, "because we knew this was going to be hard. But governments monitor everything we do. And you have to be able to put on an event like this and have it be the strongest, most potent attack. If it isn't, it can just be dismissed. There are countries where people are in prison and being tortured, and we know that they would be released if these artists went onstage for us."

ABOUT TWO AND A HALF YEARS ago, Jack Healey paid a visit to Denver concert promoter Barry Fey to discuss Amnesty International's accelerating campaign against torture. During the meeting, Fey came up with an unusual idea—a train that would go from one end of America to the other, flying the flags of all the countries where torture was allowed or condoned. Pictures of victims would also be displayed on the train, and Fey suggested staging a concert at every whistle stop, "even if it's just someone singing with a guitar," along with speeches from prominent politicians and authors about human-rights abuses.

"By the time you get to the end," Fey told Healey, "you'll have stopped torture in some countries because they'll be so damned embarrassed to have their flag up there."

"It was a great idea," Healey exclaims. It was so great that Healey used it as the model for his Amnesty rock & roll caravan. Initially, U2 and Amnesty had hoped that all the performers would travel together from show to show, creating a sort of communal feeling that would carry over into the concerts. At press time, however, Healey's attempts to acquire a free airplane from one of the major airlines to ferry the entire concert troupe had proven unsuccessful, and travel arrangements were still sketchy.

The format of the shows was also up in the air. At the time they were interviewed, Bono, Sting and Bryan Adams had no firm idea of exactly what they would play at the concerts. Sting, at least, was well rehearsed; he's been on the road with his current jazz-pop fusion band since last summer. "I have an idea of maybe performing with U2," he adds, "kind of a trade-off for the time Bono got onstage with the Police. It was at a festival in my home town, Newcastle. He got onstage and we sang 'Invisible Sun' together. It would be nice to return the favor."

Other than that, superjams are still a question mark. Set lengths for the main acts will probably be a maximum of thirty minutes for the arena shows, just enough time for most of the artists to run through a few big hits. "The concert is to make people aware of what Amnesty International is doing," Bryan Adams explains. "It's not necessarily important for everyone to have a song about Amnesty International. If they do, great. But the idea should be entertainment for the day, not preaching."

Nevertheless, Jack Healey feels the Amnesty tour is true to Barry Fey's antitorture-train idea "because the whole teaching element is still there." Indeed, the lessons have already begun. When Sting asked his touring band if they would join him for the Amnesty benefit shows, they had no idea what Amnesty International was. So he handed out a few Amnesty pamphlets he carries on the road. "After five minutes of reading this stuff, they were convinced."

ASIDE FROM BEING IRISH, Jack Healey and Bono have something in common—their belief in the power of rock & roll to inspire average people to do great things. A former Franciscan monk who worked for the Peace Corps in southern Africa for five years, Healey, 48, first got the rock & roll bug as a teenager in Pittsburgh. His brother-in-law operated a string of jukeboxes in local bars and gave Healey a lot of his used records. "When I heard Presley and Fats Domino, that was the first explosion in my brain."

He got a similar buzz from U2 when he saw the 1984 benefit at New York's Radio City Music Hall. "Bono sang with such driving strength and commitment. There was such a force to it that you had to figure it was either straight manipulation or true strength. And I decided it was true strength and that they really believed in what they were singing. As an Irishman myself, I wanted to believe in my own."

His faith has been well placed. The band and McGuinness have been aware of Amnesty for quite some time. Before managing U2, McGuinness had worked in an Irish film-production company run by Tiernan Mac-Bride, son of Amnesty founding member Sean MacBride. Bono's introduction to the organization was Amnesty's 1979 London benefit show, the Secret Policeman's Ball. "So any criticism of this tour being ineffective in raising awareness is unfair," Bono notes. "I'm the perfect argument against that."

In U2, Healey has the perfect Amnesty band. Sting, too, is the ideal Amnesty representative—both popular and politically aware (he performed at the Secret Policeman's Other Ball in 1981). Peter Gabriel has written and recorded one of the strongest rock-music indictments of apartheid with "Biko," his 1980 song about South African martyr Steve Biko. But the question remains: will the nearly 200,000 fans who see the Amnesty shows, not to mention the enormous June 15th radio and television audience, go home with something more than memories of a great rock show?

"I don't underestimate our audience," says Bono. "They're a smart bunch, they're into the music and into what's behind it. They're going to be pretty effective. And I know it. Because I was part of that audience once. I saw *The Secret Policeman's Other Ball* [a film account of Amnesty benefit highlights], and it became a part of me. It sowed a seed."

■ **RANDOM NOTES** "SELF AID" (July 3, 1986)

Self Aid. It sounds more like leftover Me Decade pop psychology than what it was—a Dublin benefit by Irish bands and artists to help Ireland's unemployed. Half a million pounds were raised during the twelve-hour show, which included sets by the Chieftains, the Pogues, Cactus World News, Clannad and Blue in Heaven. Bob Geldof, who's about to begin a solo career, played what may have been his last show with the Boomtown Rats. "It's been a very good ten years," he told the crowd. "Rest in peace." Elvis Costello played with the Attractions, dedicating a song to his fiancée, Calt O'Riordan of the Pogues. Van Morrison previewed his upcoming album with a new song, "Town Called Paradise." But the show really belonged to U2, who did a medley of Bob Dylan's "Maggie's Farm," John Lennon's "Cold Turkey" and Elton John's "Candle in the Wind." Bono eschewed his customary leap into the audience, but added a back flip off the drum riser to his repertoire of stage moves. The show's emotional highlight was a special tribute to the late Phil Lynott. His band, Thin Lizzy, performed, with Geldof filling in as lead singer.

1986 MUSIC AWARDS

February 26, 1987

READERS PICKS:

BEST BAND
Genesis
Van Halen
R.E.M.
The E Street Band
U2

BEST BASS PLAYER
John Taylor (Duran Duran)
Michael Anthony (Van Halen)
Geddy Lee (Rush)
Sting
Adam Clayton

BEST GUITARIST
Eddie Van Halen
Eric Clapton
Mark Knopfler (Dire Straits)
The Edge
Steve Stevens (Billy Idol)

BEST LIVE PERFORMANCE
Bruce Springsteen and the E Street Band
Genesis
Van Halen
U2
R.E.M.

ANTHONY DeCURTIS

U2 RELEASES *THE JOSHUA TREE*

Band says new material "more in focus"; music
incorporates blues, country

"WE STARTED WRITING SONGS with this record, and we're determined not to stop," says U2 lead vocalist Bono about the band's new LP, *The Joshua Tree*. "It's our most literate record by far, because I just felt it's time to come clean."

The eleven songs on *The Joshua Tree* come clean on a wide range of subjects, including the problems of British miners ("Red Hill Mining Town"), the harrowing effects of heroin addiction ("Running to Stand Still"), the untimely death in a motorcycle accident of U2's personal assistant, Greg Carroll ("One Tree Hill"), crises of spiritual faith and personal relationships ("Where the Streets Have No Name," "With or Without You," "I Still Haven't Found What I'm Looking For"), the atrocities of repressive governments ("Mothers of the Disappeared") and the wild beauty and violent underbelly of America ("In God's Country," "Exit," "Bullet the Blue Sky," "Trip Through Your Wires").

Despite the range of subjects and styles—blues and country music, for example, are evident in U2's sound for the first time—bassist Adam Clayton says there's an attitude and feel that hold the LP together. "We definitely went in saying we're not going to make heavy weather out of this," Clayton says. "If a song is happening, we're not going to mess with it too much and we're going to try to get it down on tape as fast as possible. If we were having trouble with a song, rather than keep working on it till it got painful, we'd say, no, fuck it, let's just work on stuff that we like. Each song is a song that every member of the band enjoyed playing."

The Joshua Tree was recorded at Windmill Lane Studios in Dublin, though demos for the record were done at a smaller Dublin studio called S.T.S. and some sessions took place at the home studios of Clayton and U2 guitarist the Edge. Like the band's 1984 LP, *The Unforgettable Fire, The Joshua Tree* was produced by Brian Eno and Daniel Lanois. "We still had more to learn from them," Edge says about the band's decision to work with Eno and Lanois again. "There was still mileage in the relationship and collaboration."

According to the Edge, U2 had very clear ideas about how *The Joshua Tree* should differ from *The Unforgettable Fire*. "On this record, the one thing we wanted to do was be more in focus," he says. "The songs should be more condensed, the kernel of each piece a bit harder, denser, a bit meatier. It would be less open-ended as a record. We would try to get more into the *song* as an art form in itself, rather than relying on breaking new ground in terms of what our pieces became."

Steve Lillywhite, who produced U2's first three albums, mixed four tracks on *The Joshua Tree* ("Where the Streets Have No Name," "With or Without You," "Bullet the Blue Sky" and "Red Hill Mining Town"), because of demands on Brian Eno's time. "We wanted to have the record out in March, because we'd been so long," drummer Larry Mullen explains. "We said we don't want to rush this and start freaking out. And Brian Eno suggested why not bring Steve in and mix some of the songs and actually get a different perspective, because everyone was tired—studio fatigue had set in."

U2 will soon launch a yearlong world tour, during which the band plans to play lengthier sets than it has in the past. The first U.S. stint of the tour will begin in the Southwest in early April and conclude around the end of May in New York. The Southwestern starting point is appropriate because the Joshua tree, which grows only in the desert, is indigenous to the region. The tree is also laden with a wide range of religious symbolism, much of which is linked with the notion of the Promised Land.

As for the tour, Bono says, "Being onstage for us all is almost like coming home. I like the kinetic energy of traveling, though sometimes it blows my head. Something that is very important to get across, I think, is that I don't want to be so deep that people have to drown in order to relate to me. Essentially, we are a *lethal* rock & roll band, and when we play live we really play."

STEVE POND

THE JOSHUA TREE ALBUM REVIEW
U2 rises to the occasion

THE STAKES ARE ENORMOUS, and U2 knows it. Its last album, *The Unforgettable Fire,* contained "Pride (In the Name of Love)," its biggest-selling single ever, and last year the band was the musical heart of Amnesty International's Conspiracy of Hope tour. Now, it seems, U2 is poised to rise from the level of mere platinum groups to the more rarefied air above. For a band that's always specialized in inspirational, larger-than-life gestures—a band utterly determined to be Important—*The Joshua Tree* could be the big one, and that's precisely what it sounds like.

That's not to say that this record is either a flagrantly commercial move or another *Born in the U.S.A. The Joshua Tree* is U2's most varied, subtle and accessible album, although it doesn't contain any sure-fire smash hits. But in its musical toughness and strong-willed spirituality, the album lives up to its namesake: a hardy, twisted tree that grows in the rocky deserts of the American Southwest. A Mormon legend claims that their early settlers called the Joshua tree "the praying plant" and thought its gnarled branches suggested the Old Testament prophet Joshua pointing the way to the Promised Land. The title befits a record that concerns itself with resilience in the face of utter social and political desolation, a record steeped in religious imagery.

Since U2 emerged from Dublin in 1980 with a bracing brand of hard, emotional, guitar-oriented rock, its albums have followed a pattern. The first and third *(Boy* and *War)* were muscular and assertive, full of, respectively, youthful bravado and angry social awareness; the second and fourth studio albums *(October* and *The Unforgettable Fire)* were moody and meandering and sometimes longer on ideas than on full-fledged songs.

But *The Joshua Tree* isn't an outright return to the fire of *War.* The band ruled that out years ago: Songs like "Sunday Bloody Sunday" and "New Year's Day" hit with driving force on the 1983 album and subsequent tour. But U2 saw itself in danger of becoming just another sloganeering arena-rock band, so the group closed that chapter with a live record and video. The band swapped longtime producer Steve Lillywhite for Brian Eno and Daniel Lanois and, with *The Unforgettable Fire,* declared its intention to no longer be as relentlessly heroic.

On the new album, U2 retains Eno and Lanois, brings back Lillywhite
to mix four songs and weds the diverse textures of *The Unforgettable Fire* to
fully formed songs, many of them as aggressive as the hits on *War*. U2's
sonic trademarks are here: the monumental angst of Bono's voice, the
driving pulse of Adam Clayton's bass and Larry Mullen Jr.'s drums and the
careening wail of the Edge's guitar. But for every predictably roaring
anthem there's a spare, inventively arranged tune, such as "With or Without You," a rock & roll bolero that builds from a soothing beginning to a
resounding climax.

The band still falls into some old traps: Bono's perpetually choked-up
voice can sound overwrought and self-important; some of the images (fire
and rain, say) start to lose their resonance after a dozen or so uses; and
"Exit," a recited psychodrama about a killer, is awkward enough to remind
you that not even Patti Smith could regularly pull off this sort of thing.

More than any other U2 album, though, *The Joshua Tree* has the power
and allure to seduce and capture a mass audience on its own terms. Without
making a show of its eclecticism, it features assertive rock ("Where the
Streets Have No Name"), raw frenzy ("Bullet the Blue Sky"), delicacy
("One Tree Hill"), chugging rhythms ("I Still Haven't Found What I'm
Looking For") and even acoustic bluesiness ("Running to Stand Still")—all
of it unmistakably U2.

But if this is a breakthrough, it's a grim, dark-hued one. At first,
refreshingly honest, romantic declarations alternate with unsettling religious
imagery. Then things get blacker. The raging, melodramatic "Bullet the
Blue Sky" ties Biblical fire and brimstone with American violence overseas
and at home. In the stomping, harmonica-spiked rocker "Trip Through
Your Wires," what looks like salvation could easily be evil seduction; "One
Tree Hill" is a soft, haunting benediction on a U2 crew member who died
in a motorcycle accident; and "Red Hill Mining Town" echoes Peter
Gabriel's "Don't Give Up" in its unsparing look at personal relationships
savaged by economic hardship—here, the aftermath of the largely unsuccessful British miners' strike of 1984.

But for all its gloom, the album is never a heavy-handed diatribe. After
the first few times through "Running to Stand Still," for instance, you
notice the remarkable music: the wholly unexpected blues slide guitar, the
soft, *Nebraska*-style yelps, the ghostly harmonica. It sounds like a lovely,
peaceful reverie—except that this is a junkie's reverie, and when that
realization hits home, the gentle acoustic lullaby acquires a corrosive power
that recalls "Bad," from the last LP.

The Joshua Tree is an appropriate response to these times, and a picture
bleaker than any U2 has ever painted: a vision of blasted hopes, pointless

violence and anguish. But this is not a band to surrender to defeatism. Its last album ended with a gorgeous elegy to Martin Luther King Jr.; *The Joshua Tree* closes with a haunting ode to other victims. "Mothers of the Disappeared" is built around desolate images of loss, but the setting is soothing and restorative—music of great sadness but also of unutterable compassion, acceptance and calm. "The Unforgettable Chill," you might call this album, and *unforgettable* is certainly the right word.

ANTHONY DeCURTIS

TRUTHS AND CONSEQUENCES

As their new album zooms to the top of the charts, the members of U2 grapple with what it means to be rock & roll superstars

"I MUST SAY, I DON'T feel very qualified to be a pop star," says Bono, U2's lead singer, one overcast February afternoon as he drives through Dublin. "I don't think I'm a very good pop star, and I feel very awkward at times in the role. I think there are other people far better suited than me."

He pauses and laughs. "I sometimes think it might have been a mistake—you picked up the wrong guy! Look, I'm built more like a mechanic or something, a carpenter. I mean, *take a look at these hands*—these are the hands of a bricklayer."

Bono has chosen a highly charged moment to begin questioning his qualifications for pop stardom. With the release of *The Joshua Tree,* U2's fifth, farthest-reaching and flat-out best studio LP, and a massive world tour in the works, Bono and his cohorts in U2—guitarist the Edge, bassist Adam Clayton and drummer Larry Mullen Jr.—will undoubtedly rise to the superstardom that has always been their goal but has always loomed as more of a promised land, ardently desired but seen from afar, than an imminent reality. Bono's half-hopeful statement that "U2 will be the band that's always coming and never arrives" is about to be proven wrong in spades.

U2's recent triumphs have raised vexing questions for Bono—artistic and personal questions all the more troubling because of the position of moral authority U2 has attained. Over the past few years, rock & roll has gone a long way toward establishing itself as a force for good in the world, and U2 has been at the forefront of the artists who have contributed to that movement. The band's 1983 LP *War* helped restore social consciousness to rock, and its galvanizing performances at Live Aid and during Amnesty International's six-concert Conspiracy of Hope tour defined the dual spirit of moral purpose and fervent celebration at the heart of those events. Success seemed to go hand in hand with significance for U2, and by the time the Conspiracy of Hope tour ended with a spectacular stadium concert last June, the whole pop-music world seemed poised for whatever U2 decided to do next.

All the while, however, as Bono saw the prominence of U2 increase, he wondered about the myths of excess and frivolous destruction that had grown up around rock & roll in the course of its history. He wondered what he and his band were supposed to represent in the context of that mythology. Was high-mindedness simply U2's "angle," an image as confining in its way as the fashion stance of the latest haircut band? As its audience and profits multiplied, what finally would separate U2 from the herd of Bands That Matter that had come down the pike and burned out or taken a sharp right turn into comfort and apathy? He also wondered about the sirenlike lure that rock-star indulgence might hold for him. This internal interrogation—a process Bono refers to as "wrestling with myself for a living"— stokes the dissatisfaction that burns at the center of *The Joshua Tree,* and within Bono himself as he stands on the verge of a potentially dangerous ascent.

"I don't accept the rock & roll mythology of 'living on the edge, man,'—I don't accept that," the twenty-six-year-old Bono says during the drive through Dublin, gesturing with characteristic intensity and making it uncomfortably clear that the point he is making is considerably more important to him than keeping his eyes on the road. "We're all pretty much removed from reality, I suppose—the reality of life and death. But rock & roll is even *more* removed from reality. Rock & roll artists who are living on the edge—what can they possibly have to offer? Their songs are written from such a removed point of view.

"We're all asleep in some way or another," he says. "I've used my music to wake me up. . . . I find now that I've been reading about them, I'm much more attracted to those old folkies, you know, like Woody Guthrie, people who work within their community. They're working, and their labor is writing a song."

LARRY MULLEN'S HOME, IN THE coastal town of Howth, is the destination of Bono's drive. Mullen's sparsely furnished but comfortable suburban-style house—complete with clothes hung in the yard and a frisky dog—sits on a small hill overlooking the Irish Sea. It's drizzling outside. Framed by a picture window, the grays and blues of the sky and the sea merge into an impressionist blur. The weather inspires such a reflective mood that Mullen will joke later on, as the Judds' sprightly album *Why Not Me* enlivens the interior of his sports car on the drive back into town: "Somehow driving along like this in the middle of Dublin in the rain listening to the Judds—it's just not *right!*"

For now, however, Bono pulls off the battered midlength gray wool coat he wore in the car and sprawls in a chair at Mullen's dining-room table. Sporting his customary black leather vest and black jeans, his shoulder-length brown hair drawn back in a ponytail, Bono is badly in need of a shave—and some sleep.

Mullen, his blond hair slicked back in a spiky cut, is, on the other hand, characteristically fresh faced and upbeat. Mullen, 25, is the quietest member of U2—and he clearly idolizes Bono. Just as clearly, Bono feels considerable affection for Mullen. The two men spend a great deal of time together—Mullen getting a kick from Bono's tireless intensity, Bono finding relief from himself in Mullen's good-natured enthusiasm and good-hearted directness.

Mullen pulls up a chair next to Bono, and the conversation turns to Joshua trees—the gnarled trees indigenous to the deserts of the American Southwest. The tree was named by the Mormons when they were settling Utah; its shape reminded them of the Biblical passage in which Joshua pointed to the Promised Land.

The imagery couldn't seem to be any more obvious, particularly for a man who confesses that the year in which he wrote lyrics for much of the material on *The Joshua Tree* was "a bit of a desert"—due to his obsession with the viability of rock & roll as a way of life, his marital upheavals and the death of Greg Carroll, U2's twenty-six-year-old personal assistant, to whom *The Joshua Tree* is dedicated. Bono, however, refuses to pin the symbol down precisely.

"We find it funny," Bono says about responses to the album's title, recalling that somebody asked, "You're not gonna change your religion *again?*" after hearing the Mormon tale. In explaining why the band chose the title, Bono for once falls short of words: "I'm not going to talk about the other reasons. You know, the symbol is a very powerful one, and you don't . . . you can't . . . you don't . . . ."

"It's supposed to be the oldest living organism in the desert," Mullen says. "They can't put a time on it, because when you cut it, there's no rings to indicate how old it is. Maybe it's a good sign for the record!"

The photos on the album's cover and lyric sheet were taken near Joshua Tree National Monument, in California, not far from where the ashes of country-rock pioneer Gram Parsons were scattered in 1973. According to Bono, however, even the band wouldn't be able to locate the exact Joshua tree that was photographed. "We stopped off on the road," Bono says, "and we went out, and we were shooting this landscape with the tree, and we just got back on the bus and drove off. Then somebody thought, 'God, say you ever want to go back to that tree? Or other people might go out looking for the tree.' And then we thought, 'No, better that people can't find it, or else some guy will arrive with it at a gig.' *'Bono, I've got the tree!'* "

"Joshua trees might be extinct by the time this album is over," Mullen says, laughing.

"The funny side of this is, like, with this album, everybody's trying to say, 'U2, the next this, the next that,' " Bono says. "You get record-industry people saying, 'As big as the Beatles—what's the name of the album?' *'The Joshua Tree.'* 'Oh yeah, oh right.' " He laughs. "It's not exactly *Born in the Joshua Tree,* or *Dark Side of the Joshua Tree.* It sounds like it would sell about three copies."

O F COURSE, 3 MILLION COPIES is more like it—and even that's a conservative estimate for what will very likely become one of the most successful, not to mention most important, records of the decade. (*The Joshua Tree* entered the *Billboard* chart at Number Seven.) The reference to *Born in the U.S.A.* is appropriate, not only because that album also lifted a populist artist to mega-stardom but because, as in Springsteen's case, the sheer aural pleasure of *The Joshua Tree* and the awesome, uplifting power of U2's live shows will probably obscure the fact that the album is as foreboding a record as can be imagined. The Joshua tree itself may be a symbol of hope and deliverance, but its twisted shape and the barrenness of its environment suggest the sort of forces that must be confronted before redemption comes.

And perhaps even after redemption comes—at least in the form in which this album will present it to U2. In the face of enormous popularity and its attendant pressures, the band will have to struggle to maintain an independent sense of self. On a much smaller but equally dramatic scale, U2 faced the issue of rock stardom and its meaning after its 1980 debut album, *Boy,* brought the band members international recognition when some of them were still teenagers.

"I think we have to own up to the fact that we really weren't that interested in being in a band after *Boy,"* Bono says about the intense period of spiritual questing that he, Mullen and the Edge undertook at that point. "We were, during *October,* interested in other things, really. We thought about giving up the band. And Adam's reaction to us thinking about giving up the band was *he* wanted to get out of the band. *October* we made with the attitude 'If people don't like it, hey, maybe that's better than if they do.' We wanted to make a record, and yet we didn't want to make a record, because we were going through a stage where we thought, 'Rock & roll is just *full of shit,* do we want to spend our lives doing it?'

"We were getting involved in reading books, the Big Book, meeting people who were more interested in things spiritual, superspiritual characters that I can see now were possibly far too removed from reality. But we were *wrapped up* in that.

"For two years, we didn't even know if we wanted to be in a band. We went on tour, and every night we had this thing: we've got to play this concert like it's our last concert. We went out with that attitude, sometimes because maybe it *could* have been our last concert.

"Steve Lillywhite [the producer of U2's first three albums, who also mixed three tracks on *The Joshua Tree*] used to say, 'Do your job,' and we were running away from doing our jobs. We wanted to do whatever—at that stage it was probably set up a mission on the street for people who hadn't got any food. We were thinking all along those lines."

Squaring the band's spiritual concerns with rock & roll's outlaw mythology was a persistent problem in the years following the release of *October* and *War*—a problem that eventually generated a contradictory response in Bono. "We were the freak show for a while," Bono says. "We felt like fish out of water. 'What are we doing in rock & roll?' We almost felt that we should do drugs out of *guilt,* to make people feel at home." Bono says he did give in to some standard rock vices. "I've kind of evened out now, but over the last few years, I've backlashed completely. Drank far too much and did far too many things out of this odd, weird reverse guilt."

Both in the rock world, then, and in dealing with the public, Bono felt removed from his own image. "Essentially, I'm a very real person, good and bad," Bono says. "And the public image is one of being very good, I suppose. But one of the reasons I'm attracted to people like Martin Luther King, Gandhi, Christ, to pacifism, is because naturally I'm *not* a pacifist. Naturally, I'm the guy that would not turn the other cheek. But when people see you're attracted to that, they think you *are* that."

By reexamining rock & roll history from the perspective of his own concerns, however, Bono began to see the tension between stardom and religious fervor not as something unique to himself or U2 but as part of an honorable tradition. "Marvin Gaye, Patti Smith, Van Morrison, Bob Dylan, Stevie Wonder—gee, I don't think there's anyone I like in rock & roll that isn't as screwed up as me in this area," he says. "I started realizing that rock & roll devoid of that spiritual confusion is the rock & roll that I don't like anyway. I started realizing, 'Hey, we're not the odd ones out. This shit on the radio is the odd stuff. It's a natural place to be.' "

W HILE WEARYING OR EVEN overbearing at times (Bono says, "I went through a period of feeling maybe the people in the band didn't like me very much; I can be obnoxious at times"), the seriousness with which Bono regards his responsibilities as a rock star is an important part of why U2 has won such a huge, devoted following. His enthusiasm was perhaps nowhere more evident than in September of 1985, shortly after Live Aid, when he felt he had to follow through on the meaning of that event by visiting Ethiopia for a month with his wife, Alison, to assist in famine-relief efforts.

The couple was determined not to let the trip turn into just another superstar's philanthropic junket. It was undertaken with no publicity—though their presence in the country was eventually discovered—and to this day Bono refuses to say much about it for fear of offending the less celebrated people who perform such work every day outside the congratulatory shine of the media's spotlight. "I don't deserve any prizes, because I could afford to go," Bono says bluntly one afternoon in a Dublin restaurant. "A lot of people would give their right arms to go to Ethiopia and help out. I could afford to."

Initially during their stay in Ethiopia, Bono and Ali helped with the hands-on physical labor and basic health care of a refugee camp. It soon became apparent, however, that communicating information about nutrition and hygiene was a crucial problem in the relief effort. Determined to assist in the best way they could, the couple came up with a month-long program that addressed one key health topic (for example, safe methods of childbearing) per week. Working at an orphanage of 300 children in the mountains of northern Ethiopia, Bono and Ali composed four songs and four playlets to familiarize the children with the European fruits and vegetables that were becoming available to them, as well as healthy first-aid techniques and proper methods of planting and reaping. The sing-along songs and plays—written with the help of African relief workers in the people's native language—were meant to encourage the children to retain their messages and pass them along.

His time in Africa with Ali left Bono flying. "I got more than I gave to Ethiopia," he says. "My head was in the clouds, and my feet were not on the ground." But Bono hit the ground hard when he returned home. "Spending time in Africa and seeing people in the pits of poverty," he says, "I still saw a very strong spirit in the people, a richness of spirit I didn't see when I came home. I had no culture shock going, but I had culture shock coming back. I saw the spoiled child of the Western world. I started thinking, 'They may have a physical desert, but we've got other kinds of deserts.' And that's what attracted me to the desert as a symbol of some sort."

ORKING TOGETHER IN ETHIOPIA was a time of particular closeness
for Bono and Ali. Bono admits they've had their share of problems since the success of *The Unforgettable Fire,* U2's 1984 album. In describing the personal strains of 1986, Bono says simply, "I live with a very strong person, and she throws me out occasionally." Bono shies away from discussing in any detail the current state of his relationship with Ali, whom he married in August of 1982 and who studies political science at University College, in Dublin. But balancing the demands of recording and touring with the emotional claims of a marriage is no easy task—and it isn't likely to become easier as U2 launches a worldwide tour that could run as long as a year. Asked how he's managed that balancing act in the past, Bono says, hesitantly, "Well, I haven't been able to manage it that well. I'm going to have to try and manage it better the next time. I have to do it. . . . We shall see." But Bono is confident he can rise to the challenge. "I'm determined to make it work, because I believe in U2, and ultimately that's what I want to do. Be in that band."

Along with such personal issues, Greg Carroll's death in a motorcycle accident in Dublin last July also darkened 1986 for Bono and U2. The band members met Carroll when they stopped in Auckland, New Zealand, on the *Unforgettable Fire* tour. They got along so well with him that they added him to their crew. When the tour ended, Carroll settled in Dublin and continued working for the band. Carroll, whom Bono describes as "like a brother," was struck by an automobile while riding a friend's bike; his friend was riding Bono's Harley, which Carroll had been minding. The band is haunted both by the suddenness of Carroll's death and by the idea that if he hadn't come to Dublin to live with them, he might still be alive.

Bono and Mullen flew to New Zealand for Carroll's funeral, and Bono wrote the exuberant memorial "One Tree Hill" about the experience. "Auckland is made up of five little volcanic mounds," Bono says, "and the tallest one is called One Tree Hill. It's sort of a landmark. Personally, I can't hear that song. I cut myself off from it, because if I didn't and somebody told me, 'Eh, now we'd like you to do the vocal again,' or 'Listen, I think that chorus is weak,' it would be iron-bar time."

For the Edge, U2's twenty-five-year-old guitarist, the impact of Carroll's death was "quite devastating." "What happened was this avalanche of questions," says the Edge one evening in London, where U2 is filming a video for "Red Hill Mining Town" with director Neil Jordan *(Mona Lisa)*. "I suppose that's the privilege of youth—you leave death to one side to be dealt with later. The uncertainty—that this person who had been so close to us was gone. . . . For a long time, *still* sometimes, I feel like he's going to walk through the door."

Not surprisingly, the Edge's response to Carroll's death assumed an unsettling spiritual dimension. "I'm struggling now to put it into words," says the Edge, whose quiet intensity—his voice is often nearly as soft as a whisper—marks a telling contrast both with Bono's driven verbal torrents and his own roaring guitar excursions. "Well, I suppose it was really . . . Is it a question of destiny? Is destiny a power? Is chance a power? . . . How does belief in God come into that? That's the thing about my spiritual beliefs, I have so many unanswered questions. A lot of my belief is . . . the truth is somewhere between"—he holds his hands apart—"here and here; you can't actually be sure about it, where it is. But 'somewhere between here and here' is enough most of the time."

AS U2'S INTERNATIONAL STATURE has grown, the band members have come increasingly to rely on their solid grounding in Dublin to lend normality to their lives. "We're still very much connected with our lives before we were successful," says the Edge. "Things have changed, but we haven't abandoned the values and ideas that we had at the earliest stage of our career. In Dublin itself, and in Ireland, people enjoy celebrities, but they're certainly not going to become sycophantic lunatics if they meet somebody who's famous."

The Edge also draws sustenance from his three-year marriage and his two young children. Of his wife, Aislinn, he says, "The great thing about her is she's really not particularly impressed with rock & roll. Although she loves our music, she's not hugely into music. She's kind of a stabilizing force. The prestige of what's going on around her—it doesn't bother her." He laughs. "It's sobering!"

Bassist Adam Clayton takes particular pride in U2's identity as an Irish band. Clayton, twenty-seven, is the most formal of the band members in his bearing and speech. He is also the one most likely to insist on U2's stature, sometimes seeming arrogant, to borrow a word he tends to use in perfectly neutral terms. "We're a bunch of noisy, rough Irishmen that are arrogant enough to drag their tails all the way round the world," Clayton says, smiling, "and I think that's something to be proud of. I think we have achieved things, and I think Ireland can stand up with its music and say to everyone, 'We're an important place.' "

Bono's relationship with his home town and homeland reflects a characteristically edgy, excited ambivalence. "I feel part of Dublin, I feel part of Ireland," Bono says. "I climb over the wall and I get out of here sometimes because the place'd make you tear your hair out. But I love its people and I love its places and as a city . . . oh, it's a very interesting city."

During the drive through Dublin, Bono notes points of historical significance with pride, but he concentrates on the toll in human lives exacted on the city by poverty, unemployment and heroin addiction, and by what Bono sees as sterile urban development that's alienating the city from its own past.

"They pulled this city down," he says. "They're pulling the beautiful buildings down. If I was ever a terrorist, if I ever were to set up my own militant organization, I'd set up a building-liberation front. I've just wanted to throw rocks through the windows of buildings in this city that they've put up. I just want to burn down so many buildings."

As Bono drives through Ballymun, the section of town where he grew up, he gestures toward the Ballymun Flats, a run-down seven-building housing project that looms over the modest one- and two-story houses in the area. "See the seven tall buildings there? They're 'the seven towers.' They have the highest suicide rate in Ireland. After they discovered everywhere else in the world that you *don't* put people living on top of each other, we *built* them here."

The Ballymun Flats provide a key image in "Running to Stand Still," the grim, dreamy antiheroin ballad on *The Joshua Tree*. "It's amazing how cheap smack did Dublin in," Bono says. "And then some of my best friends started. . . . It all got a bit messy then: I wrote 'Bad' out of that, and on this record I wrote 'Running to Stand Still': 'Sweet the sin/But bitter the taste in my mouth/I see seven towers / But only one way out. . . . I took the poison, from the poison stream / And I floated out of here.' It's almost the only way out of here.

"There's this thing, if you're really desperate in Dublin, you can risk all or nothing on a 'run.' If you've got a really bad habit, you can go to Amsterdam or Pakistan or wherever and risk smuggling in a big bag. You either go down for life or you get rich quick."

There's a bright spot in the neighborhood, however, which Bono mentions as he drives along a quiet street lined with small, working-class houses, where he grew up and lived for twenty years. "There's about a hundred bands on this street now," he says, bursting into laughter, delighted at U2's evident influence. "It really is rock & roll all the way here."

DESPITE U2'S FIERCE ATTACHMENT to Ireland, *The Joshua Tree* is full of images of America—a locale that also came in and out of focus amid the murky dreamscapes of *The Unforgettable Fire*. The wild beauty, cultural richness, spiritual vacancy and ferocious violence of America are explored to compelling effect in virtually every aspect of *The Joshua Tree*—the title and cover art, the blues and country borrowings evident in the music, the imagery that pervades songs like "Bullet the Blue Sky," "In God's Country" and "Exit" (which drew its original inspiration from *The Executioner's Song,* Norman Mailer's book about Gary Gilmore's murderous odyssey in the American West). Indeed, Bono says that "dismantling the mythology of America" is an important part of *The Joshua Tree*'s artistic objective.

"You know, America's the promised land to a lot of Irish people," Bono says. "I'm one in a long line of Irishmen who made the trip to the U.S., and I feel a part of that. That's why I embraced America early on, when a lot of European bands were throwing their noses up. And America, indeed, seemed to embrace us. Of course, my opinions have changed from utter stars in the eyes." The band's new attitude toward America finds roaring expression in moments like the Edge's Hendrix-like guitar solo at the end of "Bullet the Blue Sky," which is the result of Bono's advice to the Edge after Bono had made a trip to Central America: "Put El Salvador through your amplifier."

The Edge is more direct about how the band's vision of America has grown more complex since the days when gaining an audience in this country seemed everything U2 could hope for. "The underbelly of America has come open to us," he says. "America seems to be everything that's great about the world and everything that's terrible about the world all rolled into one. . . . For us, it's the contradictions of the place, the paradoxes, the strangeness—that's what 'Bullet the Blue Sky' is all about.

"There is a tradition in America, which for a long time seemed to be pretty much dead," he says, "of people in rock & roll holding a mirror up to what was going on around them. Asking awkward questions, pointing out things. I suppose *The Joshua Tree* is in that sort of tradition."

Bono sometimes seems overwhelmed by the task of confronting the monumental problems in America and the world. "I wrestle with everything," he says, shaking his head. "Maybe I'm just one of those people. Politically, I'm looking around—there's elections coming up all over the place, in England, in the U.S. I'm sick and tired of party politics. You know, the left, the right—I'm sick of the left, I'm sick of the right. Even the *liberals* are giving me a pain in the ass. We need new solutions to new problems." He quotes from *The Joshua Tree*'s "In God's Country": " 'We need new dreams tonight.' Where are the new visionaries—the people who dream new dreams?

"We're entering into a whole new era here, a frightening new era, akin to probably what the Industrial Revolution was. Massive unemployment—

machines don't ask for pay raises, they don't go on strike, they work seven days a week, twenty-four hours a day. I can see there's going to be a lot of people out of a job. There's that. There's spiritual issues, the complications of your spiritual life. So what do you do?

"I nearly feel like just going, 'Tutti frutti,' at the moment, 'be-bop-a-lula,' " he says, laughing. "I'm starting to think that actually says *more,* because words are failing me at the moment, they're really failing me. That album is wrestling not just with myself, but wrestling with everything. Searching, and all that—on all those levels, I'm unhappy. There isn't a level I'm happy on, really."

The willingness to engage large, open-ended issues in their art and lives—and maintain both their sanity and their sense of humor—is finally the band members' best qualification for superstardom. It's why they don't need to indulge the empty rock & roll mythology of "living on the edge."

"I am finding that the real world is far more dark, far more dangerous," Bono says. "To cop out of it is cowardice."

STEVE POND

ON THE ROAD WITH U2
Band bounces back after shaky start; album rockets up the chart

T HE DAY BEFORE THE START of the most important tour of U2's career, Bono stood in a backstage hallway in the Activity Center at Arizona State University, in Tempe, Arizona, and unwittingly but unerringly summed up what would be a tumultuous, extraordinary opening week of shows. "I'll tell you," said U2's singer quietly, "being in a big band is a pain in the ass."

That's not the only place it hurt during the first week of U2's current American tour. The band had to deal with political controversy, injuries and a vocal problem that caused the first postponed show in U2 history. In addition, there were some exceedingly high expectations brought on by the success of the group's new LP, *The Joshua Tree,* which had entered the charts at Number Seven, making it the first U2 album ever to dent *Billboard*'s Top Ten. Most shows on the six-week, thirteen-city tour sold out immediately, and in some places scalpers were asking upward of $150 a ticket.

When U2 arrived in Arizona for its first three shows, the band had more on its mind than just music. After taking office in January, Arizona's new Republican governor, Evan Mecham, had promptly issued an order to rescind the state's holiday in honor of Martin Luther King Jr. In protest, the Doobie Brothers recently moved a planned Phoenix concert to Nevada. Deciding that Mecham didn't speak for the people of Arizona, U2 opted not to move its shows. Instead, the band met with and donated money to the Mecham Watchdog Committee, a group behind a recall effort. U2 also released a statement calling the governor "an embarrassment to the people of Arizona," and during a potent opening-night version of the King elegy "Pride (In the Name of Love)," Bono issued an understated but unmistakable call to arms: "I think the people of Arizona know what to do, so let's not talk about it."

Twenty-four hours before that opening show, on April Fool's Day, politics weren't worrying Bono as he stood backstage at Arizona State. "We've got a lot to live up to tomorrow," he said, his voice slightly hoarse from intensive rehearsals. "And we've already decided that the only way we can do that is by not trying to live up to anything. We are not together yet, so tomorrow's gonna be a rehearsal in front of 15,000 people."

Frowning, he walked to the stage to join U2 guitarist the Edge, bassist Adam Clayton and drummer Larry Mullen Jr. They played a gentle version of Curtis Mayfield's "People Get Ready" and some off-the-cuff, off-the-wall oddities, including a medley of Johnny Cash's "I Walk the Line" and "Folsom Prison Blues." Then they began to run through the show with a fervent version of "Where the Streets Have No Name." The few friends gathered in front of the stage cheered loudly; Bono shouted, as if to a full house, "I bet you say that to all the bands passing through here!" and things seemed in good shape.

But two songs later, midway through "Bullet the Blue Sky," Bono picked up a portable spotlight and began walking up a ramp to a raised platform at stage right. Suddenly, he slipped and fell onto the spotlight. When he stood up, his chin was covered with blood and he seemed dazed and hesitant. U2's manager, Paul McGuinness, ran onstage with a towel and hustled him into the dressing room; half an hour later, a pale and wobbly Bono was led out of the dressing room and into a waiting ambulance, the blood-soaked towel clutched to his chin. So much for U2's final rehearsal.

But the next night, as John Lennon's version of "Stand by Me" faded from the P.A. and U2 rolled into "Where the Streets Have No Name," Bono's stitches, covered by makeup, were invisible to most of the crowd; his voice, however, was clearly hurting. As the band ripped through material from the new album—which supplied six of the night's first eight songs—Bono strained to hit notes, his voice ravaged, cracked and almost reduced to a whisper at times. The intensity was there, and the presence of so many *Joshua Tree* songs gave the set an edgy, almost angry feel—but the singer could barely sing.

"When Bono has problems with his voice, he usually gets stronger during a show," the Edge said later. "But that night he got worse and worse. When he tried to sing the high notes in 'Bad,' I could tell that it took all he had. After that, there was nothing left."

So the audience supplied what the singer could not, making "Stand by Me" seem like the most fitting overture imaginable. When Bono clutched his throat in pain and stopped singing, the crowd took over. It sang the choruses of "Gloria" and "Sunday Bloody Sunday," but it also sang the new songs as lustily as if they'd been old favorites. "I knew things would work out," said an amazed Paul McGuinness afterward, "when they sang the melody to 'Running to Stand Still.' I mean, the record's only been out for ten days, and that's the fifth or sixth most popular song at radio."

Added the Edge, "It was a brilliant show, but not because of us. If it had been a different audience, we could have been in serious trouble." This is the tour on which U2 is expected to prove, night after night, that it's the best rock & roll band in the world; in Tempe it wasn't the best, but it was undoubtedly the most moving, and for one night that meant more.

But it didn't bode well for the tour. The next day, the band canceled its first show ever and worried that a week of shows might have to be scrapped. Bono's main problem, however, turned out to be a short-lived virus that causes laryngitis; two days later he was able to do the rescheduled show at what the Edge estimated as eighty percent of what Bono usually has, and the tour was back on. (The extra time enabled the band to fly to Las Vegas and catch the Hagler-Leonard fight and a Frank Sinatra concert.)

By the fourth concert of the tour, in Houston, Bono's voice was so strong that a local critic dismissed his vocal problems as "rumors." His voice broke a few times late in the show, but there were few signs that he ever held back, and the band performed its full two-hour show, not the abbreviated version it'd been forced to do in Tempe.

The Houston shows didn't have the overpowering drama of the shows in Arizona, but U2 packed a stronger punch musically, mixing the old and new to better effect than on opening night. "In God's Country" was a fearsome rocker; "Bullet the Blue Sky" included barbs at Jimmy Swaggart and Oral Roberts; "Bad" was a show stopper, with lines from "Ruby Tuesday," "Sympathy for the Devil" and "Don't Let Me Down" included the second night; "With or Without You" had even more insinuating grace than on vinyl, and Bono introduced it once by saying, "Does this sound like a hit record?" Encores included "People Get Ready," with an amateur guitarist pulled from the audience, and a stomping overhaul of Neil Young's "Southern Man," which the Edge said the group last performed in 1981, when it played a Dallas nightclub "as support act to a wet-T-shirt contest."

After the second Houston show, the Edge sat on the arm of a couch backstage and summed up the week with a small grin. "The start of this tour has been weird," he said quietly, "but we're very pleased with the progress we've made in three dates. It normally takes three or four weeks for us to really sound hot, but I feel like we're getting a handle on it. And it's only gonna get better."

With that, the Edge headed for the hotel—and, the next morning, for New Mexico, then on to Nevada and California. U2 will wind up the first leg of its tour with five mid-May dates at New Jersey's Brendan Byrne Arena, outside New York City; by then, the band may well find itself on a new level of stardom. But the tour's most indelible moment may well have come on its first night, when Bono, covered with sweat and clearly in pain, stood on a riser and gazed at the crowd roaring out the chorus to "New

Year's Day." In that moment, his tension and pain seemed to dissipate into profound relief. He broke into a smile and silently mouthed a single phrase to an audience determined to make him part of a very big band, indeed: "Thank you."

■ **RANDOM NOTES** "KINDRED SPIRITS" (June 4, 1987)

During a recent U2 show in Los Angeles, Bono began a version of Bob Dylan's "I Shall Be Released," which he dedicated to Amnesty International. Then Dylan himself walked onstage and took the second verse. "I used to make up my own words to Bob Dylan songs," Bono said when they finished the tune. "But Bob said it was okay." After a quick huddle, they launched into Dylan's "Knockin' on Heaven's Door"—complete with some of Bono's improvised lyrics.

STEVE HOCHMAN

A CELEBRATION
U2 fans join the club

"**U2** FANS ARE A SPECIAL GROUP, there's a special link between us," says Laurie Wong, a seventeen-year-old high school student from Pasadena, California. "It's more than the music. It's the meaning behind the music. What U2 says is what we want to be."

That's the kind of line we've heard from fans of everyone from Elvis to Elton, from Bruce to the Bay City Rollers. Every kid wants to believe that the bond between his or her favorite band and its audience is somehow unique. But judging by the unusual setting in which Wong made her statement, it would be hard to deny that there is something unprecedented about U2's relationship with its fans.

Wong is one of the regulars at A Celebration, a gathering of U2 fans that for the last year has taken place at Hollywood's funky, little Lhasa Club on the first Sunday of each month. Surrounding her are about 250 people, representing the whole range of U2 fandom. It is, undeniably, a mixed bag: at one table four youngsters sit and work on coloring books while their mother talks of her concern about the "satanic" message communicated in most rock music. Nearby is a group of guys in their twenties, hard at work on a case of beer. Back in the corner of the room is a man sporting long hair, a tie-dyed shirt and —among a lot of Beatles buttons—a heart-shaped pin that reads LOVE-IN '87.

That the music of U2 could draw these people into the same social setting along with the young, fresh-faced folks who make up the bulk of the crowd would be enough to support claims that U2's appeal is a singular phenomenon. But the nature of A Celebration (the name comes from an early British U2 single) adds even more support to the claim.

For one thing, how many nonprofit nightclubs do you know of? Here the five dollars each patron pays at the door is a donation rather than an admission fee, and whatever is left after overhead goes to Amnesty International and the sponsorship, through the Christian ministry organization World Vision, of two third-world children.

In the past year the club has contributed approximately $1200 to

Amnesty and $900 to World Vision. Fueled by the sounds and ideals of Dublin's favorite sons, A Celebration represents the sunny flip side of a Los Angeles underground club scene that's still marked by the darkness left by the initial punk explosion of the Seventies.

"In the club we feel it's on two levels," says Celebration cofounder Corey Lesh, a twenty-four-year-old commercial photographer. "It can be strictly entertainment, but we were hoping we'd reach people on another level. They'd be able to hear about Amnesty and sponsor children. It's like U2's music—it's more than just pop music."

Says his partner, twenty-three-year-old Ellen McCurdy, "Bono's always said, 'We're just asking you to get up and do something, just do something to make a difference.' " That was the same thought that motivated McCurdy, who works as a publicity assistant at MGM/UA, and Lesh when they first formulated the idea for the club while attending a U2 concert in December 1984.

Struck by the ease with which U2 fans seemed to communicate with each other and by the band's socially and spiritually conscious messages, the pair organized an informal get-together in a Los Angeles park for the first L.A. date of the *Unforgettable Fire* tour the following March. They asked all who came to bring a can of food to be donated to L.A.'s homeless. A notice of the gathering that appeared in the *Los Angeles Times* drew a crowd of about seventy-five. Six months later Lesh and McCurdy decided to repeat the event in a pizza parlor. The next spring, the pair were joined by Julie Borchard, a twenty-one-year-old communications student at UCLA, who became a codirector in the club. The monthly Lhasa nights began in May 1986, drawing as many as 200 eager fans to each meeting.

The result is as strong a testament to U2's ideals and influence as the band could hope for. When first informed of the club, Bono declared that it "more than anything made me feel good as a performer, as a songwriter and as a member of U2. . . . The biggest compliment anyone can pay U2 as performers is to get out there and do something themselves."

On the surface, A Celebration might appear to be a cross between a U2 fanatic's refuge and a Christian youth group. In fact, it's neither. "We have a lot of contact with fanatics," sighs McCurdy. "They search us out, and we let them know right away that we're not even going to talk to them if they act that way around us." The club discourages many typical hardcore fan activities. "We don't encourage scalping tickets," explains Borchard. "If you're going to sell a ticket here, you sell it at face value. And we don't have a table where people exchange boot recordings. We don't encourage that at all."

Actually, one could spend an evening at the club without even talking about U2, since much of the music played is by other stylistically related artists, like the Alarm, Cactus World News and the Waterboys. And they are booking local musicians to perform at A Celebration. Still, there is a certain sense that for anything other than U2 music to get much play, it has to have been "blessed" by the Dublin lads.

As for the Christian angle, the club directors are adamant that although three members of U2—and a club codirector—identify themselves as Christians, the club itself has no religious overtone. "We're definitely a secular club," says Borchard. "We have no affiliation with any church or religion or value system, although World Vision is a Christian-based organization. I see a bunch of middle-class kids with middle-class values, and if those are Christian then, yeah, that's what you might see."

With a year's experience under their belts, the Celebration organizers are looking for ways to broaden the club's scope. Though reluctant to sacrifice the club's intimacy, they hope to spread the concept across the country. They've already been consulted by a woman who recently started a Celebration-inspired gathering in Boston Common, and a regular Boston club is set for the fall. But the three insist that if A Celebration never added another person to its roster, they'd still be satisfied with what they've accomplished thus far.

Lesh, with near-evangelical zeal, says, "Every month [Amnesty International] petitions are being signed. Every month money's going to Amnesty and World Vision. Every month we get up and explain about different injustices. So if it stayed on the level it's on now, it would be a success to us.

"Cynics say, 'I can't change the world.' I *can't* change the world, but I can change the world for one person. I can go down to McDonald's and find a homeless person and buy him food and change his life for one day. That's the idealism we believe in. That's what U2 said all along. This is right. This is true."

■ **RANDOM NOTES** "ROBBIE ROBERTSON: SOLO BUT NOT ALONE" (August 13, 1987)

Robbie Robertson's first solo album—three years in the making—is due this September, and Robertson has no intention of picking up where the Band left off. "This is just the way I feel now," he says, "just the way I *hear* now. I don't know if it's what's expected of me or if it's going to be shocking. You just do what your heart tells you to do." Though Robertson plays guitar and keyboards and handles all the lead vocals, he's not completely on his own. Peter Gabriel joins him on "Broken Arrow," the Wisconsin rockers the Bo-Deans sing backup on "Showdown at Big Sky" and "American Roulette," and U2 sits in on "Sweet Fire of Love" and "Testimony." "That was a challenge," he says of his collaboration with the Irish rockers, "mixing two worlds of music together. I didn't know U2 was going to become the biggest band in the world this year." In fact, U2 worked with Robbie well before the release of *The Joshua Tree* and the ensuing furor. "It was just an experiment, and whether we're successful or not . . . we'll see."

■ **RANDOM NOTES** "PARIS MATCH" (September 10, 1987)

What were David Bowie and U2's Bono doing out together at a Paris club? "We sat and talked most of the evening about comparative experiences—shows and things," says Bowie. The following night, Bono, the Edge, Larry Mullen Jr. and Adam Clayton attended Bowie's concert at a stadium in Paris and visited him backstage. U2 played there the following night. Bowie's elaborately choreographed stage show is said to have gotten a mixed reception from some European audiences. At any rate, he's had no trouble selling tickets for his first dates in the States. "I really wasn't sure how American audiences would take to the show," he said after a sold-out New York appearance, "but the response from the crowds has been just terrific." U2 is also thinking big these days: when the Irish band returns to the U.S. in September, it will be playing several stadiums as part of an Eastern swing. Planned dates include New York's Shea and Philadelphia's J.F.K.: shows are also slated for Montreal and Toronto.

DAVID BRESKIN

BONO: THE Rolling Stone INTERVIEW

"**D**ARLING, I WOULD LOVE TO take you by the hand, take you to some twilight land," sings the country songwriter, his voice wistful and cracked. He struggles through the verses, faltering a bit, forgetting, humming here and there, just pickin' his guitar and tappin' his foot gently in the corner of the darkened room. Finally, in a mood of wizened woe, he finishes the last chorus, "Am I left to burn and burn eternally? She's a mystery to me."

Now, what makes this particular moment in the history of tearful country ballads (a man, a guitar and PAIN!) a bit more fetching is that the lonesome critter over there in the corner, the sad-eyed young man who done wrote the song, who is sitting quietly at home in his modest castle—which is, in fact, an ancient seaside watchtower built with seven-foot-thick walls of granite and oxblood mortar to withstand shelling from hostile navies—happens to be the same fellow who usually spends his time fronting the world's most popular rock & roll band.

And when done crooning "She's a Mystery to Me," the strange and lovely song he's writing for Roy Orbison, he launches into "When Love Comes to Town," an uptempo chugger he figures might fit B.B. King. Barely pausing, he plunges into "Prisoner of Love," which features a handy doo-wop break in the chorus, and then assays his beloved ballad "Lucille," his first-ever country song, written way, way back in the spring of 1987. And so here we have Bono, at home outside Dublin, during a short break on a long tour. Well, shucks!

We met a few days earlier in Cardiff, Wales, where U2 gave a spirited outdoor sing-along for 55,000. (Angst ridden and angst driven, the band's shows have become—for its fans—forceful, friendly rituals: sort of like Up With People, with an edge.) Immediately thereafter, a police escort whisked the band members away from the exiting mob toward the little white jet—the one with OUT OF OUR TREE TOUR painted on its fuselage—waiting at the airport to bring them home. And there, over the course of two days in late July, first in my hotel room, with the gulls wheeling and crying outside the window, and then in his watchtower, with John Coltrane's recording "A Love Supreme" snaking up the spiral staircase, Bono and I talked.

He often spoke in little more than a whisper, his voice strained from recording B sides of singles until early-morning hours on nights offstage. What he revealed beneath his well-defined and carefully controlled surface was an enthusiast in the grips of reason; a wishful idealist stimulated and confused by his own contradictions; and a young man who quite honestly has not found what he's looking for—and may never. Chances are if he ever does find it, he'll know it when he sees it, stop briefly to enjoy the view, and move on.

*L*ET'S DO A RADICAL THING AND *go back to before the beginning. Your grandparents.*

My grandfather—my dad's dad—was a comedian at Saint Francis Xavier Hall, in the center of the city. He was a morose man. So I think this idea of laughing a lot and then biting one's own tongue is something that runs in the family.

My grandmother on my mother's side was a really big laugh. Which disguised the fact that beneath her dress, she had a big stick with which she reared, I think, eight kids. She used to joke that the contraceptives, which were banned in Ireland, were intercepted at the post office, and—too late!—another kid was born, another mouth to feed.

My mother was the oldest of her family and quite petite. Really a delicate flower, but she took on the responsibility of bringing up the younger kids.

Both my mother and my father were from the center of the city, what they call Dubs. My mother was a Protestant, and my father was a Catholic, and they grew up on the same street. Their love affair was illicit at the time. Ireland was just being born as a country, and the Protestant-Catholic rivalry—the bigotry—was at a pitch. But it didn't mean anything to them. They faced the flak and got married.

It was a bit of a difficult thing to do.

In a mixed marriage the children had to be brought up Catholic. The Protestants made up only about ten percent of the population at that time, and it was an anathema to them. My mother decided to bring us up in the Protestant church, and my old man went along with this. So my old man would drop us off at one place of worship and go on to another one. And I really resented that. I was always fighting with him. Always fighting. We were too alike.

Was he a disciplinarian?

He attempted to be. He was a very strict man. But I was one of those kids who was almost impossible to tie down, from the very beginning. People used to—and family people still sort of—put up the cross [*crosses index fingers*] whenever I come in. They used to call me the Antichrist [*laughs*]. How many kids on your block were nicknamed the Antichrist?

What's the first thing you can remember?

I remember having my photograph taken with my brother and not liking it. I was around three years old. I think we had two little leopards, like ornaments on the mantel, and at the end of the session there was only one leopard left, and I was put away for that.

Do you have any idyllic childhood memories?

None at all. The little pieces that I can put back together are, if not violent, then aggressive. I can remember my first day in school. I was introduced to this guy, James Mann, who, at age four, had the ambition of being a nuclear physicist, and one of the guys bit his ear. And I took that kid's head and banged it off the iron railing. It's terrible, but that's the sort of thing I remember. I remember the trees outside the back of the house where we lived, and them tearing those trees down to build an awful development. I remember real anger.

What of your mom and dad and the way they got on?

To be honest, I don't remember that much about my mother. I forget what she looks like. I was fourteen or fifteen when she died, but I *don't remember*. I wasn't close to my mother or father. And that's why, when it all went wrong—when my mother died—I felt a real *resentment,* because I actually had never got a chance . . . to feel that unconditional love a mother has for a child. There was a feeling of that house pulled down on top of me, because after the death of my mother that house was no longer a home—it was just a house. That's what "I Will Follow" is about. It's a little sketch about that unconditional love a mother has for a child: "If you walk away, walk away I will follow," and "I was on the outside when you said you needed me/I was looking at myself I was blind I could not see." It's a really *chronic* lyric.

There was not a lot of closeness, physically?

Not really. I have just found out bits and pieces about my family in the last year or two. Now I want to know. Before I didn't. Trying to talk to my old man is like trying to talk to a brick wall.

Even now?

Even now. Do you know, the first time he really spoke to me was the night of his retirement from the post office. I went to his send-off party. I used to hear all the names, Bill O'This and Joseph O'That, and I never knew who they were, and I didn't really know what he did. But at this party a year and a half ago, I met all these people. And they were amazing. It was at a pub, and there was a guy with a fiddle, and they were all singing songs. There was a guy who had painted on a Hitler mustache who introduced me to his daughter, and I said, "Who are you?" And she said, "The Hitler youth." It was like a Fellini movie. It was a world, a world of Irish in Dublin. And afterward, he showed me the place he worked, where I had never been. And he showed me the seat that he used to sit in. And already someone else had moved into that seat. And that night, I got to talk to my old man for the first time. We had a glass of whiskey, and he began to tell me a few things about what it was like growing up.

It's been said that artists never get over their childhood, and perhaps, in some ways, it's because they don't that they remain artists.

I think maybe it should be said that a lot of artists never grow up [*laughs*]. I think it's certainly true in rock & roll. Rock & roll gives people a chance not to grow up—it puts them in a glass case and protects them from the real world of where they're gonna get their next meal. Who is it—Camus?—who said, "Wealth, my dear friend, is not exactly acquittal, just reprieve." But in the end, I don't know if being a pop star is any less real than being a city clerk. Is suburbia the real world? Is the real world half the population of Africa that is starving? I haven't worked it out yet. I always wondered, "What am I? Am I Protestant or Catholic? Am I working-class or middle-class?" I always felt like I was sitting on the fence.

Well, the very fact that you were fifteen when you lost your mom and yet can't remember her suggests that there is a lot that you've blocked out. When you were a teenager, you were very angry and uptight, and I wonder how much of that is a result of her death.

I don't know. As I've said before, the fact that I'm attracted to people like Gandhi and Martin Luther King is because I was exactly the opposite of that: I was the guy who wouldn't turn the other cheek.

Let's say you scuffled a bit.

[*Laughs*] "Scuffle" is a beautiful euphemism.

Okay, you beat the crap out of people.

Well, I'd never start a fight, but I'd always finish it.

You were a contentious little S.O.B.

It was the way we grew up. Street fights were just the way. I remember picking up a dustbin [garbage can] in a street fight, and I remember thinking to myself, "This is ridiculous. I'm not going to hit someone with this." And right then, this guy came up with an iron bar and brought that iron bar down so hard on me. And I just used the lid to protect myself. I would have been dead, stone dead, if I hadn't had that thing. But when you're singing songs, people think you are like the songs you sing about. I think we need to let some air out of that balloon.

The songs may represent you because you need to be like the songs you sing—not that you are yet those things.

Yes. You want to be.

And what kind of feeling did you have inside after these violent episodes?

I never liked it. Never. I would worry sick about having to go out on the street, in case a guy I had been in a mill with would come back for more.

And yet I can remember—not so many years ago—we were playing in a local bar here, and some guy threw a glass. And the glass just missed slashing Edge's arm. And I knew the guy that threw it. There was resentment, because Adam and Edge came from a sort of middle-class background, and people thought, "Oh, U2, they're not really punks!" But I *knew* where this guy lived. And he lived in a bigger house than I did. And it took all my energy to stop myself from driving a car through his front door that night.

Were you curious as a kid, but not in an academic way?

I was curious, but I never knew what I wanted to be. One day I'd wake up and want to be a chess player—the best. I'd read a book on it, and at twelve I studied the grandmasters, and I was fascinated. The next day I'd think, "No, I'll be a painter." Because I'd always painted, since I was four years old. So I was just wandering. And I'm still wandering, I suppose. But see, I want it all and I want it now [*laughs*].

You were the first punk in your class—haircut, pants, chain, et cetera. Did you really feel it, or was it just theater?

It was theater. I had gotten interested in Patti Smith and then the Sex Pistols. And the great thing about the Ramones was you could play Ramones songs all in three chords—which was all I had then and, in fact, is about all I have now [*laughs*]. Before that, I was interested in Irish folk music. It was around my family. There was a lot of singsong. And my brother taught me those three chords. He used to play [the Kenny Rogers and the First Edition classic] "Ruby, Don't Take Your Love to Town." I'm still fascinated by that song.

And my old man was into opera, which, as far as I was concerned, was just heavy metal. I like those bawdy opera songs: the king is unfaithful to the queen, then he gets the pox, they have a son, the son grows up and turns into an alligator, and in the end they kill the alligator and make some shoes for the king. But because it's sung in Italian, people think it's very aloof. Not at all.

And when the now-famous note went up on the now-famous bulletin board, asking for members to form a band, did you think, "Ah, this is it"?

No. At that stage, I was interested in the theater. When I was younger, I ran away from home one day to book myself into an acting school. But there was no acting school. My father used to act at a theater, and I would sit in the front row. When I was thirteen or fourteen, I set up a theater company in the school I was in, because there was none. I don't know if I would be a good actor. Now, I'd almost like to write for the stage more than to be on the stage. So when the note went up, I had to be talked into it by a friend.

Was being onstage the lure?

Yeah. And in one of the plays, I sang. I remember the feeling of singing through a microphone and hearing it bounce off the walls. I got a bit of a *belt* off of that—sort of an electric shock. But even after we started, Adam was the only reason we went any further. He'd say, "I think I know where we can get a gig." And I'd say, "What's that?" He'd say, "A place where we can play." I'd say, "You mean *in front of people?* But we're crap." He'd say, "So are the Sex Pistols." [*Laughs.*]

There'd been a precedent for people who couldn't play.

Yes. You see, the roundabout had just slowed down enough for us to jump on. Any other time, and it wouldn't have worked out. 'Cause before that it was all the worship of the instrumentalist, and you had to be able to play. All we had was raw power.

The acting fell by the wayside. And I got a job as a petrol-pump attendant so that I could write when the cars weren't coming in. But then we had the oil crisis, and we had these queues for miles, and the cars just kept coming, so I quit.

Are Edge, Adam and Larry guys you would have chosen for your friends if you didn't have the music among you?

No. No. Now I would, but not then.

You claim you're socially inept.

I'm very awkward, I'm not a very good pop star. [*At this point, room service knocks. A young attendant brings in six Heinekens, and seeing Bono, he almost drops his tray. He nervously asks for an autograph and is obliged.*]

See, your regal presence totally disarmed this poor guy. You seem like a perfect pop star.

Well, I don't feel like a pop star, and I don't think I look like one.

What's a pop star supposed to feel like?

Well, I don't know. But I *imagine* if you're a pop star, that you don't feel like me. If I was a good pop star, I wouldn't be telling you about the way I grew up, because I'd want to keep those things from the public. I'd want people to believe I just came out of thin air. Sometimes I wish I were that way. At the moment, actually, I'm going for bastard lessons.

Where do you begin—Refusing Autographs 101?

Like when the twentieth caller knocks on the door to my house, I'm just going to tell them, "Fuck off! Leave me be!" instead of bringing them in for a cup of tea. Which I do, which is just dumb. I think the thing I least like about myself is that I'm *reasonable*. And being reasonable is a very un-pop-star trait. So I am taking bastard lessons.

In 1979 you said, "We're determined to achieve a position where we have artistic freedom and where we can affect people the way we want to affect them. That position derives from money and success, and we'll work very hard to get there." So you did, and now you're here: pop stars.

It's true, we did work long and hard to get rid of the anonymity that we now need in order to live. It's an interesting irony. I can remember thinking, back in '77, "Yeah, we are going to take this all the way." Do other people think those things? Was it blind faith or just stupidity? And if your dream comes true, is it dangerous to think that all of your dreams will come true?

Well, two tragic things can happen: one is to not get what you want, and the other is to get what you want.

Yeah. But we really haven't gotten what we want. You see, we live in a culture where the biggest is often equated with the best. And now people say we are the biggest band in the world. So what? That means nothing to me. No, it must mean something. But our want is to be worthy of the position we've been put in. To be the best—to make a music that hasn't been made before. And I don't know that we'll get to that point.

Can you assume it's even possible to get there, playing to crowds of 60,000 people? Aren't the limitations imposed on communicating to that many people contrary to the notion of experimentation? In this context you become a "product" no matter what your intentions.

Well, live is not the place to experiment. U2 has always been a very different act live than in the studio. Part of rock & roll is about raw power, and that's what we are about live. In the studio we have experimented, and we will continue to. I suppose what we're looking for is a better synthesis of the two.

In the studio you usually build from improvisations, and yet when you present the material live, it's very formal, structured, repetitive.

Yes. U2 live is much more like theater: there is a beginning, a middle and an end. On this last tour, we have been experimenting with that form more than ever.

I must say, there is a real thrill to being onstage in front of 50,000 or 60,000 people. The event is much larger than the group and the audience. It's an amazing thing to see people united and in agreement, even if only for an hour and a half.

Does it ever frighten you, seeing that?

No, because I never underestimate the intelligence of the U2 audience en masse. I actually feel that they know more about the group than we do.

We were in the audience when the Clash played Dublin. We just got up out of the audience ourselves and played. So I feel very close to the audience. There's no separation in my own mind. And I know if I told them all to stand on their heads, that they'd tell me where to go.

But you clench your fist in a particular way, and all 60,000 will clench their fists accordingly. Is there not something within this gesture that gives you pause?

When a Japanese man bows to another man, and the other man bows in response, that's nothing but a sign of consent. When people respond, or when they sing a song I've asked them to sing, they are just being part of a bigger theatrical event. The idea that they are rather moronically being lemmings, following Adam, Larry, Edge and Bono off the cliff's edge with their fists in the air, does not pay them enough respect.

But there is a power inherent in your position, and it would take a certain amount of duplicity or false humility on your part to suggest that there's not. And that power . . .

Can be taken advantage of. Maybe.

And you never have intellectual or emotional hesitations about that kind of power?

That kind? No. There are other kinds of power—the kinds that are not seen—that worry me. If you could see into the dressing rooms and the offices of a lot of bands in our position, you would see the real abuse of power. Like making a promoter crawl because you are paying his wages; like making the road crew wait for four hours because you are late for a sound check; like the sexual abuse of people who are turned on by your music. I don't know whether I am guilty of all of those. Maybe I am. But that is the type of power I worry about in rock & roll.

On your tour of the States in 1981, you had, for the first time, people grabbing at you for autographs, and you felt like a commodity and were quite depressed by the whole "gladiators, dinosaur rock" thing, you called it. And then when the group first broke through in the States, a few years back, you said, "I believe in U2 in audiences up to 20,000." And yet now you are playing to fifty, sixty, seventy thousand people.

We have to. To do a tour that lasts three years in length would be the end of us as artists. And to do a short tour [playing arenas], where we just ignore people and make them pay scalpers for tickets—I don't like it. I've even said from the stage, "Don't pay those prices." But they do. They will pay $100 to see U2, and U2 is not worth $100. So on this tour, we've tried to strike a balance of playing indoors and outdoors, so the ones that really want to see us indoors get a chance, *and* we can play to other people. I think U2 can actually do it. People invented the idea of "stadium acts"—you think of these great chord-crashing dinosaurs. But Stevie Wonder is a stadium act, the Beatles were, Bob Marley was.

Let's go back to where we started on this, that is, the sort of public power you are able to exercise at the moment. You've stated a number of times that the goal of all U2 songs is to make people think for themselves.

To inspire people to do things for themselves. To inspire people to think for themselves. But that's *not* why I'm in U2: I'm in U2 because it inspires *me*. I'm here because I couldn't find work anywhere else. And the real reasons to be in a rock & roll band are probably much closer to ego, and to be onstage and have people look at you and think you're a great guy. Those are the real reasons—at least when you're fifteen and sing into a microphone. On the way, since that time, we've thought about what we're doing—and we've accepted some of the traditions of rock & roll and rejected others.

Let me play devil's advocate: it seems like standing among an audience of 60,000 people, all singing the same song, can in no way encourage one to think for oneself.

I disagree. They *do* think for themselves is my point. But the problem is that in the world we live in, in the West, the doctrine of personal peace and prosperity prevails. If you've got a fridge, a car or two, a vacation once a year, you're okay. And you'll agree to anything, such as voting for whoever can preserve this. People are subject to a lot of influences that attempt to send them to sleep. There is media. People's reaction to violence onscreen: the difference between what is real on the news and what is surreal on *Miami Vice* has become blurred. We are in a big sleep, where I'm okay, you're okay. And we don't ask questions that have difficult answers.

And if U2 is throwing cold water over that kind of thinking and people are waking up—that's fine. But that's not the reason we're there. We're there because this is the way *we feel* about the world. Now people have to choose: they go to the supermarket and choose what brand of cornflakes to buy and what detergent. They have to make choices. And U2 is just one choice.

Isn't there a worry for any serious artist that he represents just such a choice— that he is packaged and sold like a detergent, that he is advertised and marketed in a certain way, that he is a commodity?

From my point of view, it's just important that we're there, that people have a choice. We are getting to the point where the choices are being dictated for us—records are being banned and choices limited. Rock & roll in the Seventies was just completely banal. I don't want to put U2 up as *the* alternative, but I think it is a good thing that a song like "With or Without You" was played on Top Forty radio.

Why?

Because I think it is provocative, both sonically and in what it suggests. When I was growing up and listening to the radio, I would hear maybe one song in every twenty or forty and fifty that I would like, that I would feel was an alternative to the music that other people deemed fit to hear on the radio. That's why I feel it's important that U2 is on the radio, that we don't leave the radio just to these product-oriented people. Because there are groups, just as there are record companies, who treat music like a tin of beans—a product to be sold.

And yet U2 is a product. . . .

I don't think of it that way.

But the record company may, and the management company must, and the advertisers do, and the promoters do, and the radio programmers do, and the T-shirt and poster manufacturers do. . . .

And that is why rock & roll is in the situation it finds itself in in 1987. Because no longer do fans of music run the music business. Fans of money run the music business.

Without being too precious about U2, let me say I'm learning to accept T-shirts; what I'm not willing to accept is bad T-shirts. There are traditions in rock & roll I am accepting, but what's important to me is the music. It would be a trap for me to spend my whole life fighting a battle about something—my knuckles would be bleeding from beating on the walls of the music business—when really what my fingers should be wrapped around are the frets of a guitar, trying to write down the way I feel and make it a song.

In some ways, intellectually, it's almost a defeat to be where you are.

Yes. Talk to Miles Davis about it.

Does this thing ever give you the blues?

Yeah. What gives me the blues more than anything is the glass case that comes with success in rock & roll. The one area of control, real control, that we have is the music, and so everything must gather around that. And our organization is set up to protect that. And in order to do that, you take on some of the excess baggage of rock & roll—like a plane—so that you can get home after a show and see your family and your friends who you haven't seen in five years. And if your motive is to protect the music, then as far as I'm concerned, those things are okay.

Let's go back to the glass case.

The glass cage, it could be called.

Now, a lot of it has to do with money, and because of who you are—what your values are—you're resistant to even deal with it.

Listen, I felt like a rich man even when I had no money. I would live off my girlfriend's pocket money or the people on the street. Money has never had anything to do with how rich I feel. But it is almost vile for me to say that money doesn't mean anything to me, because it means a lot to many people. It means a lot if you don't have it.

But how do you deal with the fact that you do have it? You've said in the past, "I just don't want to see it," which sounds like the first stage of reacting to anything that's traumatic, and that's denial.

Yeah [*pauses*]. Oh, boy. All money's done is remove me from my friends and family, which are my lifeblood. It has cut me off. People have said, "You've changed." But sometimes it's not you who has changed but the other people in their reaction to you. Because they are worrying about the price of a round of drinks, and you're not. It's the butt end of stardom. And this fits in perfectly with the U2 sourpuss image—you know, U2 is number one, and they're too *stupid* to enjoy it [*laughs*].

Well, as W.C. Fields said, "Start off every day with a smile, and get it over with." Maybe you're the W.C. Fields of rock.

[*Laughs, almost defensively*] Well, I do enjoy being in a number-one band, and I do enjoy the jet so I can get home while on tour, and I do enjoy hearing the record on the radio, so I don't want to come across as being down-in-the-mouth about being number one. I am on top of the world, it's just that something else is on top of me.

Your great couplet from "New Year's Day" doesn't only apply on a macro level to society but on a micro level to the band: "And so we are told this is the golden age/And gold is the reason for the wars we wage."

Yeah, and I'm starting to see the value of being irresponsible. You know, you read about the excesses of the rock & roll stars of the Seventies—driving Rolls-Royces into swimming pools. Well, that's better than *polishing* them, which is the sort of yuppie pop-star ethic we've got in the Eighties [*laughs*].

Brian Eno says something interesting about money. He says that possessions are a way of converting money into trouble. You can almost trace the downfall of some of the great rock & roll bands by the rise of their consumerism. They were consumed by it. You can see that when they got fat and settled down, their music wasn't the same. And I don't want that to happen in U2, 'cause it's the music that is the center of our world—and I don't want that to be replaced by either, one, material wealth, or two, the worry about it.

It's said that there's never been a true artist who couldn't handle failure, but that many have run aground on the rocks of success.

I suppose I just don't see U2 as a success. I just see U2 as a whole list of failures: the songs we haven't written and the concerts we haven't played.

I don't know if we will make it through. I suppose the chances are that we won't. But maybe if we know that, we will.

What could stop you? The fact that you and Edge are the focus musically, and you are the leader lyrically?

It's true that the two of us are becoming more interested in the craft of songwriting, as opposed to the band's overall interest in improvising. But I think we've gotten it right in the past—there are four of us, and we are committed to that. What would a U2 song be without Larry playing the drums? "Pride" started with Larry and Adam. Adam just about wrote the backing for that.

Do you ever feel limited being in U2?

Well, if you want to be in a band, I think U2 is the best band to be in. But sometimes you become restless. You think, "Wouldn't it be interesting to write a play or a book or to work with Miles Davis?" Sure. But to be in a band is an amazing feeling, both in its fraternity and fun and frolics, as well as its musical achievement. See, only about ten people in the world make me really laugh, and four of them are in the band—including Paul [McGuinness], our manager.

Before 'The Joshua Tree,' you had an album in your head you said U2 almost couldn't play. Did you put a lot on the shelf in making 'The Joshua Tree'?

We did about thirty songs, so there's a lot in gestation. There's a few records we still want to make, and maybe some of these songs will be completed.

Rock & roll, it seems, is caught up in juvenilia. Relationships are at the level of sex in the back seat of a Chevrolet. Now I'm interested in what happens further down the road—the violence of love, ownership, obsession, possession, all these things. And I think rock & roll is wide-open for a writer who can take it all down. And take it to the radio. "With or Without You" is a really twisted love song, and it's on the radio.

Let's go back a few years. During the 'War' tour, you said that you thought rock & roll was full of shit, and that you were fed up with it.

And the question is: Do I still think rock & roll is full of shit? Yes, I do. It was full of shit then, and it's still full of shit, and it's always been full of shit. For me, rock & roll has always been as black as a mine—but you could find a jewel down there that made it all worthwhile. At that time, we just didn't seem to fit in. I had to ask myself, What is it about? Elvis Presley shooting at the television while reading his Bible; Jerry Lee Lewis believing in God and playing the devil's music with his fourteen-year-old bride at his side; John Lennon at the peak of his success singing "Help." Rock & roll is almost *about* the confusion. So I see now that there is a place for my own confusion and my own contradictions—my own desire to do something relevant with my life, as well as my own enjoyment of driving down Park Avenue in a limousine.

I guess I've just accepted the contradictions: being in a privileged position and writing about those without privilege; being in a position of *having* and writing about those that *have not;* being fully employed and writing a song about unemployment. These are contradictions, and they're awkward at times.

Do you feel lonely?

More and more, over the last years. I feel cut off. I used to go out the back of the venues, and there would be some people hanging around, and we'd chat, maybe sign some bits of paper and go back to their places and sleep on the floor, talk through the night. Or I'd have people come to my room. One time I had thirteen people sleeping in my room, on the floor. Now I go out, and I don't know who I can talk to. I've got people who want to kill me, people who want to make love with me, so they can sell their story to the newspapers, people who want to hate you or love you or take a bit of you. So you end up going back to the hotel and back to your room, and even if it's a suite in the finest hotel, after being onstage in front of 10,000 or 100,000 people, it's almost a prison cell. But, hey, if you can't stand the heat in the kitchen, then get out.

But I have fewer friends now than I did five years ago. I know more people. I'm a lot of people's best friend.

Has this made you cynical?

No, I don't want to be cynical. Maybe lesson number two in How to Become a Bastard will teach me to be cynical [*laughs*]. I'm open.

The challenge of your position is, How do you make it not a prison?

Imagine what it would be like being a solo performer. At least we've got each other. We're a band, a real band. I can always drag Edge out of bed and talk.

I hardly saw Ali, my wife, for a year. Nineteen eighty-six was an incredibly bad year for me. It's almost impossible to be married and be in a band on the road—but Ali is able to make it work. Then you tell the press that she is her own person and very smart and not some dolly girl and that she doesn't take any shit from me, and they read into it a marital breakdown. And I think, "Well, what sort of women are they married to?"

Have you thought about having children?

I'm both frightened and excited by it. I feel just too irresponsible. The kid would end up being my father. I'm the sort of guy where the son is sent out to fetch his dad and bring him home. But I think Ali would be an amazing mother, and it might be exciting to see new life. I'd just be afraid that if it were a boy, it would turn out like me.

Is Greg Carroll's death the most significant thing that's happened to you in the last few years?

Yes, yes it is. It was a devastating blow. He was doing me a favor, he was taking my bike home. [Carroll, a U2 employee, died in July 1986, at the age of twenty-six, in a motorcycle accident.] Greg used to look after Ali. They would go out dancing together. He was a best friend. I've already had it once, with my mother, and now I've had it twice. The worst part was the fear, and fear is the opposite of faith. After that, when the phone rang, my heart stopped every time. Now when I go away I wonder, "Will these people be here when I get back?" You start thinking in those terms. We've never performed "One Tree Hill" [a song about Carroll's funeral], and I can't. In fact I haven't even heard the song, though I've listened to it a hundred times. I've cut myself off from it completely. I want to start singing it soon.

How much of 'The Joshua Tree' was written after Greg died?

I don't know.

Because it clearly stands above your other records in its openness, its willingness to reveal and not conceal.

I agree with you. I think so. It's a very personal record. Greg's death brought us together in a way. That's what always happens. It becomes *the family* again.

So much of fashionable pop has been presented with coolness, distance.

It was sad for us in U2 to discover when we were eighteen that the Sex Pistols were a "good idea" that someone had thought up. Because when we were sixteen we had *believed* in it, we believed in rock & roll. Often it is a sham. And it can be entertaining or even enlightening as that, but that's not what I like. I like it to be loose, to laugh at itself. Tutti-frutti, yes, but being manipulated by an artist, no.

There have been times when your work has not been so revealing. I think one reason some folks had problems with 'The Unforgettable Fire' is because some of it seemed not ambiguous but confused, and confusion is irritating, such as on "Elvis Presley and America."

There is confusion in that. That is genuinely confused. But we were not at all confused in making the decision to put it there. A jazzman could understand that piece. He would just listen to it. Was it self-indulgent? Yes. But why not? *The Unforgettable Fire* was a beautifully out-of-focus record, blurred like an impressionist painting, very unlike a billboard or an advertising slogan. These days we are being fed a very airbrushed, advertising-man's way of seeing the world. In the cinema, I find myself reacting against the perfect cinematography and the beautiful art direction—it's all too beautiful, too much like an ad. And all the videos have the same beauty and the beautiful shadows and . . .

Your videos, too!

Yeah. And if I had made a film a few weeks ago, it might look like that. But something is happening in me that makes me want to find a messier, less-perfect beauty. I'd like to see things more raw.

Is it harder to please yourself now? Are you tougher on the lyrics?

I used to see words as music and my voice as an instrument. It was the sound of the words as much as the sense that interested me. The way they bumped against each other, not necessarily their meaning. The idea of a couplet I think I discovered about two years ago, talking with Elvis Costello. But my writing at best is still sort of subconscious. "Running to Stand Still" is pretty much as I wrote it the first time, as a sort of prose poem.

You take a stance against cliché, and yet there are clichéd images throughout 'The Joshua Tree.' Through the storm we reach the shore, mountains crumble, rivers run to the sea.

Yes. I was rooting around for a sense of the traditional and then trying to twist it a bit. That's the idea of "I Still Haven't Found What I'm Looking For."

But there are other places where clichés are used without the sense of irony they have in that song, and they just come across as stock images or metaphors, whereas a few albums ago, before you had developed as a lyricist, they wouldn't have been noticed.

Umm. There are two rival instincts in me as a word writer. One is an interest in writing subconsciously, almost in a half sleep, which is the way I wrote "One Tree Hill." And the other instinct is a desire not to be self-indulgent and not to use clichés the way rock & roll music has always used them. The Beatles were experts at it, every single song: "Please Please Me," "The Long and Winding Road."

Do you think it's more important to be good or to be original?

I think it is more important to be good. But rock & roll is at its most exciting when it's pushing at the parameters a bit. When it stands still for too long, it gets stagnant.

Have you ever felt dry? Like you were operating in a closed loop of your own devices and had nothing new to say or a way to say it?

No. When I was at school, I remember we were talking about William Butler Yeats and the different periods in his life. And the teacher told us about a period when he felt he had nothing left to say, and how this often happens to poets. I said, "Yeah, but why didn't he write about the fact that he had nothing left to say?" And that is what I have always done—started with what I feel. As it says in the Bible, know the truth, and the truth will set you free.

You're never frustrated with your own limitations?

I'm so undisciplined and untidy, and the everyday doings of my life are such a mess, that I get frustrated. I write on the bus, on the backs of cigarette packets or on the table mats in restaurants and lose them. I lost a song I wrote with Bob Dylan, in the early-morning hours after a gig in L.A., during our last tour. I've got to own up to being a writer and just write. So now I'm trying to develop the craft of songwriting, so that what I do neither dries up nor blows up in my face. And all of us are committed to thrashing about in the studio.

Do you think you've gotten past shouting now—and are finally a singer?

I'm becoming a singer, I think. I'm not a soul singer yet, but I think I've got soul. We may not be accomplished musicians, we are raw, but I think all I want is that soul. Because, now, as we listen to Coltrane, if that didn't have soul, I wouldn't listen to it. I'm not impressed by the jazzman's technical ability, but rather I'm impressed by the way he can use his skill to tell a story, to create a mood, to make me believe. That's the ability to reveal and not conceal, and that's what I want.

You have been insisting in interviews all through this tour that you take the music seriously, but not yourself. It's almost defensive, as if in this age it's not cool to take yourself too seriously. Why the dichotomy?

It's just that we have this image of po-faced young men. Severe and serious. Like the album covers. I mean, are these guys too stupid to enjoy their success? Don't these guys ever go down to the pub or take the piss out of each other? Of course we do. There is a somewhat unbalanced impression of U2, and that's where that comment comes from.

It's my suspicion that you do take yourself rather seriously. What's wrong with that? This is the age of Lite beer and lite music and lite politics, so why be defensive about being heavy?

I have to be careful that people don't manipulate our public image into something we're not. When we come offstage, we're just four guys in the dressing room. I think it's okay to be serious as long as you're not boring.

Well, if you don't live it, it won't come out of your horn.

Is that a jazz phrase? I understand it. See, I'm a guy with no midrange. I'm all bottom and all top, emotionally. I let people take advantage of me way past the point others let people go. But when I break, I really break. Watch out.

So your "reasonableness" is a defense against losing it?

Yeah, and I'm sick of it. It leads me to make a lot of bad decisions. I just wish I could be a little more testy or say, "Stop," to someone who is doing something I don't like. I put up with it. There are some hilarious examples of this. When I first got married, I put up with an alcoholic house painter for two weeks, who painted rooms in the colors he wanted—but then he painted the front door *silver*. I told him, "I don't like silver." He said, "Everybody is going for the chrome-door look." At which point I took him and all his paints and threw them out of the house.

Do you weary of the missionary vibe that has come to surround you—that you are some sort of savior for Irish youth, or some kind of quasi-political, quasi-religious figure to your fans in the States? How do you deal with this?

[*Long pause*] Oh, boy. I don't have an answer to that. But I know that I have to find the answer. On one level, it's exciting. Amnesty International doubled its membership because of that tour. But it's not so exciting having a psychopath call you up day after day because he thinks you're left-wing politically. Writing a song is one thing, but a song can't save anybody's life.

You're talking about the differences between art and action. Can you imagine a time or a condition where you would feel the need to put down the guitar and pick up a gun?

You mean, is there a point where instead of singing about apartheid you should be on the street demonstrating? Should you be tying yourself to the gates of the South African embassy? I don't think an artist has that responsibility; his responsibility is to his art, ultimately.

Don't you feel an artist's responsibility, above and beyond his art, is ultimately to his fellow human beings?

I need a few cornflakes before I answer that. [*Eats out of the box*] No greater love has a man than he shall lay down his life for his friends. Who said that?

"You can get much farther with a kind word and a gun than you can with a kind word alone." Who said that?

[*Laughs*] It wasn't Jesus.

It was Al Capone. Come on, Bono, let's say you were around in the Forties instead of the Eighties. It's one thing to write songs about how the Third Reich is in general a bad idea, and it's another thing to fight it. What would you have done?

You have to give me a few weeks before I can answer that.

Is it all war you oppose, or is there anything that you would fight for?

For instance, would I defend my home and my country? Would I defend my family with violence? [*Pauses*] Two guys once walked by the door of a beach house where I was staying. They were wearing green berets and carrying rifles. They just came down the driveway. They did not look like policemen. It was just after "Sunday Bloody Sunday," so I didn't know what was happening. And before I got a chance to think about it, I had a large knife in my hands that I took from the kitchen. And that *sickened* me, because I felt like a hypocrite. But that was natural instinct. That's all I can tell you. That's about as far as I've gotten on this one. This is a very interesting question, and I don't have an answer for it.

Okay, let's broach the frequently covered but still murky subject of your relation-ships to religion and spirituality.

Well, religion has torn this country apart. I have no time for it, and I never felt a part of it. I am a Christian, but at times I feel very removed from Christianity. The Jesus Christ that I believe in was the man who turned over the tables in the temple and threw the money-changers out—substitute TV evangelists if you like. There is a radical side to Christianity that I am attracted to. And I think without a commitment to social justice, it is empty. Are they putting money into AIDS research? Are they investing in hospitals so the lame can walk? So the blind can see? Is there a commitment to the poorly fed? Why are people left on the side of the road in the United States? Why, in the West, do we spend so much money on extending the arms race instead of wiping out malaria, which could be eradicated given ten minutes' worth of the world's arms budget? To me, we are living in the most un-Christian times. When I see these racketeers, the snake-oil salesmen on these right-wing television stations, asking for not your $20 or your $50 but your $100 in the name of Jesus Christ, I just want to throw up.

And your religious background and education in Ireland?

In Ireland we get just enough religion to inoculate us against it. They force-feed you religion to the point where you throw it up. It's power. It's about control: birth control, control over marriage. This has nothing to do with liberation.

And what's a Christian to do about liberation? Social action?

Well, I am not sitting here with flowers in my hair, chanting away. I do have responsibilities, and actions speak louder than words. That's why I don't feel guilty about the money we've made. I sometimes feel embar-rassed, but not guilty. I am in a situation where the actions sometimes do not equal the words, and I would like them to. Charity is a very private thing.

What about liberation theology, which promotes social action on behalf of the poor?

I think the danger of liberation theology is that it can become a very *material* ethic, too material. But I am really inspired by it. I was in the Church of St. Mary of the Angels, where liberation theology has a base, in Nicaragua. I did not like the romanticization of the revolution that I found there. Because I think there is no glory in dying a bloody death. I attended a mass, and the priest asked all those who had lost a loved one for the revolution, fighting the *contras* or whatever, to stand and come forward and call out the name of your loved one. And all these people stood, and called the names one by one, including sons and daughters. And with each name the congregation would cry, *"Presente!"*—meaning they are present. It was amazing to see such solidarity. If you are not committed to the poor, what is religion? It's a black hole.

Let's get more mundane here. Where are you going next—film, theater, other music, writing?

The most exciting of all those possibilities is to see where U2 can go. I'd like to see if I can stretch U2 to take words that I am hearing. I'm really excited about being in the band, and in fact, this is the first time all four of us have been excited about being in the band at the same time. The key for us as a band is to reinvent ourselves.

Despite your interest in the band, are there other things you're interested in pursuing?

The fact is, there are very few things I am not interested in. I am a very curious man.

I am writing a play with one of my best friends, Gavin Friday, who is a performance-artist-singer-writer. We're writing a play called *Melt Head*. I'm interested in theater, in Irish theater and Brechtian theater and Kurt Weill's music.

I've a whole pile of writing I may one day publish, just bits and pieces. I also painted during *The Joshua Tree*. A friend and I are having a show together in a Dublin gallery. But instead of paintings, I am going to show some photos I took the last week I was in Ethiopia—because I want to keep the awareness of that alive.

There is also a project I am interested in writing or co-writing with Edge, which would be like a play to be filmed. As far as acting, I've turned down a few roles. I find it hard to look at myself on the television, much less a big screen, and yet, if the right role turned up, I'd take it. I'm interested in the mentality of violence; terrorism interests me. Because it's the everyday Holocaust of our times. The idea that two IRA men were blown up because they stood too close to the bomb they had set—because they wanted to see the carnage—is beyond my understanding, and I'm fascinated by it. Terrorists are ordinary men who have the ability to take the lives of other ordinary men because of the way they see the world. I am talking about the ability to knock at the door of a man's house in Belfast, and when he answers the door, to shoot him ten times in the head in front of his children. This is something that I would like to understand. I think I could play the part of a terrorist.

Are you ever at peace with yourself?

I'm happy to be unhappy. I'll always be a bit restless, I suppose. I still haven't found what I'm looking for [*laughs*]. Let's go for a ride in the car, okay?

DAVID BRESKIN

TWENTIETH ANNIVERSARY SPECIAL
Bono Q&A

IN ROLLING STONE'S special twentieth anniversary issue (the last of four), editors chose thirty-three individuals "whose work has stood out and whose voices have often been heard in the pages of ROLLING STONE, to talk about their experiences during the past two decades, their understanding of what has survived and what they see ahead." Bono was selected as one of those "who have helped to shape rock & roll, as well as American culture and politics," a list which also included Bruce Springsteen, Jesse Jackson, Pete Townshend, Tom Wolfe, William Burroughs, Lou Reed, Bob Dylan, Sting, Keith Richards, Mick Jagger, Paul McCartney, and George Harrison, among others.

MANY EUROPEANS—BRITS AND IRISH, artists and intellectuals—have wrestled with America, first as the New World, then as the British colonies and then as the United States. Now you, too, are part of that same process. How does it feel?

I think the only reason we get away with our criticisms of America is because people know that we love to *be in* America. U2's attitude doesn't come from a typical European eyes-down-the-nose look at American life or a blinkered look at American life.

Some have come over and "put down" America. You may criticize, but you don't condescend.

No. Because what I feel is a mixture of love and anger, and love and anger do not condescend. Miles Davis and Bob Dylan and Janis Joplin and Jimi Hendrix and the great bluesmen and the gospel singers and the wide-open spaces and the great writers like Tennessee Williams and poets like Robert Hayden and Sterling Brown would not let me—because America has given me much more than I could ever give it.

More than a complicated reality of specifics, America has always existed as a dream—both for its citizens and for outsiders.

Yes, the American dream. But we mustn't sleep in the comfort of our freedom. Rock & roll has woken a lot of us up out of a sort of big sleep and has the power to keep us awake. I think of Jimi Hendrix playing the "Star-Strangled Banner."

You said "strangled," not "spangled"—a perfect slip!

[*Laughs.*] When I think of Vietnam, I think of two things: Hendrix playing the "Star-Spangled Banner" and the photo of that child running after a napalm strike. The things that affect me most about Vietnam both happen to be conveyed through a creative medium. So I think rock & roll can make *real* the situation a country finds itself in.

You've said that when you first came over, you found Americans more honest and more innocent than the people you were used to.

I found the people *open*. This to me was and is an endearing quality of the American people. They wanted to be positive rather than negative. But this sort of openness makes Americans quite vulnerable to manipulation, vulnerable to what I call the new fascism. The new fascism will come with a warm handshake, with gold fillings and a smile. And through the media, people will be manipulated en masse. The potential is there. A nation as powerful as the United States surely must not elect a leader because of his suitability for television. Surely this is not just a sign of our times but a warning for times to come.

Do you ever feel the need to get America out of your system, almost as if it were a stage in your development?

No, because there is no end in sight for me with American music. I didn't discover John Lee Hooker until I was upstairs in the Rolling Stones' studio in New York, in 1986. That opened up a whole new world to me. I didn't discover the Miles Davis of *In a Silent Way* and *Sketches of Spain* until 1985, and now there is John Coltrane and Art Pepper and gospel music and so on. We in U2 are hearing all this for the first time—our ears are fresh. We're looking to the past to find the future.

America's music is really the world's music, at least popularly.

That's right. It's just a shame that in 1987 there are sixteen-year-olds who have never heard of Jimi Hendrix or Janis Joplin. Look, if Bob Dylan walked into a record company in 1987 and played them "Subterranean Homesick Blues" and told them it was a hit record, they'd show him the door. If Jimi Hendrix came along now, he wouldn't get a deal. The companies would file him under Black and Confused and Out of Tune. That is an example of the difference between now and then. Radio is so tightly formatted because this apartheid exists in the music business between black and white music.

Though you came late to black American music, you've been deeply affected by it.

As an Irishman, I feel a real closeness to the black man because we were both the underdog, because we both have soul and the spirit to spit it out, because we both are too raw to sit nicely on the stiff upper lip of the intelligentsia, wherever they may be found in art circles. The Irish have been described as white niggers, and I take that as a compliment. A lot of my heroes happen to be black artists. It would be wrong for me to imitate their actual form, but the spirit of it is something I wish to imitate and to learn from. Bob Marley was a huge, huge influence on U2. To hear B.B. King sing, which I did a while back, and to hear his voice break—I mean, I wanted to give up singing. The spirit of abandonment, which I see as part of black music, is also part of U2. I must admit, I find it hard to think in terms of color, because it's not an issue for me. [*Laughs*] It's just a bummer— me buying all these black records and them not buying any of ours.

How do you think technology will affect the music?

I think we will all need to get back to the roots. In the Nineties, I think people will be listening to traditional Irish music or Cajun music or old soul music. I find myself being drawn away from art-school rock and toward people like Johnny Cash and Willie Nelson—people like Dylan, Van Morrison, Patti Smith. There's a humanness to their work. Dehumanization is a part of life in the cities in the 1980s, and I find myself reacting against that and looking for that human moment, which I call soul. Which is not to say I want to throw stardust on the past and be a revivalist. I want to go forward.

Are you implying that there will be a rejection of technology?

It would be wrong to rule out the use of this technology, but if it doesn't have a spark of soul, let's dismantle it. It's not the machines I worry about, it's the machines who play the machines. I believe the future lies in a marriage of both acoustic and electronic, because instruments like the violin and the guitar and the saxophone are the most expressive. How the traditional and technological will cross is on my mind a lot.

How do you think the future of rock will come out of its past?

In the Fifties rock & roll had a cool haircut and a curled lip. In the Sixties it wore tie-dye and discovered distortion and electric-guitar power and ran away with that for a few years—but at least it held up a placard and exploded now and then. In the Seventies it rediscovered some of its underlying folk values and ran with that—and everyone grew their hair and ate magic mushrooms and believed in Mother Earth. But it got fat and put on lipstick.

Then it discovered minimalism in '76, nihilism and punk, and again the idea of rock & roll as revolution. Then rhythm was rediscovered, from George Clinton into the Talking Heads, and I think now there is a rediscovery of songwriting. I also see a resurgence in jazz.

At the time you guys started in the garage, punk was considered a naive revolution, but in retrospect, it seems as calculated as anything today.

You could say that the Sex Pistols were the ultimate designer rock & roll group. They were *assembled* with a view toward subversion. It wasn't like the Beatles, where John called round to Paul's house. It was more like Malcolm [McLaren, the Sex Pistols' manager] made the phone calls. But at the same time, they made a wonderful, big and nasty noise, and it woke me up. There was a cynicism and a manipulation involved in some of those punk groups, and we were blind to that. For us, it was truth.

Eventually, you came to feel that punk had warped the positive potential of rock & roll, that power had corrupted the music.

I still feel power corrupts the music. I see it at the edges of U2.

So rather than identify yourself with the bands that came out of punk, what groups do you feel akin to?

The Who. Because of that three-dimensional quality: sexual, spiritual and political.

It's interesting that you pick a group that came out of the Sixties.

It's true that we rewrite history and glorify the Sixties—and I *do* glorify the Sixties—because rock & roll was *exploring* in some way. I hope what I feel is not just nostalgia for something I missed—but rock & roll is too rational right now. It waits and it watches instead of jumping right in: taking a chance is not high on the list of priorities. There is an environment in which music can live and breathe, and right now the environment is suffocating. When we look back at this decade, we'll have to say that in the Eighties rock & roll went to work for corporations and got up at 6:00 A.M. to go jogging. And it wasn't just to keep fit. It was to *get ahead:* to improve the prospects of the corporation.

Do you think rock & roll in the Sixties was really an engine of change, or that it merely reflected the changes going on in the culture around it?

I think those things are bound up in each other. It could be said that the lack of response in the generation now is due to the fact that the inspiration is not there—the inspiration to be part of change.

Perhaps one reason for the difference is that the Sixties was a time of prosperity, and people had a chance to look further than material things. Perhaps the Sixties was the product of a generation of spoiled children who could afford to drop acid and set off for Peru.

Well, how do you reclaim the past triumphs of the form without being overly conservative?

In looking back at itself, rock & roll can make use of everything it has. For instance, why is it only a heavy-metal band that plays with fuzz boxes and distortion? Why is it only a funk band that uses beat-box machines and rap? Why is it that folk musicians stick together and write about fear in the

big city and the rivers and hills? Why is it all so cut up and compartmental-
ized? Why can't we have it all! Why can't rock & roll dance like Elvis
Presley, sing like Van Morrison, walk like the Supremes, talk like John
Lennon, roar like the Clash, drum like Keith Moon and play guitar like Jimi
Hendrix? Why?

JIMMY GUTERMAN

PERFORMANCE REVIEW

Giants Stadium, East Rutherford, New Jersey,
September 14, 1987

FROM SHAKY START TO POWERFUL finish, U2's two-hour performance at Giants Stadium—the first outdoor concert on the group's
fall tour—showed both the problems and promise that the band
faces in adapting to larger arenas.

A portentous taped introduction announced the opening number,
"Where the Streets Have No Name," with the band members staking their
positions quickly: drummer Larry Mullen and bassist Adam Clayton establishing the beat, guitarist Edge and vocalist Bono steering the band's melodic course. Creating the band's omnipresent signature rhythms, Edge
rocked slowly and seductively from the waist, his few flourishes probing
rather than flashy. But all eyes were on Bono. The vocalist's every gesture
was greeted with roars of approval as he sang from a lowered platform.

Handicapped early in the program by a muddy sound mix—even by
football-stadium standards—and a dragging version of the show's second
song, "I Will Follow," there were reasons to doubt Bono's boast that "if
we had a roof, we'd blow it off anyway."

Sensing the show was in danger of slipping away, U2 moved to bridge
the gap created by the huge arena. Although the sound problems never
cleared up, the performance turned back to the band by the sixth song, a
version of "The Unforgettable Fire" far more muscular than on the wobbly
album of the same name.

Energetic solos by Edge stomped out any lingering reservations: on
"Bullet the Blue Sky," his furious guitar thrashes allayed any pretension that
could be found in Bono's spoken sections. Encouraged by the crowd, Edge
became a progressively stronger visual foil to Bono, his guitar playing
increasingly wild and less studied. The response from the audience was
immediate and absolute—supportive during the concert's tentative opening, the crowd became unequivocally adoring as the show improved.

A cover of the Impressions' "People Get Ready" proved a highlight,
with the set peaking on an extended and angry version of "Exit." Playing
off each other, Mullen and Edge piled tension between drums and guitar

higher and higher until Edge slashed everything down with one brazen chord. Bono slipped in bits of other songs, including smidgens of the Doors' "Riders on the Storm" and Van Morrison's "Gloria" (the band didn't play its own song of the same name), before resolving into a thrashing, bare-bones version of "Silver and Gold," Bono's contribution to the *Sun City* project. During a winding version of their own "Bad," Bono interpolated the Rolling Stones' "Ruby Tuesday" and "Sympathy for the Devil," as well as Lou Reed's "Walk on the Wild Side," emphasizing U2's formative links with other bands. The set ended with a plaintive "Pride (In the Name of Love)."

Starting its first encore by ripping through "One Tree Hill," the band turned sultry and understated on "With or Without You." Preceding the second encore—their usual finale "40"—Bono told the audience the band had decided to play stadiums "so scalpers don't rip you off." Asking if those far from the stage would prefer a video screen earned the night's only mixed response.

Even if the band's success was qualified, U2 is a group that has always prided itself on communicating with its audience, and appears intent on not allowing the necessity of performing in large arenas to create new barriers. The band members still haven't found what they're looking for, but they're hunting it down like few other bands today.

■ RANDOM NOTES "ALL-STARS GATHER FOR CHRISTMAS LP" (December 3, 1987)

Look at all of you guys in town!" exclaimed Bruce Springsteen as he greeted Bono and Sting. A few feet away, John Mellencamp and his wife, Vicky, tended to their daughter Teddi Jo, while Julianne Phillips Springsteen chatted with the Edge. The occasion was a New York photo session for *A Very Special Christmas,* the Jimmy Iovine-produced album to benefit the Special Olympics. (Iovine's wife, Vicki, works with the group, which offers sports programs for the mentally retarded.)

Springsteen's arrival signaled the start of the session. "It's interesting how all of the Europeans got seats up front," remarked U2's Adam Clayton.

"Lately I've been turning a lot of stuff down," said Sting. "But I'm very much in favor of this group. I'll do Amnesty, and I'll do this." Bono, still nursing his injured left arm, said that U2 recorded "Christmas (Baby Please Come Home)" because it made him laugh. "If U2 sings a Christmas song," he said, "it better be lighthearted." Mellencamp had the same logic with "I Saw Mommy Kissing Santa Clause." "Everybody was doing serious songs," he said. "I thought I'd do something lighter." The members of Run-D.M.C. said they're making a video for their contribution, "Christmas in Hollis." When "Hollis" played over the speakers, Bono, Annie Lennox and the Edge started to groove.

Asked about his Christmas plans, Sting announced, "I'm Father Christmas when I go home." Does that mean he dons a white beard and red suit? "No, I make sure the kids know it's *me* who buys all of this shit."

And Bono's holiday plans? "When I was a boy," he said, "I worked as a postman at Christmas to get money. That's what I *won't* be doing this year!"

■ RANDOM NOTES U2 TOUR FILM, LP PLANNED FOR SPRING (December 3, 1987)

Fans who couldn't get enough of U2 on the group's extended worldwide tour this year have something to look forward to in 1988: The Irish quartet is planning spring releases for a concert film and a mostly live double album.

The documentary film, expected to cost $5 million, is being directed by Steven Spielberg protégé Phil Joanou, who directed the recent feature film *Three O'Clock High* and two episodes of the television series *Amazing Stories.* Financed by the band, the as-yet-untitled film will be entirely improvised and will include scenes from backstage and on the road as well as in concert. Plans call for U2's upcoming performance in Buenos Aires—slated for the third week of December—to make up the lion's share of the movie's concert footage.

U2 spokesman Paul Wasserman says the group declined financing offers from several studios in order to retain control over the final cut. "They are going to do it entirely themselves," he says, adding that distribution has yet to be arranged. A final cut isn't expected until late spring.

Also in the works is a double album, which, like the film, is without a working title. Although most of the album will be devoted to live material, U2 is slated to enter a Dublin studio in January to record four new songs for the package. The album will be the group's third collection of live recordings.

■ YEAR-END RANDOM NOTES (December 17–31, 1987)

March   "It's our most literate record by far," says Bono of U2's album *The Joshua Tree*. But that doesn't stop it from going triple platinum by year's end.

April   With the success of *The Joshua Tree*, U2 hits the United States for the first leg of its eighteen-month world tour.

September   **Bruce Springsteen** joins U2 onstage at JFK Stadium, in Philadelphia. At an earlier gig in Washington, D.C., Bono takes a tumble onstage and ends up with a sprained shoulder.

November   U2 records Woody Guthrie's "Jesus Christ" at Sun Studios, in Memphis. The track is a contribution to the upcoming Guthrie-tribute album.

December   "Why don't we sing 'Jingle Bells'?" says Sting during the photo session for the holiday album *A Very Special Christmas*. Proceeds will benefit the Special Olympics, an organization that offers sports programs for the mentally retarded. Produced by Jimmy Iovine, the album features Christmas songs from Sting, Bruce Springsteen, Eurythmics, Run-D.M.C., John Mellencamp, Bob Seger, Madonna, Bon Jovi, Stevie Nicks, the Pointer Sisters, Whitney Houston, Bryan Adams, Alison Moyet and the Pretenders. A highlight is U2's cover of "Christmas (Baby Please Come Home)."

"U2 would like to write a Christmas song of our own sometime," says Adam Clayton. Maybe next year.

TOP 100 ALBUMS OF 1987

December 17–31, 1987

1 BON JOVI
Slippery When Wet—Mercury

2 MICHAEL JACKSON
Bad—Epic

3 U2
The Joshua Tree—Island

4 WHITNEY HOUSTON
Whitney—Arista

5 PAUL SIMON
Graceland—Warner Bros.

6 BEASTIE BOYS
Licensed to III—Def Jam/Columbia

7 WHITESNAKE
Whitesnake—Geffen

8 ANITA BAKER
Rapture—Elektra

9 STEVE WINWOOD
Back in the High Life—Island

10 GENESIS
Invisible Touch—Atlantic

11 BRUCE HORNSBY AND THE RANGE
The Way It Is—RCA

12 EUROPE
The Final Countdown—Epic

13 JANET JACKSON
Control—A&M

14 THE ROBERT CRAY BAND
Strong Persuader—High Tone! Mercury

15 MADONNA
True Blue—Sire

16 BRUCE SPRINGSTEEN
Tunnel of Love—Columbia

17 CINDERELLA
Night Songs—Mercury

18 FLEETWOOD MAC
Tango in the Night—Warner Bros.

19 POISON
Look What the Cat Dragged In—Enigma/Capitol

20 PETER GABRIEL
So—Geffen

21 KENNY G
Duotones—Arista

22 BANGLES
Different Light—Columbia

23 EXPOSÉ
Exposure—Arista

24 LUTHER VANDROSS
Give Me the Reason—Epic

25 PINK FLOYD
A Momentary Lapse of Reason—Columbia

26 LISA LISA AND CULT JAM
Spanish Fly—Columbia

27 CLUB NOUVEAU
Life, Love and Pain—Warner Bros.

28 L.L. COOL J
Bigger and Deffer—Def Jam/Columbia

29 HEART
Bad Animals—Capitol

30 SUZANNE VEGA
Solitude Standing—A&M

31 MÖTLEY CRÜE
Girls, Girls, Girls—Elektra

32 BOSTON
Third Stage—MCA

33 CAMEO
Word Up—PolyGram

34 GEORGIA SATELLITES
Georgia Satellites—Elektra

35 FAT BOYS
Crushin'—Tin Pan Apple/PolyGram

36 R.E.M.
Document—I.R.S.

37 LA BAMBA
Soundtrack—Slash/Warner Bros.

38 PRINCE
Sign o' the Times—Paisley Park/Warner Bros.

39 FREDDIE JACKSON
Just Like the First Time—Capitol

40 THE GRATEFUL DEAD
In the Dark—Arista

41 CROWDED HOUSE
Crowded House—Capitol

42 DEF LEPPARD
Hysteria—Mercury

43 BEVERLY HILLS COP II
Soundtrack—MCA

44 BRUCE SPRINGSTEEN AND THE E STREET BAND
Bruce Springsteen and the E Street Band Live/1975–85—Columbia

45 JOHN COUGAR MELLENCAMP
The Lonesome Jubilee—Mercury

46 THE PRETENDERS
Get Close—Sire

47 LOS LOBOS
By the Light of the Moon—Slash/Warner Bros.

48 THE WHISPERS
Just Gets Better with Time—Solar

49 WHO'S THAT GIRL
Soundtrack—Sire

50 GREGORY ABBOTT
Shake You Down—Columbia

51 THE CURE
Kiss Me, Kiss Me, Kiss Me—Elektra

52 TESLA
Mechanical Resonance—Geffen

53 SAMMY HAGAR
Sammy Hagar—Geffen

54 HUEY LEWIS AND THE NEWS
Fore!—Chrysalis

55 LIONEL RICHIE
Dancing on the Ceiling—Motown

56 DOLLY PARTON, LINDA RONSTADT AND
EMMYLOU HARRIS
Trio—Warner Bros.

57 ERIC CLAPTON
August—Duck/Warner Bros.

58 METALLICA
The $5.98 E.P./Garage Days Revisited—Elektra

59 ATLANTIC STARR
All in the Name of Love—Warner Bros.

60 BARBRA STREISAND
One Voice—Columbia

61 JODY WATLEY
Jody Watley—MCA

62 OZZY OSBOURNE AND RANDY RHOADS
Tribute—CBS Associated

63 BRYAN ADAMS
Into the Fire—A&M

64 BILLY IDOL
Whiplash Smile—Chrysalis

65 TOM PETTY AND THE HEARTBREAKERS
Let Me Up (I've Had Enough)—MCA

66 THE POLICE
Every Breath You Take: The Singles—A&M

67 PSYCHEDELIC FURS
Midnight to Midnight—Columbia

68 CYNDI LAUPER
True Colors—Portrait

69 THE GREGG ALLMAN BAND
I'm No Angel—Epic

70 HERB ALPERT
Keep Your Eye on Me—A&M

71 AEROSMITH
Permanent Vacation—Geffen

72 KATE BUSH
The Whole Story—EMI

73 READY FOR THE WORLD
Long Time Coming—MCA

74 OUTFIELD
Bangin'—Columbia

75 ECHO AND THE BUNNYMEN
Echo and the Bunnymen—Sire

76 BRUCE WILLIS
The Return of Bruno—Motown

77 TALKING HEADS
True Stories—Sire

78 BILLY VERA AND THE BEATERS
By Request: The Best of Billy Vera and the
Beaters—Rhino

79 STAND BY ME
Soundtrack—Atlantic

80 DURAN DURAN
Notorious—Capitol

81 CARLY SIMON
Coming Around Again—Arista

82 GREAT WHITE
Once Bitten—Capitol

83 RATT
Dancing Undercover—Atlantic

84 CUTTING CREW
Broadcast—Virgin

85 DAVID AND DAVID
Boomtown—A&M

86 SAMANTHA FOX
Touch Me—Jive/RCA

87 HANK WILLIAMS JR.
Born to Boogie—Warner Bros.

88 THE LOST BOYS
Soundtrack—Atlantic

89 LEVEL 42
Running in the Family—Polydor

90 SIMPLY RED
Men and Women—Elektra

91 GLORIA ESTEFAN AND MIAMI SOUND MACHINE
Let It Loose—Epic

92 STEVIE RAY VAUGHAN AND DOUBLE TROUBLE
Live Alive—Epic

93 NEW ORDER
Substance—Qwest

94 THE PAT METHENY GROUP
Still Life (Talking)—Geffen

95 STEPHANIE MILLS
If I Were Your Woman—MCA

96 ALEXANDER O'NEAL
Hearsay—Tabu

97 THE CARS
Door to Door—Elektra

98 LEVERT
The Big Throwdown—Atlantic

99 HOOTERS
One Way Home—Columbia

100 WARREN ZEVON
Sentimental Hygiene—Virgin

DAVID FRICKE

YEAR-END REVIEW OF *THE JOSHUA TREE*

"T HE MONEY TREE" WAS more like it. With their fifth studio album, the fighting Irish reaped the harvest of almost a decade's blood, sweat and tours. Yet if *The Joshua Tree* was for U2 the best of times, it was also in a sense the worst of times, the band's bleakest vision yet of a world at war with itself. The barren landscapes and monochromatic photography on the cover accurately reflected the ravages of the album's themes: economic hardship ("Red Hill Mining Town"), emotional torment ("With or Without You") and desperate confusion ("Where the Streets Have No Name"). The haunting Brian Eno–Daniel Lanois production, with its echoey evocation of cold winds blowing through a Western ghost town, didn't chill the band's inner flame, though. Bono's voice and the Edge's clanging guitar rose in outrage throughout the album. With their backs against a wall of despair, the members of U2 cracked the mainstream this year in incomparable style.

■ **RANDOM NOTES** "PAINTING THE TOWN" (January 14, 1988)
During the California leg of U2's recent tour, Bono's activities ranged from street scrawling to Hollywood reveling. For the grand finale of a free noontime "save the yuppie" concert in downtown San Francisco, the singer climbed onto the nearby Vaillancourt Fountain, where he jubilantly spray-painted the slogans "Stop the Traffic" and "Rock n Roll." This didn't go over too well with local authorities, and the graffiti was sandblasted off.

In a letter of apology to the S.F. district attorney, Bono said, "I hope that the real street artists of San Francisco will not suffer because of a scrawler like me."

Following their Bay Area spectacle, Bono and the band were the guests of honor at a party at the Santa Monica home of Jane Fonda and Tom Hayden. "We wanted to give them an opportunity to make some new friends and meet some new people," says Hayden, who admits to having played *The Joshua Tree* "about a thousand times." Among the 300 guests were Eddie Van Halen and Valerie Bertinelli, David Crosby, Graham Nash, Quincy Jones, Bob Seger and Annette Sinclair, Charlie Sheen and Charlotte Lewis, Martin Sheen, Oliver Stone and Julianne Phillips Springsteen. "A good time was had," says Hayden, especially by the members of U2, who were the last to leave.

STEVE POND

U2 ON LOCATION

"**H**ERE WE ARE AGAIN, back where it all started."

It's a chilly, cloudy December day in the Arizona desert, and Bono stands at the entrance to a resort hotel near Tempe, the town where U2 began its worldwide *Joshua Tree* tour nearly nine months and 12 million albums earlier. The tour, which along the way turned into the rock & roll event of 1987, has returned to Arizona for two concerts that will do more than simply play to 120,000 more fans: They will be the core of U2's first movie.

But with nearly nine months of touring behind him and two shows to go, Bono looks like one of the walking wounded. You can still see the scar on his chin that he received the last time he was in Arizona, when he fell on a portable light during a rehearsal; more than that, though, he's visibly weary after those months on the road, and at the moment he's frustrated at trying to mix rock & roll with motion pictures.

The night before in Sun Devil Stadium, he recalls, U2 rehearsed its entire show in a raging thunderstorm that had everyone thinking of *Under a Blood Red Sky,* the 1983 U2 concert video shot in a downpour at Red Rocks Amphitheater, near Denver. Although the rain made for a dramatic video back then, nobody came to Tempe expecting or wanting another night of wet cameras and drenched fans. But the Arizona weather turned bad, and the cameras had trouble keeping up with the band members during rehearsal—suddenly, ending a triumphant tour by making a movie doesn't seem like such a bright idea.

Bono thinks of the problems and sighs deeply. "It's like *Apocalypse Now,* without so many helicopters."

A FEW HOURS LATER, U2 is back onstage at the stadium, running through the opening moments of its show for the benefit of director Phil Joanou's cameras. This, the opening sequence of the still-untitled movie, is also its one staged moment: to make sure the band members' entrance onstage is effectively captured, the film crew will shoot the sequence again and again. Before, the band fools around: Bono sings snatches of the Beatles' "Dear Prudence," the Edge plays "Stairway to Heaven" on his guitar. Every time the band members stop to converse, they're surrounded by cameras, technicians and movie folks—including one skinny, long-haired youth who appears to be a typical U2 fan but turns out to be Phil Joanou, the twenty-six-year-old director, whose credits include two episodes of Steven Spielberg's TV show *Amazing Stories* and the feature film *Three O'Clock High*.

Finally, they begin the sequence, entering one by one as the somber opening strains of "Where the Streets Have No Name" resound. The Edge, bassist Adam Clayton and drummer Larry Mullen Jr. take their places and begin playing, two formidable "lightning boxes" throw bursts of light across the stage, and Bono slowly walks on, waving to the nonexistent crowd. At the end of one take, he stops and steps to the mike. "Listen, Philip," he says to Joanou, "I mean, what's my motivation?"

U2's motivation? The band's manager, Paul McGuinness, supplies a few reasons. "We can't get to the audience that wants to see the band," he says, "and we didn't want to do a four-year tour. Second, everyone's sick to their back teeth of Red Rocks by now. It crops up endlessly on TV, and it's become quite embarrassing. The only way to get rid of it is to replace it. Everyone's nuts about the movies, and we came to the point where we thought we could make a great movie."

That decision came early in the *Joshua Tree* tour, when it was clear that 1987 would be U2's breakthrough year. The band hired its longtime video producer, Michael Hamlyn, to handle production chores for the movie and then started meeting with name directors in New York and Los Angeles. Joanou wasn't on anybody's list, but he was a die-hard U2 fan. He had a mutual friend arrange for an introduction, then flew from L.A. to Connecticut at his own expense to meet the band.

"The first thing Bono said to me," says Joanou, "was, 'If you were to make a movie with U2, what kind of film would you make?' And I said, 'What kind of film do *you* want to make?' I think it was the first time somebody had said that back to them, and they all perked up and launched into all these ideas. We talked until about four in the morning."

Joanou got the job and went to work shooting the black-and-white documentary footage that is to constitute about a third of the planned movie, which is expected out in the fall. "The main criteria for being in the movie is that it's music," says McGuinness; that means Joanou shot U2 recording at Memphis's Sun Studios and onstage with blues musicians in Texas but didn't get any shots of the band getting out of limos or eating breakfast.

Which is not to say that Joanou—whom the band came to call E.T.— wasn't aggressive. In Washington, D.C., for instance, Bono separated his shoulder onstage, finished the show and then was hustled to a hospital.

"They put me into the ambulance, and I was weak from the pain," he says. "And I look up, and there's E.T. standing over me with his camera and his lights. I said, 'E.T., what the fuck are you doing in my ambulance?' And he said, 'Hey, you wanted me to make a documentary!'"

Unless Bono okays it, though, that sequence won't be in the movie. "I always felt that this is as much their movie as it is mine," says Joanou. "This is a movie made by myself *and* U2. If they don't like something, it will be out. I will fight for what I believe in tooth and nail, but if Bono says, 'I hate that shot of me,' it will go out."

The heart of the movie will be two concert sequences: color footage from Tempe and black-and-white footage shot on two consecutive nights at an indoor venue in Denver (where by all accounts the first show was dismal, the second terrific). The Tempe shows are especially crucial, because they are being lit specifically for the film under the supervision of noted cinematographer Jordan Cronenweth, who shot Talking Heads' *Stop Making Sense*. That means a crew of 70 film people and 120 tour staffers—and higher costs. "There's no faster way of spending money," says McGuinness, who adds that U2 is financing the movie because the studios the band approached thought that $5 million was too much to spend on a concert movie. The gate won't offset much of the costs: tickets for the Tempe shows were priced at five dollars each, partly to ensure the band would draw a crowd in a city it had already played and partly to compensate the audience for the filmmakers' intrusions.

With so much riding on the show, the pressure and frustration are apparent. Onstage, U2 runs through the beginning of "Where the Streets Have No Name" several more times. It's classic movie-set drudgery. At one point, U2 passes the time between takes by playing "Walk to the Water," one of the B sides to "With or Without You." But in place of the original's hushed narration, Bono uses a gravelly, Tom Waits-style mumble—and at the end of the song, he adds some new, seasonally appropriate lines.

"She asked him what he'd like for Christmas," Bono rasps. "And he said, 'I'd like the movie to be fuckin' *over,* that's for sure.'"

THAT NIGHT, IT TAKES BONO only fifteen minutes to throw the camera crew into a panic. The fourth song of the set is supposed to be "MLK," U2's somber elegy to Martin Luther King—but Bono, who says he decided the band needed to be looser before going into that tune, calls for the up-tempo rocker "Out of Control" instead. Phil Joanou tries to tell his cameramen about the change—but with twelve cameramen and as many assistants, all with their microphones open so they can talk to each other, the communications system is a complete disaster. Joanou gets through to some of them to let them know this is an unrehearsed addition to the set, but he can't reach others, including the stagehand whose job it is to bring out a big black cross—"the *Blade Runner* fan," they call it—and slowly rotate it during "MLK."

"Halfway through 'Out of Control,'" says Bono with a laugh, "I looked over to the side, and there's the guy turning that *Blade Runner* fan real slow. The poor guy probably thought, 'They're sure doing this song a lot *faster* than they did it in rehearsal.'"

Bono makes a few other changes in the set list and spends a good deal of time on an eighty-yard ramp that extends into the audience (the ramp serves as a runway for a giant camera-toting crane). On the whole, though, it's not an exemplary U2 show. With the darker, moodier movie lighting and the twelve cameras trying to follow the band's every move, it's hard for the audience to see some parts of the show—and the rain, which begins early in the set, doesn't help matters any.

Afterward, nobody is especially happy. "I felt torn when I was out there," says Bono. "On one hand, I really want to reach out to the people who've come to the show. But that part of me is directly conflicting with the side of me that knows that on film it'll look completely over the top if I do that."

Delivering a post-mortem to his crew, Phil Joanou is even unhappier. "We can't have this happen again, guys, or we will not get the concert," he says. "We *did not* get it tonight. In my opinion, we got three songs. To me, it was an utter fucking disaster."

Only producer Michael Hamlyn seems calm—partly, perhaps, because he's just met with three Paramount Pictures executives, who've flown in to show how serious they are about making a distribution deal. "I haven't slept in three days," Hamlyn says with a grin. "I go to bed and lie there thinking, 'Oh, God, we're spending a million dollars in the next two days.'"

He shrugs. "But tonight, I'll sleep. This was about like the first night in Denver."

And how was the first night in Denver?

"Uh . . . the second night in Denver was very good."

IS THERE ANY WAY WE CAN make this so I don't see a television show, guys?"

It's the second night in Tempe, and Phil Joanou is in his backstage headquarters looking at the bank of video screens that show him what his cameras are shooting. Most of them are working fine—except the monitor for camera ten, which is showing *Murder, She Wrote.*

When that's corrected and the show starts, Joanou moves into action, scanning ten screens simultaneously and shouting into his headset and a walkie-talkie. "Here comes Bono, two!" he screams to that cameraman. "Go into Bono! Get in there, two, c'mon! Seven, you can start tightening here. Give me something on the drummer, yeah, nice and easy. Nice. Stay with him. . . . C'mon, two! You gotta give me *movement,* guys!"

At the end of the first song, he sits back and nods. "Beautiful," he says softly. "Beautiful."

Problems crop up throughout the set—the man on camera two, for instance, runs over his cable and severs it, cutting off all communication with Joanou—but within half an hour it's clear that U2 is playing one of its best sets of the tour, it's not going to rain, and Joanou's cameras are capturing the show exceptionally well. Slowly, the director starts smiling more often, sometimes pounding his heels or his fists in delight at an especially good shot or yelling, "Whooo!" at the end of a song.

The band adds a fearsome version of "Helter Skelter"—"a song Charles Manson stole from the Beatles," says Bono in his introduction—and follows it with a gorgeous, hushed version of "Help," then an epic rendition of "Bad" that causes record producer Jimmy Iovine to run into the control room and scream, "Was 'Bad' fuckin' *great* or *what?*" Iovine has recorded close to twenty concerts for a live disc that will make up half of the movie's two-record soundtrack album; the release will probably also include a side of newly recorded songs, plus odds and ends that U2 cut during the tour, among them a gospel version of "I Still Haven't Found What I'm Looking For" and a tune recorded with B.B. King.

Onstage, U2 launches into a dramatic "Bullet the Blue Sky," incorporating fireworks, a helicopter, Jimi Hendrix's version of "The Star-Spangled Banner" and Bono's most pointed barb. "Turned on the TV," he shouts. "But I see no difference between the *CBS News* and *Hill Street Blues* and a preacher on *The Old Time Gospel Hour* stealing money from the sick and the old." He pauses deliberately. "The God I believe in isn't short of cash, *mister.*"

At the end, they play "Christmas (Baby Please Come Home)" for the first time live; the crowd then serenades the band with "Jingle Bells." "We're a very serious band, and you guys are out there having a party," says Bono with a big grin. "As the spokespeople of this generation, we've had a very hard year carrying the weight of the world on our shoulders."

AFTERWARD, MICHAEL HAMLYN is beaming. "The best show of the tour, and we got it on film."

Phil Joanou is delighted. "Last night caught a lot of people off guard, but tonight we had everything covered. Bono forces a movie crew, who are used to having a very controlled environment, to take risks. That makes it hard for me, but if you don't have a guy that's gonna climb onto the camera crane, if you've got four guys who stand there in their spots, what am I gonna do after two songs? The greatest concert films have fought that: four guys stand in the same place and you light them with blue, then red, then green. . . .

"I'm so effusive about how great it was tonight, I'm making it sound like we just shot *The Godfather*. And we haven't. It's a concert movie. But I am so hyped and so pumped, because it was a great show and we nailed it visually and they nailed it musically and the crowd was great."

And an hour or so after the show, Bono stands on the stage and looks out at the empty chairs and litter of Sun Devil Stadium. "We had problems with this movie, but tonight I think we did it right," he says quietly, then gazes at the debris that's all that remains of the tour that made U2 the year's foremost rock & roll band.

"You know, in one way this is all like a kid's game," he says. "Tallest building, fastest train, biggest band. And in that sense, this last year hasn't meant that much. But in another sense it's very important, because this is the first time that all of the members of U2 have been on fire at the same time.

"I mean, this is really the *beginning* of something for us, and the only way that we'll see what comes of it is to go home and start writing songs."

■ **RANDOM NOTES** "IRISH EYES SMILE ON U2" (February 25, 1988)
After making headlines around the world, the members of U2 were back on the front pages (twice in one week, no less) in their home town of Dublin. The band, along with other esteemed Irish artists, received a *Sunday Independent*/Irish Life Arts Award, one of the country's highest honors. Later that week Bono was in the papers again, this time for the opening of an exhibition of his photography at a Dublin gallery. The show, titled A String of Pearls, features photos he took in 1985, when he and his wife, Ali, spent a month working in a relief camp in Wello, Ethiopia. The photos are for sale at 1000 Irish pounds each (about $1600) or 20,000 pounds a set. All proceeds will go to an Ethiopian charity.

"The Ethiopians are very beautiful people," says Bono, "and it was the strength of their spirit that I tried to capture. I wanted to focus on their dignity, humanity and sexuality. Not in order to forget the famine but to make their tragedy even more poignant."

U2 is now working on the soundtrack to its forthcoming film. Two tracks being considered are "When Love Comes to Town," which the band recorded with B.B. King, and "Prisoner of Love," written with Bob Dylan. The film, says the Edge, will be "like seeing U2 from the best seats in the house."

1987 MUSIC AWARDS

March 10, 1988

For the first time in four years, Bruce Springsteen was not named Artist of the Year in the ROLLING STONE Readers Poll. That honor, and numerous others, went to U2. A record number of readers—23,000, up by 4,000 from the previous year—voted in the 1987 poll, and Bono and company won in almost every conceivable category, including Artist of the Year, Best Album *(The Joshua Tree),* Best Single ("With or Without You"), Best Songwriter (Bono), Best Band, Best Live Performance, Sexiest Male (Bono) and even Best Album Cover. Best Rap Act, oddly enough, eluded them.

READERS PICKS:
ARTIST OF THE YEAR
U2
R.E.M.
Madonna
Bruce Springsteen
Bon Jovi

BEST ALBUM
The Joshua Tree, U2
Document, R.E.M.
Tunnel of Love, Bruce
 Springsteen
A Momentary Lapse of
 Reason, Pink Floyd
Whitesnake, Whitesnake
Hysteria, Def Leppard
Sign o' the Times, Prince
Tango in the Night,
 Fleetwood Mac
. . . Nothing Like the Sun,
 Sting
Bad Animals, Heart

BEST SINGLE
"With or Without You," U2
**"Where the Streets Have No
 Name," U2**
**"I Still Haven't Found What
 I'm Looking For," U2**
"The One I Love," R.E.M.
"Here I Go Again,"
 Whitesnake
"Brilliant Disguise," Bruce
 Springsteen

"Touch of Grey," the
 Grateful Dead
"Alone," Heart
"I Want Your Sex," George
 Michael
"Learning to Fly," Pink Floyd

BEST BAND
U2
R.E.M.
Fleetwood Mac
Whitesnake
The Grateful Dead

BEST MALE SINGER
Bono
Bruce Springsteen
Sting
John Mellencamp
George Michael

BEST PRODUCER
Daniel Lanois and Brian Eno
Quincy Jones
Jimmy Iovine
Jimmy Jam and Terry Lewis
Robert John "Mutt" Lange

BEST SONGWRITER
Bono
Bruce Springsteen
Sting
Prince
John Mellencamp

HYPE OF THE YEAR
Michael Jackson
U2

The Beastie Boys
Madonna
Rap Music

BEST VIDEO
**"Where the Streets Have
 No Name," U2**
"With or Without You," U2
"Learning to Fly," Pink Floyd
"The One I Love," R.E.M.
"Touch of Grey," the
 Grateful Dead

BEST ALBUM COVER
The Joshua Tree, U2
Tango in the Night,
 Fleetwood Mac
A Momentary Lapse of
 Reason, Pink Floyd
Hysteria, Def Leppard
Kiss Me, Kiss Me, Kiss Me,
 the Cure

BEST LIVE PERFORMANCE
U2
Pink Floyd
Madonna
Mötley Crüe
David Bowie

BEST GUITARIST
The Edge
Eddie Van Halen
Eric Clapton
Peter Buck (R.E.M.)
Prince

BEST BASS PLAYER
Adam Clayton
Sting
Geddy Lee (Rush)
John Taylor (Duran Duran)
Nikki Sixx (Mötley Crüe)

BEST DRUMMER
Larry Mullen Jr.
Phil Collins
Neil Peart (Rush)
Sheila E.
Tommy Lee (Mötley Crüe)

BEST-DRESSED MALE ROCK ARTIST
David Bowie
Sting
Bruce Springsteen
Bono
Jon Bon Jovi

SEXIEST MALE ROCK ARTIST
Bono
George Michael
Jon Bon Jovi
Sting
Bruce Springsteen

CRITICS PICKS:
ARTIST OF THE YEAR
U2

BEST ALBUM
Tunnel of Love, Bruce
  Springsteen
The Joshua Tree, U2
Sign o' the Times,
  Prince
Robbie Robertson, Robbie
  Robertson
Pleased to Meet Me, the
  Replacements
Bring the Family, John
  Hiatt
By the Light of the Moon,
  Los Lobos
Document, R.E.M.
Franks Wild Years,
  Tom Waits
Babble, That Petrol
  Emotion

BEST BAND
U2

BEST PRODUCER
Daniel Lanois

BEST GUITARIST
The Edge

ARTISTS PICKS:
Larry Mullen Jr.
Bring the Family, John Hiatt
Poetic Champions Compose,
  Van Morrison
T Bone Burnett, T
  Bone Burnett
Introducing the Hardline
  According to Terence Trent
  D'Arby, Terence Trent
  D'Arby
Lord of the Highway, Joe
  Ely
Out of Our Idiot, Elvis
  Costello
Hillbilly Deluxe, Dwight
  Yoakam
Sign o' the Times, Prince
Document, R.E.M.
Lyle Lovett, Lyle Lovett

JAMES HENKE

THE EDGE: THE ROLLING STONE INTERVIEW

NESTLED AMONG WAREHOUSES in the drab Dublin dockside, Windmill Lane Studios would, under normal circumstances, hardly qualify as a tourist attraction. Since the ascension of U2 to the highest levels of rock stardom, however, the scene outside Windmill Lane has changed dramatically. The building, which functions as a sort of command center for the group's activities, has been covered with graffiti—"Italy Loves U2"; "Edge, I Think You're Brill"; "Dear U2, I've Been Here '40' Times and 'I Still Haven't Found What I'm Looking For' "—while dozens of faithful fans patiently stand watch along the street, hoping to catch at least a glimpse of rock's reigning heroes.

On one particularly rainy, windswept day in mid-January, their perseverance pays off when U2's guitarist, the Edge, arrives in his 1971 Volkswagen Beetle. As a security guard looks on, Edge rolls down his car window and obliges a few fans with autographs. Then another fan, in his 'mid to late' twenties, approaches and asks for money to get home. Edge gives him seven pounds, then realizes it's time to move on. "It's kind of hard to deal with," he says of the adulation. "I find it a little embarrassing."

Though Bono is the more public face of U2, Edge—whose nickname resulted in part from his tendency to observe things from the sidelines—has quietly played a key role in the band's journey to the top. His minimal, echo-laden style of guitar playing has virtually defined the group's sound and spawned a legion of imitators. He is also responsible for writing the lion's share of the group's music, as well as contributing a few key lyric ideas.

Born Dave Evans in East London in 1961, Edge moved to Dublin with his family when he was a year old. Settling in the middle-class suburb of Malahide, the Evanses, Protestants of Welsh heritage, felt a little like outsiders in largely Roman Catholic Ireland. That sense of not quite fitting in led Edge to music—he took up guitar when he was nine—and when U2 was formed in late 1978, he finally found a focus for his energy. "It became an obsession pretty quickly," he recalls. "We all realized that we really liked doing it. We loved playing together and writing songs together."

And that feeling is now stronger than ever, Edge insists. "I've found out recently that I really want to be in this group," he says. "I don't want to write screenplays or soundtracks or do anything else. I want to write songs, and I want to record them, and I want to go on the road with those songs."

Before embarking on another road trip, though, U2 has to complete work on its feature-length concert movie, which was filmed during last year's American tour, as well as an accompanying soundtrack double album, which will feature four or five previously unreleased studio tracks. Those projects will take Edge to London and the United States, away from his wife of four years, Aislinn O'Sullivan, and their two daughters, Hollie, 3, and Arran, 2.

"Keeping a marriage going can be kind of hard, and you gotta work at it," Edge says. "But I think it's so much more true of anybody in a band, because being in a band is almost like being married anyway. I'm so close to the other three guys in this group that sometimes it feels like a marriage."

Over the course of two days, Edge elaborated on that second marriage in interview sessions at the group's offices and in a nearby pub. "It's only in later life that the lure of the pint of Guinness has really drawn us into the pubs," he says, adding that, especially on the road, "a few drinks can really put things in perspective."

W*HEN THE BAND WAS STARTING OUT, did you ever imagine that U2 would become this successful?*

Well, I don't know if I ever really thought about it too hard. You know, this year's been a dangerous year for U2 in some ways. We're now a household name, like Skippy peanut butter or Baileys Irish Cream, and I suppose that makes us public property in a way that we weren't before. And that's a bit weird, because we're getting so much mass-media attention. We've seen the beginning of the U2 myth, and that can become difficult. Like, for instance, Bono's personality is now so caricatured that I worry whether he'll be allowed to develop as a lyricist the way I know he can.

What's the greatest danger U2 faces?

Going cold. Because there are too many distractions now. I spend most of my time trying to avoid distractions.

What kinds of distractions?

All sorts of things. Financial things. Once you have money, it has to be taken care of. As much as you try and forget about it and let someone else deal with it, there are times when it just has to be faced up to. I think it was Eno who said that possessions are a way of turning money into problems. And so I've tried to cut down on anything like that.

My lifestyle, and that of the rest of the band, is pretty straightforward.

I don't want to get fat. I don't want to get lazy. Money can bring great freedom, because it means you can travel, you can go into the studio whenever you want. You can pretty much do whatever idea comes into your head. But a lot of groups have not survived financial success. So there's a potential problem.

I also think being taken too seriously is a problem. It seems that no matter what we do, people place this huge weight of importance on it. Importance out of the realm of music, whether it's political importance or something cultural or whatever. I think that can be bad.

I assume that's what you were talking about when you referred to "the U2 myth." In the past year you've suddenly become "the spokesmen for a generation."

[*Laughs*] Well, it gets tough, you know, running Amnesty International, organizing summits between superpowers. It gets pretty exhausting. I sometimes feel sorry for Bono, because he seems to get the worst of that. But we try and not let it affect us, because we'd probably be inclined to do something really stupid in order to prove that we're just like ninety percent of the musicians in other bands.

But ninety percent of the musicians in other bands don't wind up on the cover of 'Time.' What was that like?

[*Laughs*] I was king for a week, I suppose. I don't know, it felt good. What I liked about it was not just that it was U2, but that music was there that week. That felt good. You know, it's nice for rock & roll to cause a stir from time to time.

You complain about being taken too seriously, but U2 certainly cultivated a more serious image than most bands. Everything from the songs to the interviews to Anton Corbijn's black-and-white photographs made it clear that this was a "serious" band.

I just never liked my smile. That was the problem. [*Laughs*] I mean, we just write songs. That's what we do. And the idea of being a leader is just so horrible. That's the last thing we ever wanted to be. But I love Anton's shots. They're kind of European. He gave us a sense of being European.

It's funny, but when you leave where you are, you get a perspective on it. When we first started touring Britain and Europe, we started seeing how Irish we were. Suddenly, Ireland became big in our songs. When we first toured America, we sensed our Europeanness. Now, with *The Joshua Tree,* I suppose we sensed the charm of America, the writers and the music.

How has your perception of America changed over the past seven years?

I like it a lot more. I didn't like it much when I first went there. We were really just passing through, and we didn't get the full picture. I left with only a superficial sense of what America was about, and that superficial level really didn't interest me. During the second couple of tours. I purposely avoided things like the radio and TV because I thought they were bad. But on the last couple of tours we've seen what I call the hidden side of America, the side that's not obvious if you're only in town for one night.

What have you found there?

Well, for instance, music that never gets played on the radio, that never gets exposed to any extent—blues and country music. And American writers, like Raymond Carver, and some Indian writers. Also the openness. American people are very open. In most big cities in Europe people are aloof, very unfriendly. It's not an Irish thing, but you find it in London and Paris. I don't find that in America, and in that way it's more like Ireland.

What do you think of the state of America now, politically, culturally?

Well, it scares me. It scares me a lot, this kind of "let's forget the Sixties" mentality, the new fascism, the new conservatism. But America's always been the best and worst rolled into one, and it's going to be very interesting to see how it goes in the next couple of years.

I'm a little fearful, but it's as bad in Europe. It's as bad in England, as far as I can see. I think in years to come, people will look back at the Sixties as a very peculiar era. We think of it as the way people should be. But if you think about the years that went before and the years that have come after, it's the Sixties that are weird, not the Seventies, not the Eighties.

Many of U2's songs, like "Bullet the Blue Sky," convey less-than-favorable impressions of America and its policies. Yet, in concert, it sometimes seems that your fans don't have a clue as to what you're trying to say.

It would be great to think that people understood what we were talking about, but the fact is that probably about half of them do—or less. The rest pick some of it up, or none of it. I think we have a pretty good balance. Some people come to shows because we're a great rock & roll band. And some people come to the shows because everyone else is going. And some people come because they understand exactly where we're coming from and they agree.

But rock & roll to me is communication. I don't just mean communication of ideas, but communication of feelings. The bands I was into when I was younger were the ones where you'd listen and get a feeling about the person, whether it was John Lennon or Marvin Gaye or Patti Smith or Lou Reed. That's the most important thing in rock & roll. It's not necessarily that your idea is great, but that it's *your* idea. That's why when we write songs, we don't sit down and say, "Let's write a song about this because this is an important issue now." We write a song because we feel we have something to say.

People always ask us if we think our songs can really change anything. And I always say that's not why we wrote the songs. We didn't write them so they would change the situation. I think it would be too much to expect

that. But they might make people think for a second, in the same way that
we stop and think.

*It always seemed that U2 was determined to become a big group. When I
interviewed Bono in 1980, he told me, "I do feel that we are meant to be one of
the great groups," and he compared the band to the Beatles, the Stones and the Who.*

Well, Adam [Clayton] and Bono used to say that a lot—and I used to
believe them. We assumed it, in a weird way, and I don't know why. We
assumed that we would achieve commercial success, and we never had any
kind of problem in going out and working for success, going for it. And
therefore that really wasn't a big issue. What was more important was
achieving musical success, and we're still trying to get that. I mean, we're
getting closer with each record.

*Though Bono writes the bulk of the band's lyrics, I understand that it was your
idea to write a song about the strife in Northern Ireland, which turned out to be
"Sunday Bloody Sunday."*

Yeah, Bono was away on holiday—I think it was his honeymoon. And
I wrote the music and hit on a lyric idea and presented it to the guys when
they got back.

Belfast is only about fifty miles up the road from Dublin, and I'd read
about it in the newspapers and seen it on TV. But going there was a bit of
an education. What was incredible was that the people of Belfast had the
most incredible warmth and friendliness and sense of humor—and there
was this thing going on that was just tearing the whole community apart.

And "Sunday Bloody Sunday"—I can't remember exactly what incident sparked it off, but I just remember sitting in this little house I had on
the sea, just bashing out this music, and it just came to me, that this should
be about Northern Ireland. And I wrote down a few lines, and Bono
instantly improved on them when he came back.

How often do you come up with ideas for lyrics?

Not that often. I might give Bono a title, like "I Still Haven't Found
What I'm Looking For." And that'll light a spark, and he'll write a song
about it.

*You and Bono seem like exact opposites—he's loud and outgoing, while you're
quieter and more reserved.*

Generally speaking, that's true. He's more at home in the public eye.
It's kind of hard for the rest of us, Larry [Mullen] and me, in particular,
because we're not naturally gregarious.

As kids, Bono was the exact opposite of me. I was a very quiet kid in
school. I think we shared a sense of humor, though, and when the band
came together, it was kind of natural that we would get on.

What was your childhood like?

Being Protestant and being English—or Welsh, in fact—in what is ostensibly a Catholic country, it felt a bit strange at times. There were times when I really did feel like a bit of a freak, and I spent a few years where I was pretty quiet. I didn't go out an awful lot. Those are the years when I listened to the most music.

When was that?

I suppose between the ages of fourteen and sixteen. That was when albums like *Horses,* by Patti Smith, came out. There were some good records around that time—Lou Reed, Bowie, the first Talking Heads records. Nobody else was really listening to those records, but they really meant a lot to me. I always remember that when someone who's sort of fifteen or sixteen comes up to me and talks about our records. I remember how I felt about records at that age.

Have there ever been any periods when you've had second thoughts about U2 or about being in a rock & roll band?

Yeah. I lost sight of what it was all about for a period. I think when a band goes on the road, unless the band is very strong, things get a bit cloudy. And that happened with us. We had to figure out who we were musically and what we were doing and where we were going. And once we had that all together, then we were fine. But for a while there, I really wasn't sure what we were up to and whether I wanted to be a part of it all.

It was kind of just after the *October* album, coming up to writing the *War* album. We'd come off the road, the album had done reasonably well, we'd done an awful lot of hard work, and we kind of had to just take stock of what was going on. I thought it was pretty healthy, actually, and I think that without that, I would be in serious trouble at this stage.

In his recent book 'Unforgettable Fire: The Story of U2,' Eamon Dunphy spends a lot of time discussing a crisis the band went through a little earlier than that, when you were making the 'October' album. He suggests that you, Larry and Bono struggled with the question of whether it was possible to reconcile your Christian beliefs with the more decadent lifestyle that has come to be associated with rock & roll.

Well, the book deals with it in a very simplistic way. It's something that's so complicated that I really feel quite inadequate to explain it fully. The *October* album was kind of our statement in that area. Maybe we're a little clearer now about what we want to be, whereas that album was probably a search. It was us trying to find out what we were doing and where we were going. And now we just want to be a great rock & roll band. And everything else is personal in a way. But it's still there, unspoken, in the music. And it should be there in the way we do things and what we are as a band.

Have you been able to come to terms with what rock & roll represents in many people's minds—the sort of "sex and drugs and rock & roll" image?

My feelings are a whole series of contradictions, and I certainly haven't been able to reconcile them. I just know that when I pick up that guitar and Bono starts to sing, I feel good about it. And that's as far as I think it needs to be justified. I'm not pretending that I've got it all sorted out. I don't think I ever will. But this band's special, and that's all I need to know.

Have you gone through any other rough periods, when you've questioned what you're doing?

No. For a while, I wanted to be this sort of Renaissance man in the group, doing soundtracks and producing other people and that kind of thing. But I tell you, being a great rock & roll band is not easy, and I've realized that if we want to be a great rock & roll group, there's little time for anything else, really.

What's the hardest thing about it?

Being brilliant. [*Laughs*] That's a bitch! No, seriously, though, there are very few brilliant rock & roll bands around. There have been a handful since rock & roll was invented. There are a lot of really average groups out there who get away with it. But that never would be good enough for us.

So you consider U2 to be a brilliant rock band?

Well, I think *The Joshua Tree* is a brilliant album. But it's not brilliant enough for me. I'm very proud of that record, though. It's the closest we've come to what we wanted to do. *The Unforgettable Fire* was a very mixed record, a lot of experiments. But with *The Joshua Tree* we really set out to write songs and work with the song as a sort of limitation. And now I don't feel nearly as much need to innovate as I would have earlier on. I feel more at home with the idea of working within classic areas.

But doesn't the magnitude of your success pose a problem for the band creatively? Now people expect a certain "U2 sound" or a specific "Edge sound."

That makes us immediately want to change it. Instantly. When we recorded the *War* album, even at that stage we were trying to kill this idea of the U2 sound. I don't mind having a characteristic style of playing, but the idea that this is a band with a sort of formula sound really appalls me. So *The Joshua Tree* had a lot of songs that were really very untypical, and that will continue, probably more so, on the next few records.

What about your guitar playing? There certainly seem to be a lot of Edge imitators out there these days.

Well, you're always going to get that, and it's flattering in a way. But I think anyone who tries to sound like me has already missed the point, really. What I'm interested in is what new guitar players sound like. It's great to hear somebody coming out with something new. Like Johnny

Marr—I thought that was an interesting thing he was doing with the Smiths. That high-life-y quality was something I hadn't heard before. I always thought the guy with Magazine [John McGeoch] was good. Again, it was something different.

I'm not a fan of the million-miles-per-second guitar player. That's more a form of athletics than anything else. It's not really about music. . . . Peter Buck from R.E.M. is also good. Good in that nothing he ever does really bowls you over—until you've heard it about twenty times. I think that's a sign of music that really has longevity, when it grows on you like that. I like R.E.M. Maybe it needs a few more records to be brilliant, but it's great now.

What guitarists did you listen to as a kid? Did you like people like Eric Clapton?

I was probably a bit young for him. My brother had a couple of Cream albums, but I really missed Clapton. I missed most of those guys. I mean, I would have been eight when Woodstock happened. So it kind of went by me. But I've been playing guitar for some time now. I got my first guitar when I was about nine years old. It took me five years to learn how to tune it. [*Laughs*] But it was easy from there on.

Was that the guitar your mother bought you?

It was the one before that. The one my mother bought me I learnt how to tune. The one I had before that was like this little Spanish guitar. It looked good. That was part of it. I mean, I liked guitars at that stage. I stopped looking at them for a while. But I've started to notice how amazing they look again.

That's one of the things that attracted me to rock & roll. Initially, there's that feeling of potential, of power, when you strap on an electric guitar. And then you learn that what it's really about is controlling that power. I mean, the guitar has been a big part of rock & roll. I just can't imagine Elvis holding a violin!

How did you develop your style of playing?

I can't really pick out influences. It's very hard. I used to mention Tom Verlaine a lot. I like him—I mean, *Marquee Moon* was a great album—but I think what I took from Verlaine was not really his style but the fact that he did something no one else had done. And I liked that; I thought that was valuable. I mean, I knew more what I didn't want to sound like than what I wanted to sound like early on, when we first formed the group.

In some ways that's why my playing is so minimal. Play as few notes as you can, but find those notes that do the most work. It became a whole way of working. If I could play one note for a whole song, I would. "I Will Follow" is almost that.

How did you start using the different effects, like echo?

Oh, yeah—the discovery of the echo unit. When we first started writing songs, I started working with what I later found out to be very Irish musical ideas, like using open strings, alternating those with fretted strings to produce drone type of things. And then when we went in to do some demos, I thought it might be neat if I got hold of an echo unit. Actually, it was Bono's idea for me to go and get it.

So I borrowed some money from a friend and got this really cheap Memory Man echo unit. We wrote "11 O'Clock Tick Tock" and then "A Day Without Me," and it just became an integral part of my guitar parts. It was really an enhancement originally, but I quite naturally got into using it as part of the guitar itself.

I tend to use effects that don't change the tone of the guitar. I don't like phasing or flanging or anything like that. I like echo. I like reverb. And Eno's been a big help in adding new sorts of treatments to my repertoire. I really think that the use of treatments and effects is one reason why U2 works so well outdoors and in these big arenas. The sound just seems to resonate through these big arenas. We've never had any problem making our music work in a big space. In fact, I think I feel more at home in a big space than I do in a small club or theater now.

U2 played quite a few stadiums on the last leg of its U.S. tour. How did you feel about that?

It was a difficult decision for us, because we've always tried to create a feeling of intimacy in any show. People said we couldn't do it in arenas, and I really believe we did. When it came to stadiums, we really had to make the move, because if we didn't, it meant playing twenty nights in an arena, which we just couldn't face. Bruce Springsteen seems to be able to do that and retain his sanity, but any more than about six shows in one town and we start going totally wacky. It becomes like a job.

There were times when I felt that we really succeeded spectacularly at the stadiums and times when I really felt disappointed. I remember one great show, in Olympic Stadium in Montreal. It was great. That's when I thought, "Hey, this can work."

But what about the fans? Do you really think someone at the back of a 60,000-seat stadium is feeling "intimate"?

With U2, it's the music that makes the atmosphere. There's no laser show, no special effects. And we always make sure that the sound is as good at the back end as it is right down in front. If we succeed or fail, it's definitely down to our own ability to communicate the music. All I can say is that some of those shows have worked really well, so it's not impossible, just kind of difficult.

Mark Knopfler recently said that any decision to play stadiums really comes down to money. You can make x million dollars by playing stadiums as opposed to only y million by playing arenas—that in the end it really has little to do with how many fans will be able to see you.

There's no doubt that if you do exclusively stadium shows, you make a lot of money if they sell out. But what we did was a mixture of stadium shows and arena shows, which is the most uneconomic thing you can do. We didn't feel confident enough to play only stadiums, but we also didn't feel that we wanted to spend six or seven months just touring the United States. I don't know what we'll do next tour. I think we could take on the stadiums. But I also feel that we've proven that we can do it, and we don't have to go any further.

In fact, two terrific stadium appearances—at Live Aid, in 1985, and at the final Amnesty International show in New Jersey in 1986—played a big role in establishing U2 as a major-league band. Do you sometimes worry that U2 has gotten too closely identified with those types of benefit shows?

Well, being the Batman and Robin of rock & roll has its disadvantages. I think we realized in the last couple of months that you can't continue to be involved in charity events. What we are, first and foremost, is a rock & roll band. If we forget that, people are going to stop listening. So at the moment my feeling is that I don't really want to do any charity shows for the moment. I think it would devalue anything else we've done.

As far as being responsible, I feel no need to be anything other than what we are. I don't feel we need to be in some way virtuous or whatever. When you reach the stage we're at, you have to learn to say no a lot more. I mean, we could do charity events solidly for the next ten years. But I don't think it would really do any good.

What about Amnesty International?

That's the one charity we really feel we can support, because its aims are so basic. You know, who can argue about human rights? It's fundamental.

In the last year it seems U2 has done everything in the book—had a Number One album and single, graduated to playing stadiums, and now a book, a movie and a live album are planned for 1988. What can you do for an encore?

Break up [*laughs*]

But seriously, how do you avoid the traps that have destroyed almost every other rock band?

By still being in love with music. I think a lot of groups that fell by the wayside just got distracted. At the moment we're so into where the band is going and what the band can do musically that the other things have really had little effect on us. It's really like we've let it wash over us without messing us up. And also because there are four of us in this group, we're all in the same position.

It must be hard being, say, Bruce or Bob Dylan. Because it's just you. There's no one else you can check with and see how they're feeling or who can keep an eye on you when you're going through a rough period. With us, when we get into the limousine and there's the four of us, it's a good feeling. There are just those four people—but it makes it a lot easier to handle, no matter what happens.

I think we're more committed to being a great group now than we ever were. For years we were insecure about our playing, about how good a band we were. But I've no doubt anymore. We're a lot less insecure. But there are still a lot of musical goals that we haven't achieved. I'm personally very excited about what's going to happen in the next three years.

So what's left for U2 to do?

I think we're about to reinvent rock & roll. That's our challenge.

■ **RANDOM NOTES** "WHO'S LATEST: ITS LAST?" (March 24, 1988)

"I'm only here for the Who," said U2's Bono at the British Record Industry Awards—England's equivalent of the Grammys—at London's Royal Albert Hall. The Who accepted this year's Outstanding Contribution Award, in honor of the band's twenty-fifth anniversary, by re-forming (for the first time since Live Aid) to play "Who Are You," "My Generation" and "Substitute." Nevertheless, Pete Townshend was quick to squelch rumors that it was more than a one-off reunion. Roger Daltrey said unhappily, "Pete doesn't want to do it. It's as simple as that. Until he does, there's no point even thinking about it." Though, of course, Roger has been. "I still think we've got a lot to offer rock & roll," he said dolefully. "It's very painful for us to go out there tonight and have a great time, because tomorrow there's nothing."

U2 collected the award for Best International Group. Bono was puffing a large cigar and wearing an uncharacteristically ornate tie—"I knew everyone *else* would be wearing leather," he said. Bono and the Edge had just spent a week in western Ireland, where they were writing songs, visiting pubs and going out on local fishing boats.

ANTHONY DeCURTIS

U2'S FORGETTABLE FLUFF

Unforgettable Fire: The Story of U2
by Eamon Dunphy

THIS BOOK IS AN EMBARRASSMENT to U2—all the more so because it is an authorized biography by a writer handpicked by the band. Eamon Dunphy, a former soccer player and now a Dublin journalist, knows virtually nothing about rock & roll, and as a result *Unforgettable Fire: The Story of U2* is littered with breathtaking inaccuracies.

Understandably, Dunphy emphasizes what he knows best: the ins and outs of Dublin and the political and religious troubles that divide Ireland's soul. This deepens our understanding of U2's origins, but it also makes for a parochial portrait of the band. Though he writes well, Dunphy describes the band members' early lives in far too much detail. The effort to make the usual traumas of growing up seem interesting over four tellings drives Dunphy to such ludicrous and romantic formulations as this, about Bono: "As a baby he'd cried all day, restless, tormented, trying to reconcile the conflicting voices in his head, the competing demons in his soul."

Like a booster in a neighborhood bar, Dunphy is always proclaiming firsts, bests and mosts for the locals. "Bullet the Blue Sky," from *The Joshua Tree,* is not merely a powerful song; it "is art, the expression of human experience through rock 'n' roll, more profound and accessible than it has ever been." Even in the book's best section a discussion of the band's struggle to square Christian principles with the worldly environment of rock—it never occurs to Dunphy that Jerry Lee Lewis, Little Richard, Marvin Gaye, Bob Dylan and countless others have experienced their own equally valid versions of this dilemma.

Then there are the simple—and simply incredible—inaccuracies. During their legendary tours of the United States, according to Dunphy, the Beatles and the Rolling Stones performed "without moving their lips or playing their instruments." Rock great Eddie Cochran's name is misspelled as "Cochrane." There were even more mistakes in the U.K. edition, in which Dunphy credited U2 with inventing the notion of onstage sound monitors and said that Bono "made up" the Velvet Underground classic "Sweet Jane" in an Atlanta bar.

As if to atone for his shortcomings, Dunphy includes an appendix of four articles on U2-related subjects by Dublin rock critics. Each is first-rate—particularly the two by *In Dublin* writer Eamonn McCann. In "U2 Pressgangbang"—about the willingness of writers to suspend their critical judgment in matters concerning U2—McCann concludes, "I think the fans are being insulted and—depending on whether and what they think of all this—maybe U2 as well." Unfortunately, that also sums up the effect of this book.

JEFFREY RESSNER

U2 SOUNDTRACK ALBUM SET

RATTLE AND HUM, THE FILM chronicling U2's 1987 world tour, will première in late October in the band's home town of Dublin, with an American debut in November. The double-album soundtrack package, composed of live and studio recordings, will be released in mid-October by Island Records.

According to the director of the film, Phil Joanou, the picture is neither a straightforward concert movie nor a traditional rock documentary. "It's more about a vibe than a story," says the twenty-six-year-old Joanou.

"This is a film about a group that's been together for ten years, capturing a moment in their lives that resulted in some new music," Joanou says, "as opposed to documenting the beginning or the end of a group, like Sting's *Bring On the Night* or the Band's *Last Waltz*."

Although a series of concerts last fall at Sun Devil Stadium, in Tempe, Arizona, and McNichols Sports Arena, in Denver, serves as the centerpiece, the movie also follows band members as they pay a visit to Graceland, work on a song in Texas with B.B. King, lay down tracks at the legendary Sun Studio and walk through Harlem before entering a church to sing with a gospel choir. Nonconcert footage makes up a third of the film's ninety-five minutes.

About twenty songs—including hits by the band, new songs like "When Love Comes to Town" and "Desire" and covers like "All Along the Watchtower"—will be heard in the movie.

"The live portion of the album is not what you'd expect," says the producer of the soundtrack, Jimmy Iovine, who previously handled the board on the band's concert LP, *Under the Blood Red Sky*. "There are different arrangements, new songs and a flow to it. It's not the greatest hits cut live—it's a real album."

As far as the studio tracks go, Bono has said *Rattle and Hum* represents U2's first genuine rock & roll-oriented work, and Iovine concurs. "It's a much more raw album than their other stuff," says Iovine. "This will be a hard-hitting, aggressive record."

TOP 100 SINGLES OF THE LAST 25 YEARS

F OR A TRIBUTE TO THE rock & roll 45, ROLLING STONE writers and editors chose the top 100 singles of the twenty-five years spanning 1963 to 1988. U2 came in at Number Forty-six, with "Pride (In the Name of Love)," which entered the *Billboard* charts on December 7, 1984. The band was interviewed for the accompanying essay.

#46 "Pride (In the Name of Love)"

" 'Pride' is the best song we've written to date," said Bono, U2's charismatic singer, after the release of *The Unforgettable Fire,* the album it appeared on. Admittedly, the song, a tribute to Martin Luther King, has some unremarkable lyrics—there's even a historical inaccuracy about King's assassination, which occurred not in the morning but in the evening. Yet Bono's fiery delivery and the Edge's fervent guitar riffs, coupled with the nobility of the subject matter, make it one of the most inspirational songs of this decade.

"With a song like 'Pride,' " said the Edge, "you can see a certain craft to the songwriting. As you get to know it better, it draws you in and becomes something personal to you."

The song was inspired by a visit to the Peace Museum, in Chicago. Next to an exhibit of paintings and drawings by survivors of Hiroshima and Nagasaki, titled the Unforgettable Fire—hence the album's name—was a collection of works dedicated to Martin Luther King. U2 had high hopes of reaching a wider audience with the single. In the U.K., it became the group's first Top Ten hit, and although it went to only Number Thirty-three in America, it set the stage for U2's phenomenal success with *The Joshua Tree.*

"Ultimately, I hope people will remember 'Pride' for what it was about," bassist Adam Clayton said. "It was important for us to have a single that said something, rather than just make a nice noise on the radio."

SONGWRITER: Bono. **PRODUCERS:** Brian Eno and Daniel Lanois. **RELEASED:** December 1, 1984. **HIGHEST CHART POSITION:** Number Thirty-three. **ALBUM:** *The Unforgettable Fire.*

■ **RANDOM NOTES** "U2: RATTLES AND TOGAS" (September 22, 1988)

"Rattle and Hum takes place in an America that might not exist in someone else's reality," says Bono, referring to U2's forthcoming film. "But it's an America that's very real to us." The movie opens with the band's searing performance of the Beatles' "Helter Skelter." Bono introduces it as a song Charles Manson stole from the Beatles, then says, "We're going to steal it back."

The film's concert footage is intended to give audiences a different perspective on the band's shows. "We want to get the moviegoer into a concert as we experience it from the stage looking out," says bass player Adam Clayton. Adds guitarist the Edge, "Our aim was to allow our audience to hear as well as see how we worked in our emotional commitment to the music we play."

U2 is now in L.A., finishing up the soundtrack album. The group recently threw a poolside toga party for Edge's twenty-seventh birthday, which one guest described as "an Irish version of *Animal House.*" Is *that* the America Bono's referring to?

■ **RANDOM NOTES** "U2: Where the streets do have names" (October 20, 1988)

"Bono wanted to get a feel of the intensity of street life in L.A.," says Richard Lowenstein, 29, who directed U2's video for "Desire," the first single from the soundtrack for the band's upcoming film, *U2: Rattle and Hum.* (The Australian director is best known for his work with INXS.) Lowenstein says the video was shot "very much on the run" on the streets of Los Angeles, from back alleys to trendy Melrose.

Prior to shooting the clip, the band collaborated on a new song, "God Part II," which will be added to the album. It's an homage to John Lennon and a putdown of sensationalist biographer Albert Goldman. The double album also features contributions from Bob Dylan, B.B. King and Brian Eno.

■ **RANDOM NOTES** "Edging in on the Blues" (November 3, 1988)

"Everybody says he's hot—everybody couldn't be wrong," said seventy-two-year-old blues great John Lee Hooker after meeting U2's Edge backstage at the San Francisco Blues Festival. "I know one thing: he's a nice person." The U2 guitarist had come up the coast from L.A. (where he was working on the band's film, *U2: Rattle and Hum*) to catch the country's oldest blues fest, now in its sixteenth year.

"He told me that I have a lot to be proud of, that I inspired a lot of people," said Hooker, who's hardly been resting on his reputation. He's just recorded an album that features Bonnie Raitt (singing "I'm in the Mood for Love"), Robert Cray, Los Lobos and George Thorogood. "It's called *The Healer,*" said Hooker—as in "the blues will heal you."

ANTHONY DeCURTIS

RATTLE AND HUM ALBUM REVIEW

U2's American Curtain Call

ATTLE AND HUM IS AN expression of U2's urge to have it both ways. A sprawling double album that incorporates live tracks, cover versions, collaborations, snippets of other people's music and a passage from a taped interview, the record is an obvious effort to clear the conceptual decks and lower expectations following the multiplatinum success of *The Joshua Tree*.

But ambition has always been U2's gift and curse, and the band clearly doesn't feel fully comfortable with its sights lowered. Consequently, if amid the rather studied chaos here, you feel moved to draw comparisons with masterpieces of excess like the Beatles' White Album or the Rolling Stones' *Exile on Main Street,* you can be sure that Bono, the Edge, Adam Clayton and Larry Mullen Jr. won't mind a bit.

This record doesn't quite ascend to those heights, but U2 does win half the prize. In its inclusiveness and rollicking energy, *Rattle and Hum* caps the story of U2's rise from Dublin obscurity to international superstardom on a raucous, celebratory note. At the same time, it closes off none of the options the band might want to pursue for its next big move—and, possibly, the album even opens a few doors.

Despite Bono's insistence in the blistering "God Part II" that "I don't believe in the 60's in the golden age of pop / You glorify the past when the future dries up," *Rattle and Hum* is in large part a paean to the tradition of Sixties artists that U2 reveres. "God Part II" itself is Bono's personal extension of "God," the dramatic track on *Plastic Ono Band* in which John Lennon shed the Sixties, his identity as a Beatle and all the idols he had worshiped. Bono's update includes a pointed attack on Albert Goldman, whose book *The Lives of John Lennon* paints a bitter, unflattering portrait of the ex-Beatle: "I don't believe in Goldman his type like a curse / Instant karma's gonna get him if I don't get him first."

Rattle and Hum evokes the Beatles right off the bat when it opens with a corrosive live version of "Helter Skelter," a song that originally appeared on the White Album. "This song Charles Manson stole from the Beatles; we're stealin' it back," Bono announces portentously before U2 tears into the tune.

Bob Dylan sings on one track (the meandering ballad "Love Rescue Me," which Dylan also co-wrote) and plays organ on another ("Hawkmoon 269"). He is further acknowledged when U2 ignites a live rendition of "All Along the Watchtower." Jimi Hendrix, the third member of U2's Sixties trinity, is resurrected when the version of "The Star-Spangled Banner" he performed at Woodstock introduces U2's searing live take on "Bullet the Blue Sky."

U2 certainly holds its own while flirting with the greats, but *Rattle and Hum* is most enjoyable when the band relaxes and allows itself to stretch without self-consciously reaching for the stars. The New Voices of Freedom choir joins the band onstage in New York for an electrifying gospel-style rendition of "I Still Haven't Found What I'm Looking For" that finds new depths in a song that was gripping the first time around.

Guitarist B.B. King teams up with U2 at Sun Studio, in Memphis, and together they tear up "When Love Comes to Town," a rousing blues rocker about the redemptive power of love. While in Memphis, U2 also brought in the Memphis Horns to help out with a soulful tribute to Billie Holiday titled "Angel of Harlem."

U2 flexes its rock & roll muscle on the Bo Diddley-inspired single "Desire," the fierce "Hawkmoon 269" and a raucous live rendition of the antiapartheid "Silver and Gold," which first appeared in a studio version on the Sun City protest album organized by Little Steven Van Zandt. A tough live performance of "Pride (In the Name of Love)," U2's anthem in honor of Martin Luther King Jr., captures the group's onstage might at its inspirational peak.

But the quieter songs on *Rattle and Hum* provide the record with introspective moments made all the more effective by the generally boisterous context of the album. The Edge turns in a fine lead vocal and accompanies himself on electric guitar and keyboards on the hymnlike "Van Diemen's Land," about an Irish nationalist poet who was exiled to Australia. "Heartland," on which Brian Eno plays keyboards, summons up a dreamscape reminiscent of the drifting, poetic songs on *The Unforgettable Fire*. And *Rattle and Hum* eases to a close with the ballad "All I Want Is You," a stirring statement of unsatisfied desire that features an eloquent string arrangement by Van Dyke Parks.

As its title suggests, *Rattle and Hum* is meant to be dynamic, rather than strictly coherent. It's intended to dramatize U2 in motion and transition and to exult in the barrage of influences the band had just begun to admit on *The Joshua Tree*. Recorded almost entirely in the United States, the album also carries forward U2's near obsession with the brave new world of America.

But for all its excitement, *Rattle and Hum* seems a tad calculated in its supposed spontaneity. The album is, after all, a soundtrack. Rather than a documentary, it's merely a document of events that often were staged and arranged for the express purpose of being filmed and recorded. The album ably demonstrates U2's force but devotes too little attention to the band's vision.

That vision, of course, has evolved impressively over the years—beginning with the dark adolescent wonder of *Boy* and moving through the mystical enclosure of *October,* the fury and poignance of *War,* the surreal imagery of *The Unforgettable Fire* and the resonant expansiveness of *The Joshua Tree. Rattle and Hum* is the sound of four men who still haven't found what they're looking for—and whose restlessness assures that they will be looking further still.

■ **RANDOM NOTES** "KEITH AND U2 JAM FOR JAMAICA" (December 1, 1988)

"Where's my mate Keith Richards?" shouted Bono midway through U2's closing set for the Smile Jamaica concert, to benefit victims of Hurricane Gilbert, at London's Dominion Theatre. Richards was already onstage behind him, preparing to add a few guitar licks and gruff vocals to "When Love Comes to Town." For the finale, "Love Rescue Me," the band was also joined by Ziggy Marley, who'd played "Jumpin' Jack Flash" during his set with the Melody Makers. Others taking part in the concert, which aired live on British TV, included the Robert Cray Band, Tom Tom Club, the Christians, Julia Fordham, Womack and Womack and Boy George.

"When we first heard about Smile Jamaica," said guitarist Edge after the show, "I thought there was no way we could play it. For a start, U2 hadn't played in a year. But the more we considered it, it seemed to be one of those events we just had to play. And when we heard Ziggy was playing the show, it gave the whole thing a new perspective. . . . It was also a good excuse to play with Keith and pinch some of the Rolling Stones licks I've been envious of all of these years."

Artists who couldn't make it to the show sent taped messages. "I can't be there at the moment," said the ever-selfless Terence Trent D'Arby during his appeal for contributions. "I'm sort of looking after my own disaster: recording my album."

■ YEAR-END RANDOM NOTES (DECEMBER 15-29, 1988)

MARCH *"Oh, God, I cried,"* said Little Richard when asked about Michael Jackson's performance of "Man in the Mirror" at the thirtieth annual Grammy Awards, in New York. "My big toe just shot up in my boot!" Though Jackson's performance of the song got rave reviews, his 'Bad' garnered him only one award (for Best Engineering).

"I hoped that I would win," said Best New Artist Jody Watley. "When I was a dancer on 'Soul Train,' I always aspired to better and bigger things." Meanwhile, U2's Bono declared, "We're slipstream, not mainstream." (The band copped two awards for *The Joshua Tree*).

AUGUST *Folkways: A Vision Shared,* the all-star tribute to Woody Guthrie and Leadbelly, was one of the year's best musical investments for two reasons. First, the album offers some stunning covers of works by the two folk legends. Most notable are the contributions by Bob Dylan, Bruce Springsteen, John Mellencamp, U2 and Taj Mahal. Second, the artists who appear on the album are donating their royalties to a worthy cause: preserving roots music. The money is being used to help the Smithsonian Institution finance its purchase of Folkways Records, the label that recorded Guthrie and Leadbelly, as well as many other folk and blues legends.

OCTOBER Keith Richards found himself onstage alongside a different frontman when he joined Bono and U2 during the band's closing set of the Smile Jamaica benefit concert, at London's Dominion Theatre. Richards and the band played "When Love Comes to Town," followed by "Love Rescue Me," during which they were joined by Ziggy Marley. The show was a fund-raiser for Jamaican victims of Hurricane Gilbert.

Others who performed included Robert Cray, Robert Palmer and Tom Tom Club. Many on the bill have Jamaican connections: U2 is on reggae impresario Chris Blackwell's label, Island (Bono spent his honeymoon at Blackwell's house in Jamaica); Richards has a home in Ocho Rios; and Tom Tom Club's Chris Frantz and Tina Weymouth, who produced Ziggy Marley and the Melody Makers' most recent album, have recorded in Jamaica.

NOVEMBER Basically it's a movie about myself, Adam, Edge and Larry—three men and a baby," said Bono at a New York press conference prior to the release of U2's *Rattle and Hum,* the band's beautifully shot concert film.

The group gave an impromptu concert before the film's première in Dublin. The Edge and Adam Clayton played acoustic guitars, Larry Mullen Jr. rattled a tambourine, and Bono led them through "When Love Comes to Town" and "I Still Haven't Found What I'm Looking For." The band also attended premières in Madrid, London, New York and Los Angeles.

In New York, the band members were asked what they thought of the film, which is certainly not lacking in hubris. "It was nice to see ourselves live," said the Edge. "We've never been to a U2 concert before," added Bono. "I thought I was much taller," said the Edge.

DAVID FRICKE

YEAR-END REVIEW OF *RATTLE AND HUM*

EVEN U2'S TRADEMARK AURA of moral righteousness and stalwart rock & roll zeal isn't enough to dispel the air of "product" that surrounds *Rattle and Hum*. You loved *The Joshua Tree*? Here's the movie of the tour, the album of the movie, the book of the whole schmear. But what really undercuts the project is an uncharacteristic lack of focus, specifically the band's inability to reconcile the difference between discovering America and conquering it. As documents of the in-concert experience, the incendiary takes of "Silver and Gold" and "Pride (In the Name of Love)" are the next best thing to being there. Not so the roots-music experiments conducted in Memphis at Sun Studio, including the awkward tribute to Billie Holiday, "Angel of Harlem," and "When Love Comes to Town," where Bono goes head to head with B.B. King, who has *lived* what he sings and lets you know it. This is a mess with a mission—Hendrix and Lennon were present in spirit, Dylan in the flesh (he co-wrote one song, appeared on two)—but a mess nevertheless.

TOP 100 ALBUMS OF 1988

December 15–29, 1988

1 GEORGE MICHAEL
Faith—Columbia

2 INXS
Kick—Atlantic

3 DEF LEPPARD
Hysteria—Mercury

4 DIRTY DANCING
Soundtrack—RCA

5 GUNS N' ROSES
Appetite for Destruction—Geffen

6 TERENCE TRENT D'ARBY
Introducing the Hardline According to Terence
Trent D'Arby—Columbia

7 MICHAEL JACKSON
Bad—Epic

8 TRACY CHAPMAN
Tracy Chapman—Elektra

9 TIFFANY
Tiffany—MCA

10 BRUCE SPRINGSTEEN
Tunnel of Love—Columbia

11 AEROSMITH
Permanent Vacation—Geffen

12 STEVE WINWOOD
Roll with It—Virgin

13 STING
. . . Nothing Like the Sun—A&M

14 DEBBIE GIBSON
Out of the Blue—Atlantic

15 MORE DIRTY DANCING
Soundtrack—RCA

16 VAN HALEN
OU812—Warner Bros.

17 POISON
Open Up and Say . . . Ahh!—Enigma/Capitol

18 GLORIA ESTEFAN AND MIAMI SOUND MACHINE
Let It Loose—Epic

19 MIDNIGHT OIL
Diesel and Dust—Columbia

20 D.J. JAZZY JEFF AND THE FRESH PRINCE
He's the D.J., I'm the Rapper—Jive/RCA

21 RICK ASTLEY
Whenever You Need Somebody—RCA

22 RICHARD MARX
Richard Marx—EMI

23 ROBERT PLANT
Now and Zen—Et Paranta/Atlantic

24 BON JOVI
New Jersey—PolyGram

25 GEORGE HARRISON
Cloud Nine—Dark Horse

26 CINDERELLA
Long Cold Winter—Mercury

27 SADE
Stronger Than Pride—Epic

28 JOHN COUGAR MELLENCAMP
The Lonesome Jubilee—Mercury

29 U2
Rattle and Hum—Island

30 ROBERT PALMER
Heavy Nova—EMI

31 WHITNEY HOUSTON
Whitney—Arista

32 GOOD MORNING, VIETNAM
Soundtrack—A&M

33 BRUCE HORNSBY AND THE RANGE
Scenes from the Southside—RCA

34 DAVID LEE ROTH
Skyscraper—Warner Bros.

35 COCKTAIL
Soundtrack—Elektra

36 BOBBY MCFERRIN
Simple Pleasures—EMI

37 ZIGGY MARLEY AND THE MELODY MAKERS
Conscious Party—Virgin

38 METALLICA
. . . And Justice for All—Elektra

39 KEITH SWEAT
Make It Last Forever—Elektra

40 WHITE LION
Pride—Atlantic

41 10,000 MANIACS
In My Tribe—Elektra

42 BELINDA CARLISLE
Heaven on Earth—MCA

43 TALKING HEADS
Naked—Sire

44 JAMES TAYLOR
Never Die Young—Columbia

45 CHEAP TRICK
Lap of Luxury—Epic

46 ROD STEWART
Out of Order—Warner Bros.

47 AL B. SURE!
In Effect Mode—Warner Bros.

48 THE SCORPIONS
Savage Amusement—Mercury

49 BOBBY BROWN
Don't Be Cruel—MCA

50 DOKKEN
Back for the Attack—Elektra

51 RANDY TRAVIS
Always and Forever—Warner Bros.

52 KINGDOM COME
Kingdom Come—PolyGram

53 STEVIE WONDER
Characters—Motown

54 ROBERT CRAY
Don't Be Afraid of the Dark—PolyGram

55 PEBBLES
Pebbles—MCA

56 HUEY LEWIS AND THE NEWS
Small World—Chrysalis

57 U2
The Joshua Tree—Island

58 NEW EDITION
Heartbreak—MCA

59 LITTLE FEAT
Let It Roll—Warner Bros.

60 UB40
Labour of Love—A&M

61 ELTON JOHN
Reg Strikes Back—MCA

62 RUN-D.M.C.
Tougher Than Leather—Profile

63 AC/DC
Blow Up Your Video—Atlantic

64 PRINCE
Lovesexy—Paisley Park

65 FOREIGNER
Inside Information—Atlantic

66 LINDA RONSTADT
Canciones de Mi Padre—Asylum

67 ROBBIE ROBERTSON
Robbie Robertson—Geffen

68 SINÉAD O'CONNOR
The Lion and the Cobra—Ensign/Chrysalis

69 JOAN JETT AND THE BLACKHEARTS
Up Your Alley—CBS

70 EUROPE
Out of This World—Epic

71 VAN MORRISON AND THE CHIEFTAINS
Irish Heartbeat—Mercury

72 JONI MITCHELL
Chalk Mark in a Rain Storm—Geffen

73 BILLY OCEAN
Tear Down These Walls—Jive/Arista

74 IRON MAIDEN
Seventh Son of a Seventh Son—Capitol

75 BILLY IDOL
Vital Idol—Chrysalis

76 INFORMATION SOCIETY
Information Society—Tommy Boy/Reprise

77 JODY WATLEY
Jody Watley—MCA

78 THE SUGARCUBES
Life's Too Good—Elektra

79 THE CHURCH
Starfish—Arista

80 JIMMY PAGE
Outrider—Geffen

81 SALT-N-PEPA
A Salt with a Deadly Pepa—Next Plateau

82 UB40
UB40—A&M

83 PATTI SMITH
Dream of Life—Arista

84 BRYAN FERRY
Bête Noire—Reprise

85 LUTHER VANDROSS
Any Love—Epic

86 OZZY OSBOURNE
No Rest for the Wicked—Epic

87 KENNY G
Silhouette—Arista

88 TAYLOR DAYNE
Tell It to My Heart—Arista

89 NEW ORDER
Substance—Qwest

90 BASIA
Time and Tide—Epic

91 ANTHRAX
State of Euphoria—Island

92 JOAN ARMATRADING
The Shouting Stage—A&M

93 FOLKWAYS: A VISION SHARED
A Tribute to Woody Guthrie and
Leadbelly—Columbia

94 MORRISSEY
Viva Hate—Sire/Reprise

95 ERIC CLAPTON
Crossroads—Polydor

96 DEPECHE MODE
Music for the Masses—Sire

97 KEITH RICHARDS
Talk Is Cheap—Virgin

98 COLORS
Soundtrack—Warner Bros.

99 DARYL HALL AND JOHN OATES
Ooh Yeah!—Arista

100 IMAGINE: JOHN LENNON
Soundtrack—Capitol

JEFFREY RESSNER

BONO LESS THAN BOFFO AT BOX OFFICE

Rattle and Hum: Ho-hum

U2'S AMBITIOUS *RATTLE AND HUM* project—encompassing a concert film, a double-album soundtrack and an illustrated paperback—rattled record stores and bookshops but received a ho-hum reception at the box office last fall.

Opening nationwide last November 4th, *Rattle and Hum* was the country's second-highest-grossing film in its debut weekend, right behind John Carpenter's creature feature *They Live*. U2's movie racked up $3.8 million at nearly 1400 theaters during its first three days, but ticket sales dropped dramatically soon afterward. By the end of Thanksgiving weekend, the picture had made only $8.3 million domestically and was being pulled from theaters for Christmas epics like *Scrooged*.

The movie, distributed worldwide by Paramount, also had trouble finding a broad audience overseas. "It's not doing too well anywhere," says Marty Kutner, Paramount's executive vice-president of foreign distribution and marketing. "Kids want to go to a concert, not a film of a concert."

Producer Michael Hamlyn defends the film's performance, however. "It did a little less than expected," he says, "but it still did better than any other rock-concert movie since *Woodstock* in terms of grosses. Films like this have a long shelf life." Hamlyn adds that the film has yet to be shown in some of the important foreign markets, like Japan.

Since *Rattle and Hum* cost $5.6 million to produce—and movies must usually gross three times their budget to be profitable—the film still has a way to go if it is to make money. Ancillary sales of cable rights and the upcoming home video, however, should help push the final tally into the black.

The imminent home-video release will "most likely" include performances of several songs not used in the theatrical version, says the film's director, Phil Joanou, with "anywhere between fifteen and forty minutes" added to the picture.

Among the tunes being considered for inclusion in the video are "New Year's Day," "I Will Follow," "One Tree Hill," "Mothers of the Disappeared," "The Unforgettable Fire" and "Trip Through Your Wires."

While the theatrical film could be considered a modest moneymaker at best, the accompanying soundtrack is a solid success. Within a month of its release, sales soared beyond the 5 million mark worldwide, with more than half that figure generated in this country. The record swiftly hit the top spot on *Billboard*'s pop-albums chart, becoming the first double album to reach that position since Bruce Springsteen's album *The River,* in 1980.

The movie's official paperback tie-in was also deemed a hit by its publisher, Harmony Books. The first press run of 40,000 copies quickly sold out, and Harmony printed an additional 25,000. In the U.K., response was even stronger, with over 125,000 copies of the book shipped to stores.

Although *Rattle and Hum* was given mixed reviews by film critics, the band intends to continue working in the medium. Jack Nicholson reportedly asked the group to score a sequel to *Chinatown,* but nothing has been firmed. Meanwhile, says Joanou, Bono is writing an original script about a New Orleans blues singer and her involvement in a sexually obsessive relationship.

Joanou's own star also seems to be rising as a result of his *Rattle* work: he's currently readying a romantic thriller entitled *The Final Analysis.*

1988 MUSIC AWARDS

March 9, 1989

SHAKE, RATTLE AND ROMP: Dublin's fab four—U2—win Artist of the Year, Best Band, Album, Single, Video and just about everything else they qualified for.

READERS PICKS:
ARTIST OF THE YEAR
U2
Tracy Chapman
George Michael
INXS
Guns n' Roses

BEST ALBUM
Rattle and Hum, U2
Tracy Chapman
Kick, INXS
Hysteria, Def Leppard
Appetite for Destruction,
   Guns n' Roses
OU812, Van Halen
Now and Zen, Robert Plant
Diesel and Dust, Midnight Oil
New Jersey, Bon Jovi
Traveling Wilburys: Volume
   One, Traveling Wilburys

BEST SINGLE
"Desire," U2
"Sweet Child o' Mine," Guns
   n' Roses
"Welcome to the Jungle,"
   Guns n' Roses
"Pour Some Sugar on Me,"
   Def Leppard
"Fast Car," Tracy Chapman
"Roll With It," Steve
   Winwood
"Need You Tonight," INXS
"Never Tear Us Apart," INXS
"Don't Worry, Be Happy,"
   Bobby McFerrin
"Love Bites," Def Leppard

BEST BAND
U2
INXS
Def Leppard

Guns n' Roses
Van Halen

BEST MALE SINGER
Bono
George Michael
Robert Plant
Steve Winwood
Sting

BEST SONGWRITER
Bono
Tracy Chapman
Sting
George Michael
Prince

BEST VIDEO
"Desire," U2
"Pour Some Sugar on Me,"
   Def Leppard
"Need You Tonight," INXS
"Sweet Child o' Mine,"
   Guns n' Roses
"Wild Thing," Sam Kinison

BEST ALBUM COVER
Rattle and Hum, U2
Appetite for Destruction,
   Guns n' Roses
Hysteria, Def Leppard
Kick, INXS
Lovesexy, Prince

BEST GUITARIST
Eddie Van Halen
The Edge
Eric Clapton
Jimmy Page
Slash (Guns n' Roses)

BEST DRUMMER
Larry Mullen Jr.
Rick Allen (Def Leppard)
Phil Collins

Alex Van Halen
Sheila E.

BEST BASS PLAYER
Adam Clayton
Michael Anthony (Van Halen)
Sting
Rick Savage (Def Leppard)
John Taylor (Duran Duran)

BEST-DRESSED MALE ROCK
   ARTIST
Robert Palmer
Sting
George Michael
Bono
Steve Winwood

SEXIEST MALE ROCK ARTIST
George Michael
Bono
Michael Hutchence (INXS)
Jon Bon Jovi
Sting

ARTISTS PICKS:
The Edge
Fisherman's Blues, the
   Waterboys
Lovesexy, Prince
Irish Heartbeat, Van
   Morrison and the Chieftains
Our Beloved Revolutionary
   Sweetheart, Camper Van
   Beethoven
Green, R.E.M.
Dream of Life, Patti Smith
Tender Prey, Nick Cave and
   the Bad Seeds
16 Lovers Lane, the
   Go-Betweens
Flag, Yello
Miss America, Mary Margaret
   O'Hara

STEVE POND

NOW WHAT?

Having conquered the world, U2 tries to figure out what to do next

"WHAT DO YOU THINK WE should do?" On a cloudy afternoon in Dublin, U2 isn't acting much like the band with all the answers. Instead, the members of the group are acting more like four guys who are themselves trying to answer a few important questions, and the main question—which Bono poses within minutes of the time he sits down in a pub and orders a pint of Guinness—is what this band should do on the heels of *Rattle and Hum*.

If they don't have an answer, at least they finally have the free time to think about it. That's something that's been in short supply for the past two years, from the release of their 1987 breakthrough album, *The Joshua Tree*, through the subsequent international tour, to the recording and filming of the controversial two-record set and motion picture *Rattle and Hum*.

"The last few years," says Bono, with his customary intensity—but also with a distracted air that suggests he's groping to put a rather deep-seated confusion into words—"have been such a merry-go-round that when you get off and you're on dry land, it keeps spinning. And we haven't quite come to terms with being at home. I have to be strapped in at night, you know? There's this thing of wanting to move. . . ."

He trails off, then looks around at his three band mates. "Wanderlust, I suppose," he says. "That's been with the group for a few years, in many ways, and I suppose it's what *Rattle and Hum* is about. Not just in terms of locations—towns and cities and places—but *musical* wanderlust. So now we're in detox.

"We would be lying, I think, if we said that everything is okay these days. Everything's *not* okay, you know? Even talking about U2, we really don't know how to talk about U2 anymore."

Bono shrugs. "I think it's really important to preface your article by saying that one of the reasons we haven't done many interviews lately is that we don't really have that much to say."

YOU VOTED THEM ARTIST of the Year and Band of the Year for the second year in a row, but lots of you are going to complain that we put them on the cover. A good number of letters, in all likelihood, will say the same thing: "Not *them* again!"

As *Rattle and Hum* the movie heads for videocassette and *Rattle and Hum* the album continues its stay in the Top Ten, it's clear that U2's problem is more than simple overexposure. After years of favorable fan and press reaction to the band's music; years of dramatic stage performances; years in which underground credibility turned into mass success; years of articles based on intense conversations with a hyperbolic, socially minded lead singer and his three more retiring band mates; years of grainy black-and-white photos of deadly serious, brooding faces, growing from dewy-cheeked youth to bestubbled adulthood; after all that, the U2 backlash has set in.

It always arrives, sooner or later, with this level of success; just ask old hands like Madonna and Michael Jackson or the newly dethroned Bruce Springsteen. But in U2's case, the backlash may have hit harder and faster than usual, and it also may be harder to shake off. And that's due, simply enough, to the way this band has always conducted itself.

From their debut with *Boy* nine years ago, the members of U2 have made it clear that they are dead serious, extraordinarily ambitious and convinced of the importance of what they achieve—or, more accurately, the importance of what they are *trying* to achieve. Emerging from the high-energy, fraying integrity and fashionable nihilism of a rapidly fragmenting punk scene, these three young Christians and the token non-believer wanted to make rock & roll matter again. Even back then, Bono was the kind of frontman who'd return a compliment like "Great album!" with a serious "Yeah, it is, isn't it?"—and what originally sounded ingenuous and endearing slowly became problematic. At the same time, though, more and more people began to agree that U2's albums were great. Two years ago, the band released the critically applauded, top-selling, Grammy-winning album *The Joshua Tree,* went on its biggest international tour and had its all-but-official coronation as the World's Biggest Rock Band.

Enter the *Rattle and Hum* juggernaut: a two-record set, part live versions of old songs and part new tunes recorded in the studio; a major motion picture, complete with a big push from the hottest Hollywood movie studio of the past few years; splashy benefit premières in Madrid, Dublin, London, New York and Los Angeles; a collection of songs written by, written about, performed by or recorded with the help of the Beatles, Bob Dylan, Jimi Hendrix, B.B. King and Billie Holiday; a work that includes shouted declarations that the band is stealing "Helter Skelter" back from Charles Manson, that it's armed with "three chords and the truth"; a souvenir book to accompany the whole thing, which, with Eamon Dunphy's *Unforgettable Fire,* makes two officially commissioned U2 books within a year; T-shirts sold in theater lobbies; and an ABC television special about the making of *Rattle and Hum,* featuring interviews and behind-the-scenes footage linked by Robbie Robertson's narration, which practically canonizes the four band members.

Trouble is, the television special never aired. (According to *Rattle and Hum* director Phil Joanou, the show was delivered to ABC too late for a timely airing.) And while the book sold well, the movie performed about as well as you can expect a concert movie to perform: It had a good opening week, but its business fell by half each subsequent week before it quickly dropped out of theaters.

In the end, the movie will no doubt recoup its $5 million cost and be remembered as a dramatic concert documentary that contributed to the air of hubris surrounding U2. Designed as a look at U2 as the band encountered America during the *Joshua Tree* tour, Phil Joanou's movie plays like a homage to U2's importance, from the backstage scene in which B.B. King tells Bono how heavy his lyrics are to the lovingly photographed concert footage. The performances are often riveting, and the camera work is remarkable, but the finished product seems more self-serving than rock films like *The Last Waltz* and *Stop Making Sense.*

As for *Rattle and Hum* the album . . . Well, it sold millions, and lots of people loved it. But it also drew the kind of flak that until now U2 had avoided. A ROLLING STONE reader wrote in to say that the album will be remembered as "the downfall of a great band." *The New York Times* greeted the album's release with a review—headlined WHEN SELF-IMPORTANCE IN-TERFERES WITH THE MUSIC—that described the album as "a mess." " 'Rattle and Hum' is plagued by U2's attempt to grab every mantle in the Rock-and-Roll Hall of Fame," Jon Pareles wrote. "Each attempt is embarrassing in a different way." And in the *Village Voice,* Tom Carson wrote, "By almost any rock and roll fan's standards, U2's *Rattle and Hum* is an awful record. But the chasm between what it thinks it is and the half-baked, overweening reality doesn't sound attributable to pretension so much as to monumental know-nothingism." Others painted a similarly unflattering portrait of U2 as a humorless, self-satisfied band, trying to boost its own image by aligning itself with the giants of American roots music.

Much of the criticism seems a vengeful reaction against a record that is, in essence, a collection of odds and ends accumulated by the band along the course of its American tour. A little bit country, a little bit rock & roll, plus a little bit blues and gospel and arena rock, *Rattle and Hum* is best read as an honest attempt by four rich and highly visible rock & roll fans to come to terms with a couple of their obsessions: their new-found preoccupation with American musical styles they'd steadfastly avoided when they started making their music, and their fixation on America itself, a country that they reflexively hated when all they knew were cheap hotels and bad nightclubs and Ronald Reagan on TV but that began to intrigue them when they got to see the inside of Sun Studio, in Memphis, and sit on the banks of the Mississippi River and go to the right blues clubs in Chicago and cruise Sunset Boulevard in the '61 Cadillac convertible Edge drove around Los Angeles during the making of the album and the movie.

Rattle and Hum is a messy but revealing collection that has some terrific songs—"Desire," "Heartland," "Hawkmoon 269," "All I Want Is You." But it doesn't say anything definitive. "The statement," says Bono, "was that there was no statement." But when you throw in a $5 million movie and a lavish marketing campaign and the book and the T-shirts and the huge posters of those four unsmiling faces that were plastered all over every city where *Rattle and Hum* was released, you get a project that demands to be taken as a Major Statement. And in the gap between what people thought U2 was promising and what the band actually delivered, you had the beginnings of a backlash, of a potential crisis in the career of a band whose seat atop the rock pile isn't quite so secure these days.

N0 SOONER HAVE THE MEMBERS of U2 settled into a small, high-walled private booth in a pub down the road from Dublin's Guinness brewery—"the snugs," these little rooms are called—than Larry Mullen Jr. is recommending U2's favorite local band. It's called the Joshua Trio.

"They're hilarious," says Bono quickly. "They do things like 'Nobody Cares': 'What about unemployment? What about the ozone layer? Nobody cares. No, wait! *Bono cares!*' "

It's a measure of the band's impact in its home town that another group exists doing nothing but U2 spoofs. Another measure is the fact that the only way the band can spend a few hours in uninterrupted conversation is to reserve one of the snugs, booths originally built so that Dublin's drinkers could sequester their wives away from the exclusively male territory of the main pub.

In fact, the fame means they have to choose their pubs more carefully, too—especially after Bono's introduction to "Sunday Bloody Sunday" in *Rattle and Hum,* in which he excoriates the Irish Republican Army and ends by saying, "Fuck the revolution." Since then, says Edge, "certain pubs in Dublin we don't feel as comfortable in. But I think our position has changed in Ireland, irrespective of that. We now drink in little boxes like this." Adds Adam Clayton, "Our world gets smaller the bigger the band gets."

As they hang up their jackets—which range from a leather New York Police Department model for Larry to a blue pin-striped number for Bono, who's looking corporate in vest, tie and gray beret—the boys in the band order a round of the locally brewed dark stout (except for Larry, who sticks to coffee) and settle into the little box. Larry thinks it's "a bit claustrophobic." Bono likes it. Adam says he feels like he's "in a men's toilet." And after listening to his band mates argue the snug's merits, Edge speaks up quietly. "It's a bit like being in U2," he says.

But if the four men who've come to this pub on a cloudy January afternoon are feeling enclosed, uncomfortable or affected by the storm that *Rattle and Hum* stirred up, they're also more than willing to talk. As usual, Bono takes center stage and summons up his characteristic fervor when the conversation turns to U2's music, but everybody chimes in when the talk deals with Ronald Reagan's place in history, or the months the band spent living in Los Angeles last year, or the band members' admiration for musicians as diverse as Jerry Lee Lewis and Nanci Griffith, or their plans for their own Mother Records label, which will soon release a record by Guy Clark and is looking to sign other veteran country and folk performers like Joe Ely and John Prine.

"I must say," says Bono, "that my heroes at this point in time all have lines in their faces. I mean, if U2 set out to see through the Fifties rebellion in the Eighties—because it didn't work, and it was stupid to think that somebody with a safety pin in their nose and a leather jacket therefore had something to say—well, then, this other idea of a generation gap is also out the window in the Eighties. The young-punk idea is nonsense. I prefer to spend a day with Johnny Cash than a week with some up-and-coming pop star."

This was precisely the kind of thing U2 began to do during the American tour that led to *Rattle and Hum*—listening to blues and gospel music, recording at Sun Studio, cutting songs with B.B. King and the New Voices of Freedom gospel singers, doing versions of "Helter Skelter" and "All Along the Watchtower." But in the process, the band drew charges that it was using past heroes to boost its own status.

"Everyone slags us off for comparing ourselves to great groups," snaps Larry Mullen, "but that's bullshit. I mean, they said that to the Beatles, as well."

When the laughs die down, Bono picks up the argument. "Seriously, folks," he says with a chuckle, "we're in this big band, but in our own heads we're still fans of the greats, from Elvis Presley and Billie Holiday to Bob Dylan to the Band to the Waterboys to whoever.

"What happened around the album is remarkable," he says, "maybe even a bigger work of art than the album. The very idea of *Rattle and Hum* was, if not to burst the balloon, to let the air out of it. Everything about it, from doing really bad cover versions, which is how we started . . . A big band should be able to be a garage band if it wants to. Being brilliant is to take risks. I don't mean taking risks in the shallow water of the avant-garde but in the deep water."

Bono takes off his beret and runs a hand through his slicked-back hair. "You know," he says, "they say in the Eighties that rock & roll is dead. I don't think it's dead, but if it's dying, it's because groups like us aren't taking enough risks. You know, make a *movie*. Put yourself up there against what's out there. *Robocop* and *Three Men and a Baby*. That's great for rock & roll, not just for U2. I think you've got to dare."

Edge cuts in. "Like Megadeth doing 'Anarchy in the U.K.,' " he says.

"Yeah!" says Bono with a grin. "We mustn't be responsible, we must be *irresponsible,* artistically speaking. Wouldn't it be awful if we said, 'Oh, we're in a big group now'? Rock & roll ought to be irresponsible, at least in the sense of being able to do a wicked cover version or say something like . . . How's it go? 'This is a song Charles Manson stole from the Beatles. We're stealing it back.' If that's gonna get up some people's noses, all the better. I don't even know what it means. It means something, though."

To many people, it means U2 is announcing itself the heir to the Beatles.

"Let's get down to the Beatles, here," says Bono, the evangelical gleam in his eye getting fiercer with each word. "We're not saying we're a better band than the Beatles. But we are *more* of a band than the Beatles. We are. There's four of us—a street gang, essentially, who drew no lines. Not Lennon and McCartney songwriting and Ringo's the drummer. When we walk onstage, it is the *band* that is the real work of art, the four of us.

"And when we were sixteen," he says, "we didn't think, 'Oh, let's not be the Beatles.' I thought, 'Fuck the Beatles, fuck the Rolling Stones.' They may have been our musical idols, but every band in the world thinks it's better than the Beatles. They are the blueprint. And we are fans and in awe of their music, but we're not reverent. It'd be childish of us to say we're better than the Beatles, or we're worse than the Beatles. I'm just saying that we're more of a band."

Larry Mullen, who fidgets as Bono grows feverish, sighs. "Back to that one again, are you?" he asks, rolling his eyes.

Edge looks over and laughs. "Oh, shut up, Ringo," he says.

Beatle jokes aside, though, it's unlikely that many of *Rattle and Hum*'s detractors would be convinced by these arguments, because for anyone who thinks U2's music is overstated or pompous, the band's interviews can seem similarly self-serving and humorless. And while it may have been daring to make a movie, that movie didn't make a case for humility.

The band members never really address this issue. They talk *about* the album but *around* the movie, other than to complain about the compromises they had to make for the cameras. "I think the movie is great for them," says Phil Joanou, "because in a way it's them, but they don't have to take responsibility for the film because they didn't make it. It takes some weight off them, and that's good."

And the relentlessly serious tone? "That's totally my fault," says Joanou. "The movie was meant to be a fairly serious depiction of their music, as opposed to a light one. I have footage that could have changed that, but my plan was to do an aggressive, grab-people-by-the-throat-and-shake-them kind of movie rather than a romp through America with U2. A romp with U2 wasn't something I could swallow, so I went for"—he chuckles—"an overly serious, pretentious look at U2. That's a fair criticism, but what the hell?"

But if the members of U2 are perfectly capable of being funny guys, Bono doesn't seem to mind the "humorless" rap. "The time we live in, nothing is taken seriously," he says. "Part of the yuppie ethic is 'Let's not take everything so seriously, man.' The fact that a third of the population of the earth is starving, let's not take that so seriously. The fact that we're moments away from oblivion because of nuclear weapons . . . You know, these subjects don't get big laughs. That's why I admire people like Robin Williams, who can make their point *and* make people laugh. That's his job. I don't know, maybe our job is to make people cry, weep, tear their hair out, gnash their teeth. . . . I mean, we are a very serious band about our work. We *are*. Deadly serious. Annoyingly, appallingly, boringly serious about our work."

And what is their work?

"To go where no band has gone before," he says, as the entire group howls with laughter. "To boldly go where no rock & roll band's gone before, to search out old soul records and steal their spirit. . . ."

The question is crucial, and history says that U2 will settle it with its next album. So far, the band has adhered to a pattern: first it makes an assertive, relatively straightforward album (1980's *Boy*, 1983's dramatic *War*, *The Joshua Tree*), then it follows it with one that's harder to get a handle on (1981's mystically minded *October*, 1984's atmospheric *Unforgettable Fire*, *Rattle and Hum*).

That might mean it's time for another more forceful and cogent LP—
except that these days the stakes are higher and the risks of overexposure
very real. "I'm sick to death of reading about U2," says Edge.

"It's a very interesting time for U2," says Bono, as the afternoon turns
into evening and the band orders another round (Larry finally shifts from
coffee to vodka). "There is a sense of 'Up drawbridge,' cut ourselves off,
and a sense of feeling misunderstood, and a sense of the antagonism toward
us. You know, *Rattle and Hum* was the end of something."

"The safe thing to do," says Edge, "would be to wait three years and
then do the next record. But I don't think I could wait that long."

"People say, 'Better not release a record within two years,' " Bono says.
" 'It mightn't sell so well.' But so what? We don't have to do anything we
don't want to do now. That is what it is to be rich—and in that sense, we
are *filthy* rich. We used to have to finish albums and go on tour just to stay
solvent, right up until *The Joshua Tree*. We don't have to do that now, so
we're just gonna play where we want to play."

If financial security means they don't have to do anything in particular,
Rattle and Hum also says that they can go in just about any direction they
choose. By being something of an undefined, sprawling mess, it gives them
freedom: instead of suggesting any one future direction, it simply shows a
band that's learning more about the roots of its music and trying to use that
new knowledge somehow.

"I do think we're slow learners," says Bono with a chuckle. "We really
move at a snail's pace. We just learned the fourth chord. We've done a lot
with three—just wait till we start using the fourth.

"There are few bands that have come so far with so little," he says. "I
think U2 has, as a white rock & roll group, broken a lot of barriers. In terms
of subject matter, even in terms of vocabulary. There are certain words that
as a writer I *own*. Lots of them. There are certain tones in the guitar, certain
approaches, which *we* own. I'm very excited about U2, looking back at
what we've done. But I'm much more excited about what we're about to
do.

"It's the end of the cold war," he says, "and I think it's also the end of
the cold wave. You know, that sort of Halloween, bogyman music, death-
march music. And we just did not fit into that, and we have been flying in
the face of that for ten years. And now I think that's ending. You see artists
in Germany, the new avant-garde, their idols are people like [nineteenth-
century romantic painter J.M.W.] Turner. It's extraordinary. To see soul
music at the center of things, Cajun music, Irish music . . ."

Not, he hastens to add, that U2 is going to become a band of roots-rock
purists. "The future is not to look back," he says. "The future is to

reinterpret the past. We didn't really reinterpret the past on *Rattle and Hum*. We gave in to it, and it was fun. But the future is to reinterpret, and preserve the spirit. That spirit is the real key, the spirit of abandonment.''

With that, Bono heads to the men's room, and the conversation lightens. The other band members, it seems, are just as happy to order a few more drinks and talk about the history of sexual segregation in Irish pubs. Then their singer returns, announcing as he steps through the door, *''All my favorite words are stolen.''*

''They are?'' asks Larry with a start.

''They are,'' Bono says. ''They're all gone, meaningless. Like *born again*. What a great idea—everyone should want to be born again, every day. But now it means nothing, because some very dangerous people got a hold of the word. Wherever I look, words have been used up. Gone. They don't mean anything. *God. Light. Sex.* And the most powerful word has got to be *love,* but the fight is on for that one.''

He sighs. ''That's the key for U2 as well,'' he says. ''With all these big ideals, we've got to bring things down to two people, really. One is good, two is better. And that's where I see us going.''

And so, in the end, we have to ask Bono the question he himself asked a couple of hours and a couple of pints ago: In 1989, after *Rattle and Hum* and everything that came with it, what should U2 do?

''I think we're really clear about one thing, maybe,'' Bono begins hesitantly. ''What we have to do is simplify. Simplify everything and just get to the center of what it is to be in a band, which is to write great rock & roll songs and perform them. We picked up so much along the way that's just extra baggage—people and houses and big motorcades and airplanes and helicopters and boats. . . .

''They're all there, but we don't need them,'' he says. ''All we need is three and a half minutes. You know, the spirit that we found that was always in our music is stronger now. It's exciting for a rock & roll band to strip itself right down, to take off all recognizable signs and just bash away and say, 'This is still us.' ''

The final question, though, is still troublesome. At this stage in their career, is it possible for the members of U2 to truly simplify themselves? They spent the last decade carefully, consciously and deliberately building themselves up to the point where they are a Big Band in nearly every sense of the term; are they really willing or able to demythologize U2 without at the same time remythologizing themselves in some other way?

''I don't know,'' Bono says simply. ''That's our dilemma. All we can do is simplify, strip away and just make shiny, bright music. Music that will . . .''

He stammers for a minute, struggling to find the right words. Finally, he gives up and shrugs. "You know, just dream it up," he says quietly. "Just dream it up."

■ **RANDOM NOTES** "I'VE BEEN RATHER . . ." (March 23, 1989)

I've been rather delighted that some of the songs I'd written a long time ago have come out so well," says Marianne Faithfull, referring to some of the tracks on her next album, *Blazing Away*. "The old associations I had with them have completely dropped away." Those associations are from the days before the smoky-voiced singer went into treatment for chemical dependency at the Hazelden clinic. "My attitude is very different now," she says. "I feel much lighter about the songs. They used to be so *deadly serious.*" *Blazing Away*, produced by Hal Willner and Fernando Saunders, also features new originals, as well as a song written for Faithfully by Bono and the Edge called "Conversation on a Barstool" and Leonard Cohen's "Tower of Song."

■ **RANDOM NOTES** "DUBLIN LOCALS . . ." (August 24, 1989)

Dublin locals Mike Scott of the Waterboys and Edge and Adam Clayton of U2 hauled out to the docks for the official launch of the Greenpeace album *Rainbow Warriors* in Ireland.

The Waterboys are now finally making their way to this side of the Atlantic: They'll begin their long-awaited U.S. tour on the East Coast at the end of September. That's also when U2 begins touring in Australia, New Zealand and Japan.

TOBY CRESWELL

U2 KICKS OFF TOUR DOWN UNDER

T O KICK OFF ITS SECOND Australian tour, U2 opened its show in Perth with the rolling Bo Diddley beat of "Desire," signaling that the band—despite what one may have expected after the over-blown film *Rattle and Hum*—had come down under for some serious rock & roll. As Bono put it at a press conference in Sydney, "Making movies, that's all the nonsense of rock & roll. Playing shows is the reason we're here. That's the real business of rock & roll."

The twenty-three-date tour has been one of the most talked-about concert events in Australia in years. Close to 250,000 tickets (priced at nearly thirty American dollars) sold out in just a few hours. Most of the band's albums have reentered the charts in Australia, and its latest single, "All I Want Is You," is currently at Number Two. The Irish quartet has brought along blues legend B.B. King and his band as special guest artists; the local band Weddings, Parties, Anything is opening all the shows.

U2 is honoring its commitment to come to Australia at the end of the 1987 *Joshua Tree* tour, when the dates were postponed because of family commitments. The band has also booked dates in Japan, New Zealand and Europe, with a final show in Dublin on New Year's Eve. While in Australia, the band will be writing songs and recording demos in a Sydney studio, with an eye toward a new album to be released by the end of 1990.

Since their arrival, in mid-September, the band members have shown they want to relax and enjoy themselves. They've spent time checking out local bands and throwing a sixty-fourth-birthday party for B.B. King on Sydney Harbor.

By the time the band members got to Sydney for the fourth show of the tour, they were clearly in gear, playing a loose but passionate set that drew heavily from the *Rattle and Hum* album and revealed the band's current fascination with R&B. Bono took command of the songs and the stage—taking time out for monologues on El Salvador and the "working girls" of Sydney. At one point he pulled a kid out of the audience to play guitar on Curtis Mayfield's "People Get Ready," and two nights later he took over on drums so that Larry Mullen could sing "Stand by Me." A tough version of Bob Dylan's "All Along the Watchtower" and an angry "Bullet the Blue Sky" were complemented by a forceful reading of "All I

Want Is You," a brief snatch of "God Part II" and a haunting "With or Without You."

Perhaps predictably, the encore featured B.B. King, whose band provided a horn section for "Angel of Harlem" and "Love Rescue Me." King's vocals powered a blistering version of "When Love Comes to Town."

Afterward, U2 seemed more than satisfied with the show. "As far as we're concerned," Bono declared, "the Eighties was just a rehearsal. I mean that."

TOP 100 ALBUMS OF THE EIGHTIES

At decade's end, ROLLING STONE editors chose the best albums of the Eighties. U2 showed up twice: in the Top Five with *The Joshua Tree* (Number Three) and at Number Forty with *War*.

#3 *The Joshua Tree*

BONO WANTED TO EXPLORE rock & roll's American roots; the Edge wanted to continue the expressionistic experimentalism of *The Unforgettable Fire*. The creative tensions between them resulted in U2's best record, a multifaceted, musically mature work. "Two ideas were followed simultaneously," says the Edge. "They collided, and this record was born."

The Joshua Tree is the rather esoterically titled album he's referring to—a title that even the typically solemn Bono could joke about. As the U2 singer said to ROLLING STONE's Anthony DeCurtis at the time of its release, "You get record-industry people saying, 'As big as the Beatles—what's the name of the album?' *'The Joshua Tree.'* 'Oh, yeah, oh, right.' It's not exactly *Born in the Joshua Tree,* or *Dark Side of the Joshua Tree*. It sounds like it would sell about three copies."

In fact, the album sold about 12 million copies worldwide, and launched the already popular Irish quartet into the rock stratosphere. But more important than the mass appeal of the album was its message of spiritual and creative yearning, articulated in songs like "I Still Haven't Found What I'm Looking For," "With You or Without You" and "Where the Streets Have No Name." Equally significant was the group's continued examination of political and social issues. In "Running to Stand Still," Bono describes the havoc that heroin use can cause, while "Bullet the Blue Sky" captures the horror and moral outrage that the singer felt about U.S. involvement in Central American politics.

"I just think the album takes you somewhere," says bassist Adam Clayton. "It's like a journey. You start in the desert, come swooping down in Central America. Running for your life. It takes me somewhere, and hopefully it does that for everyone else."

The Joshua Tree is "an album of contrasts," says the Edge. "Bono had fairly strong ideas. He'd been taken with American literature and music.

Lyrically, he wanted to follow the blues and get into America. I'd written off white blues in 1978. I was trying desperately to figure out ways to play without using white blues. I wanted to push the European atmospherics. But listening to Robert Johnson and other early blues, I could see what was there. I warmed to the idea."

Both Brian Eno and Daniel Lanois, who coproduced the album, made major contributions. "Brian strongly suggested that we do it all ourselves," says the Edge. "We felt inclined to bring people into the sessions—at times it would have been nice to have pedal steel or background vocals. But he always felt we could do it. There was a great wisdom in that decision."

There was no attempt to make *The Joshua Tree* a commercial album. "If anyone had even *breathed* that idea . . . ," says Clayton. "We wanted to make music. The thing is to challenge radio. To get 'With You or Without You' on the radio is pretty good. You don't expect to hear it on there—maybe in a church."

Before recording began, the group spent time rehearsing at Clayton's house in Dublin, and the atmosphere was so comfortable that they decided to record there. "Just this big, high room," he says. "One of the biggest rooms I've ever seen in a house. With windows and natural light. Pretty much all of it was recorded at my house." The band spent about three months on the album, interrupting the sessions to headline Amnesty International's Conspiracy of Hope Tour in the U.S. Some recording was also done at Dublin's Windmill Lane Studios, at the Edge's house and at another Dublin studio, S.T.S.

Approximately seventeen songs were worked on. Some of the material that didn't end up on the album—such as "The Sweetest Thing," "Spanish Eyes" and "Deep in the Heart"—became B sides of singles.

Lanois credits Eno with sparking many of the music's more adventurous moments. "They had found the experimental side of working on *The Unforgettable Fire* tiring," says Lanois. "But if you work with Brian, like it or not, he's gonna weird things up."

Yet the sessions often had a relaxed, off-the-cuff feel. Of "Running to Stand Still," the Edge says it was "almost improvised to tape." And "I Still Haven't Found What I'm Looking For" originally had a different melody and was called "Under the Weather."

One of the album's best tracks, "Where the Streets Have No Name," proved extremely difficult to record. At one point Eno became so disillusioned with it that he tried to destroy the tape; the engineer told the Edge, "I just had to stop Brian from erasing 'Streets.' "

"It took forever to get that track," says Lanois. "We had this giant blackboard with the arrangement written on it. I felt like a science professor, conducting them. To get the rise and fall, the song's dynamic, took a long time."

Does the band consider *The Joshua Tree* one of the best albums of the Eighties? "With *Joshua Tree,* we wanted to make a really great record with really great songs," says the Edge. "We became interested in songs again. We put abstract ideas in a more focused form. It's the first album where I really felt Bono was going where he was aiming with the lyrics. Bono is more of a poet than a lyricist. With *Joshua Tree,* he managed, without sacrificing the depth of his words, to get what he wanted to say into a three- or four-minute song."

"Important?" muses Clayton. "I don't know. It was important for *us.* Suddenly we could do so many different things musically. It gave us a great freedom. I think we were able to stretch and do things we didn't really understand before. It captured a musicality for us that we'd never gotten on record before."

PRODUCERS: Daniel Lanois and Brian Eno. RELEASED: March 1987. HIGHEST CHART POSITION: Number One.

#40 *War*

"**P**UNK HAD DIED," says the Edge. "We couldn't believe it had been swept to the side as if it had never happened, and *War* was designed as a knuckle buster in the face of the new pop."

Indeed, at the time of the album's release in 1983, the anger and anarchy of the late-Seventies punk movement had been replaced by the new romanticism best typified by Duran Duran and Spandau Ballet. Into such tepid waters, U2 dropped its bomb: *War* is a powerful fusion of politics and militant rock & roll, an album that anticipated the political awareness that would come back into vogue as the decade progressed.

With two of U2's best sing-along anthems, "Sunday Bloody Sunday" and "New Year's Day," *War* became something of a *Who's Next* for the Eighties. The album's aggressive sound is highlighted by what bassist Adam Clayton calls "all those helicopter guitars."

Following U2's first two albums, the delicate and ethereal *Boy* and the moodier and disjointed *October, War* arrived with the force of a jackhammer ripping into concrete. Rough, hard and metallic, it remains U2's most overt rock album.

"We loved the Clash's attitude early on," the Edge says. "And Richard Hell and the Voidoids, the Pistols. Guitar bands that didn't use blues clichés. I was listening to Tom Verlaine to figure out how to make tough music."

The title itself was arresting, as were its politically inspired songs. "We wanted a record people couldn't just write off," says Clayton. "It was an unsettled time, a year of conflict. Poland was on the news at the time. You looked around and there were conflicts everywhere. We saw a lot of unrest on TV and in the media. We focused on that."

Still, U2 wanted to leave listeners with a feeling of hope. "We wanted love *and* anger," says the Edge. "We wanted a protest record, but a *positive* protest record."

War was recorded in about six weeks at Windmill Lane Studios, in Dublin, with most of the songs written in the studio. Vocalist Bono improvised lyrics to completed tracks, then refined them. "Bono would sing, and whatever came out would be the starting point," says producer Steve Lillywhite.

Completing the songs was difficult. "It's always hard to finish them," says Clayton. "It takes Bono a long time to commit to a lyric. 'New Year's Day' was a tough one. We had arguments over the vocals. At one stage it wasn't even on the record."

The album's final track, "40," which takes its title and lyrics from the Fortieth Psalm, was literally finished at the last moment, even as the next band scheduled to use the studio cooled its heels. "We were trying to get lyrics down and mix it with people pounding on the door," says Clayton.

PRODUCERS: Steve Lillywhite and Bill Whelan. RELEASED: March 1983. HIGHEST CHART POSITION: Number Twelve.

■ **YEAR-END RANDOM NOTES** (December 14–28, 1989)

March When B.B. King came through Dublin in March on his tour, he was joined onstage by local favorites Bono and the Edge to play "When Love Comes to Town," the song that the boys from U2 had penned for King and performed in *Rattle and Hum*. The Dublin show was a dress rehearsal for U2's own tour with King later in the year.

September Being so successful as a producer, Daniel Lanois had to put his first solo album aside twice—to work with the Neville Brothers and Bob Dylan. But the dreamlike *Acadie* (with guest appearances by the Nevilles, members of U2 and Brian Eno) was worth the wait.

October Making movies, that's all the nonsense of rock & roll," said Bono, almost apologizing for U2's bombastic film *Rattle and Hum* at a press conference in Sydney, Australia. "Playing shows is the reason we're here. That's the real business of rock & roll." U2 was touring down under with B.B. King while also recording demos for its next album.

Family Affairs U2's family tree grew two branches. Bono and wife Alison had their first baby, Jordan, on May 10th. The Edge and wife Aislinn had their third daughter, Blue Angel.

THE TOP 100 ALBUMS OF 1989

December 14–28, 1989

1 BOBBY BROWN
Don't Be Cruel—MCA

2 NEW KIDS ON THE BLOCK
Hangin' Tough—Columbia

3 PAULA ABDUL
Forever Your Girl—Virgin

4 FINE YOUNG CANNIBALS
The Raw and the Cooked—I.R.S./MCA

5 GUNS N' ROSES
G n' R Lies—Geffen

6 MILLI VANILLI
Girl You Know It's True—Arista

7 TRAVELING WILBURYS
Volume One—Wilbury/Warner Bros.

8 TOM PETTY
Full Moon Fever—MCA

9 GUNS N' ROSES
Appetite for Destruction—Geffen

10 EDIE BRICKELL AND NEW BOHEMIANS
Shooting Rubberbands at the Start—Geffen

11 SKID ROW
Skid Row—Atlantic

12 BON JOVI
New Jersey—PolyGram

13 MADONNA
Like a Prayer—Sire

14 RICHARD MARX
Repeat Offender—EMI

15 R.E.M.
Green—Warner Bros.

16 BEACHES
Soundtrack—Atlantic

17 PETER GABRIEL
Passion—Geffen

18 ANITA BAKER
Giving You the Best That I Got—Elektra

19 TONE-LOC
Loved After Dark—Delicious Vinyl/Island

20 THE CURE
Disintegration—Elektra

21 LIVING COLOUR
Vivid—Epict/E.P.A.

22 DEF LEPPARD
Hysteria—Mercury

23 GREAT WHITE
Twice Shy—Capitol

24 ROY ORBISON
Mystery Girl—Virgin

25 10,000 MANIACS
Blind Man's Zoo—Elektra

26 DON HENLEY
The End of the Innocence—Geffen

27 TRACY CHAPMAN
Tracy Chapman—Elektra

28 KENNY G
Silhouette—Arista

29 PRINCE
Batman—Warner Bros.

30 ENYA
Watermark—Geffen

31 THE CULT
Sonic Temple—Sire/Reprise

32 U2
Rattle and Hum—Island

33 WARRANT
Dirty Rotten Filthy Stinking Rich—Columbia

34 POISON
Open Up and Say . . . Ahh!—Enigma/Capitol

35 BONNIE RAITT
Nick of Time—Capitol

36 ELVIS COSTELLO
Spike—Warner Bros.

37 GLORIA ESTEFAN
Cuts Both Ways—Epic

38 THE B-52'S
Cosmic Thing—Reprise

39 INDIGO GIRLS
Indigo Girls—Epic

40 PINK FLOYD
Live: Delicate Sound of Thunder—Columbia

41 JOURNEY
Journey's Greatest Hits—Columbia

42 COCKTAIL
Soundtrack—Elektra

43 LOU REED
New York—Sire

44 L.L. COOL J
Walking With a Panther—Def Jam

45 SOUL II SOUL
Keep On Movin'—Virgin

46 LOVE AND ROCKETS
Love and Rockets:—Beggars Banquet/RCA

47 FLEETWOOD MAC
Greatest Hits—Warner Bros.

48 SIMPLY RED
A New Flume—Elektra

■ **RANDOM NOTES** (February 8, 1990)

U2's New Year's Eve gig at Dublin's Point Depot was broadcast in Western and Eastern Europe. Bono dedicated "Pride (In the Name of Love)" to "the people of East Germany, Poland, Czechoslovakia and especially Romania."

■ **RANDOM NOTES** (February 22, 1990)

It's not difficult to trace the musical influences of Dublin's Joshua Trio. "We have a simple message to the world," says drummer Arty Mathews. "Listen to Bono. We are but vessels for his words."

The band's members, who perform a sly satirical tribute to Bono and company, say they're haunted by the prospect of becoming bigger than U2. Following in U2's footsteps, the Trio is making a movie, *Beyond Sexuality,* about a fifteenth-century peasant boy who finds a *Rattle and Hum* CD in a field.

1989 MUSIC AWARDS

March 8, 1990

Without a 1989 album or American tour, U2 still managed to win entrance into several categories of ROLLING STONE's readers poll.

BEST BAND	BEST MALE SINGER	BEST SONGWRITER
The Rolling Stones	Tom Petty	**Bono**
R.E.M.	**Bono**	Billy Joel
U2	Don Henley	Tom Petty
Fine Young Cannibals	Mick Jagger	Tracy Chapman
Guns n' Roses	Richard Marx	Don Henley

■ RANDOM NOTES (May 17, 1990)

Eighties nostalgia already? In the preface to his book *U2: The Early Days,* Irish rock critic Bill Graham says the book is "a biographical sketch in words and pictures," based on the memories of those who saw U2 in the beginning. (Graham introduced the band to its manager, Paul McGuinness.)

But even the author admits that the photographs are a more reliable source than certain recollections. As one U2 follower told him, "I can't remember a thing. . . . I was drunk all the time."

Still, for U2 fans, the book is a treasure-trove of anecdotes and photographs from the band's club days, when Bono, the Edge, a bushy-haired Adam Clayton and a pouty-faced Larry Mullen fraternized with the transvestite band the Virgin Prunes, played covers of Thin Lizzy's "Dancing in the Moonlight" and didn't take themselves quite so seriously. Most comical among the photos are a series of ill-fated publicity shots that have (understandably) never before surfaced.

■ YEAR-END RANDOM NOTES (December 12–27, 1990)

January   This is a very posh event," said Ray Davies from behind the podium at the fifth annual Rock and Roll Hall of Fame induction dinner at New York's Waldorf-Astoria. "And we're all tarted up to be here. I realize that rock & roll has become very respectable. What a bummer." Davies, who, with the rest of the KINKS, was inducted this year into the Hall of Fame, obviously hadn't gotten a good look at the members of U2. When Bono, the Edge, Adam Clayton and Larry Mullen took the stage to induct the Who, they cut a decidedly casual figure in jeans, work shirts and boots. But Bono soon shifted attention away from attire, turning instead to *physical* attributes. "It's written in rock & roll that all you need is love," he said. "But you also need a great *nose.*" The reference to Pete Townshend's profile got a good laugh from the crowd.

February   *A Clockwork Orange* debuted on the London stage; U2's Edge wrote the score.

1990 MUSIC AWARDS

March 7, 1991

Out of sight, out of mind . . . almost. In hibernation, U2 just barely managed to make it into the readers poll this year. The group moved down to fourth place in the Best Band category.

BEST BAND	**BEST BASSIST**	**BEST DRUMMER**
Aerosmith	Paul McCartney	Phil Collins
Depeche Mode	Geddy Lee of Rush	Tommy Lee of Mötley Crüe
Living Colour	Nikki Sixx of Mötley Crüe	Neil Peart of Rush
U2	Michael "Flea" Balzary of the	**Larry Mullen Jr.**
The Black Crowes	Red Hot Chili Peppers	Jason Bonham
	Adam Clayton	

■ **RANDOM NOTES** (June 27, 1991)

Bootlegs of U2's rehearsals and demos for the band's upcoming album have surfaced in Germany and England, causing Island Records to counter with a stern warning against any pirating activity.

BRIAN ENO

BRINGING UP BABY

COOL, THE DEFINITIVE EIGHTIES compliment, sums up just about everything that U2 isn't. The band is positive where cool is cynical, involved where it is detached, open where it is evasive. When you think about it, in fact, cool isn't a notion that you'd often want to apply to the Irish, a people who easily and brilliantly satirize, elaborate and haggle and generally make short stories very long but who rarely exhibit the appetite for cultivated disdain—deliberate noninvolvement—for which the English pride themselves. The Irish are storytellers, pattern makers, great salesmen and inspired fantasists, and they remake their world by describing it—several times a day. Temperamentally, they aren't inclined to remain spectators to someone else's idea of how things are: They'll jump right in and make it up for themselves. Reality, that arid bottleneck of European thought, comes to seem much more relative and negotiable—something to be continually reinvented, even at the cost of occasionally losing touch with it completely. It is this reckless involvement that makes the Irish terminally uncool: Cool people stay 'round the edges and observe the mistakes and triumphs of uncool people (and then write about them).

So here I am, writing about this record with which I had a tangential involvement, still hopefully warm from the experience. U2 had asked Dan [Lanois] and myself to produce this album with them, but I'd already made plans for much of the period. The role I thus ended up with was luxurious: I came in now and again for a week at a time, listened to what had been going on and made comments and suggestions. I could point to something and say, "This doesn't do much for me," and suggest how it could be done otherwise without being made aware that I was casually dismissing three weeks' work. On the other hand, I could come in and try to reexcite everyone about something that had, for whatever reasons, fallen out of favor. I can think of worse jobs than hearing something you like and then telling the people who made it why they ought to like it, too. But the solid backbone of the producing work was down to Dan and [engineer] Flood, who stayed with it through months of ups and downs and twists and turns and maintained their concentration and good humor. And, of course, the band members themselves, whose dogged optimism and good-natured perseverance infect everyone who works with them.

Which is just as well, for working on a U2 record is a long and demanding process. The pattern seems to go like this: A couple of weeks of recording throws up dozens of promising beginnings. A big list goes up on the blackboard, songs with strange names that no one can remember ("Is that the one with the slidy bass or the sheet-of-ice guitar?"). These are wheeled out, looked at, replayed, worked on, sung to, put away, bootlegged and wheeled out again, until they start to either consolidate into something or fall away into oblivion. The list on the blackboard begins to thin down, although Bono, the Mother Teresa of abandoned songs, compassionately continues arguing the case for every single idea that has ever experienced even the most transitory existence: "We *have to have* a song like this on the record." "This will be *fantastic* live." "Imagine *this* coming out of your car radio." But as the weeks pass, and the seasons turn outside the studio windows, some things seem to start holding a shape while others get passed over.

And a language starts to evolve. It's a language of praise and criticism, the first flagpoles marking out the landscape within which this new music is being made. Buzzwords on this record were *trashy, throwaway, dark, sexy* and *industrial* (all good) and *earnest, polite, sweet, righteous, rockist* and *linear* (all bad). It was good if a song took you on a journey or made you think your hifi was broken, bad if it reminded you of recording studios or U2. Sly Stone, T. Rex, Scott Walker, My Bloody Valentine, KMFDM, the Young Gods, Alan Vega, Al Green and Insekt were all in favor. And Berlin itself, where much of the early recording was done (nostalgically, for me—we were in the same room where Bowie's *"Heroes"* was made), became a conceptual backdrop for the record. The Berlin of the Thirties—decadent, sensual and dark—resonating against the Berlin of the Nineties—reborn, chaotic and optimistic—suggested an image of culture at a crossroads. In the same way, the record came to be seen as a place where incongruous strands would be allowed to weave together and where a probably disunified (but definitely European) picture would be allowed to emerge.

The emotional scope of the record was prefigured in the scope of its inspirations: psychedelia, glam, R&B and soul. These earlier eras of pop music, however, were characterized not by the search for perfection but by bizarre enthusiasms, small budgets, erratic technique, crummy equipment and wild abandon. The dichotomy between that and the way in which we were working gave rise to a lot of questions. Given the choice, how much do you allow a record to exhibit warts-and-all spontaneity, and how much do you repair? Are you really making a record that's recorded in a garage, or are you making a record that reminds you of the feeling of records that are made in garages (the way a filmmaker might use a hand-held camera to give the impression of documentary urgency)? Does it make a difference if people hearing the record say, "That record sounds like trash," rather than, "They've deliberately chosen to make a record that sounds like trash"? Can you use that kind of detached, craftful irony and yet come over as emotionally sincere at the same time? On the other hand, is "sincerity" important, or are we here as actors, purveying credible *impressions* of sincerity? Should a record be a picture of where you are now or of all the places you could just as likely be?

And then another crop of questions: If you know you're probably going to sell several million albums on the strength of your track record, should you remain consistent to that track record? Are you deceiving people by moving off in new directions? Do people value you for your consistency or your surprises? It's easy for a theorist (normally someone who isn't selling 20 million records) to answer these questions: Naturally, he or she will recommend the supposedly riskier choice, releasing the weirdest and most extreme album possible. But this apparently heroic stance is based on a romantic view of what artists do: the idea that they drag benighted publics into shocking new worlds for their own good. There's a certain medicinal note to the whole process—if you don't like it, it must be doing you good. Pop music has never really been like this: Its practitioners don't usually shield themselves behind the shimmery veils of High Art, dividing the world into insiders and outsiders; they expect to be liked (or at least talked about) by significant numbers of people. They want to be part of a world that excites them, not way out beyond it. Actually, I can't think of any artist I know who is not concerned about the reactions of his or her listeners: not with a view to pandering to them, but with a view to not disappointing their trust.

So now you start to get the picture: We left the songs in Berlin three long paragraphs ago and digressed into a series of "What are we actually *doing?*" discussions. This is quite normal. It can take four or five hours a day, two or three days a week. U2's records take a long time to make not because the band members are stuck for ideas but because they never stop talking about them.

Records that are made over an extended period (this album, *Achtung Baby,* took about a year), however, court the curse that I call Hollywoodization. This is the process where things are evened out, rationalized, nicely lit from all sides, carefully balanced, studiously tested against all known formulas, referred to several committees and finally made triumphantly unnoticeable. It's the Dunhill-lighter approach to culture, grafting a miserable concept of polish onto a conceptually croaky frame, where deficits of nerve, verve and imagination meet surfeits of glitz and gloss. The only

reason that pop hasn't fallen completely into this trap is that few investors—
and thus, few opinions—have traditionally been involved in the making of
a record. Compared with the returns that a big-selling band like U2 can
expect, the actual cost of recording is traditionally quite small. And compared with film, music is technically relatively simple: A record is usually the
result of a small, tightly knit team working in very close contact and with
a continuity of attention. Thus "big" records still keep appearing that are
genuinely surprising, that haven't been whittled down to normalcy,
kitsched out or democratically neutered.

I have a feeling that whatever else people accuse this record of, it won't
be those things. It's a long step taken with confidence. U2's state of mind
going into this record was similar to that before *The Unforgettable Fire:* ready
for something bigger, rebelling against its own stereotypes. When you listen
to the result, it all makes sense, sounds coherent. You might be forgiven for
thinking that the band members knew just what they wanted before they
began, but I don't think that's true. I doubt anyone ever does until they run
into it, and even then it might take a while to recognize. There's a very
general compass bearing when you start out, a few pointers and code words
that get you going, some musical oases that you'll hope to visit on the way.
But those are just hints: They don't tell you where you're headed, just what
you're likely to pass. On the other hand, though, you can know what you
don't want, and a lot of the process of making a record comes to be the task
of finding a cultural space that isn't already ringing with unwanted reso-
nances and overtones. This can be a new space, one that no one had
identified before, or it can be an old one that suddenly sounds fresh again.
Pop is a lot to do with reevaluation, tapping into the periodic cycles of
energy that things radiate as they recede into history. Occasionally there are
memorable moments of vision, powerful lights to head boldly toward, and
when they happen, they supply the drive for a whole new slew of work.
Although no one sits around *waiting* for them (nothing comes to him who
waits), if your attention is somewhere else, you can miss them. That's why
rough mixes are so important: They allow you to postpone your attentive-
ness.

Attention is noticing where you are, as opposed to where you thought
you'd be. It's easy to get stuck in the detailed work of overdubbing, fiddling
and tweaking, but it often doesn't get you far from where you started.
Bigger jumps take a type of nimbleness, the agility to switch back and forth
from detail to big picture, from zoom to wide angle. The advantage of
working in company is that you don't have to do both yourself. With U2
it's very rare that *everyone* in the room is using the same lens at the same
time. Larry [Mullen] and Adam [Clayton] are reliable wide anglers when

things start to lose perspective or become too narrowly focused: They become the voice of musical conscience. Edge, the archaeologist of the rough mix, delves back through earlier strata in the song's development, emerging triumphantly with a different vision on a battered cassette. Steve Lillywhite, a welcome addition at the mixing stage, comes in fresh and enthusiastic, free of history, and trusts his gifted ears. Dan listens to feel, to the skeleton of the song, and draws attention to things that everybody else has stopped noticing. Flood reawakens sleeping songs with brilliantly original mixes after we've all gone home. I trust my instincts, wax doubtful or enthusiastic, grumble Englishly and liberally contradict myself. All these shifts of perspective make the development of a song very nonlinear: From the inside, the process often feels chaotic, jumping from one identity to another, stretching the song this way and that, until it all falls apart, then picking up the bits and starting over.

But the bottleneck (in most records, probably) is lyric writing. Why? It's because the lyricist assumes the really specific job of focusing the music, of pointing it somewhere. Words are very sharp objects. On a vocal day Bono appears with numerous written sheets that he fans out over the floor of the control room. Dan, as always, will have made the situation as conducive as possible: usually no headphones, a hand-held mike, loud monitors, nice reverb, good lighting—and regards the ensuing technical difficulties as his problem, not the musician's. Bono gets singing, jumping physically and conceptually through the emerging song, weaving lyrical threads into bigger patterns. The vocal glides gracefully between recognizable language and fluent Bongolese—semilinguistic scat forming temporary bridges over lyrical gaps. Meaning is chiseled out bit by bit, polished, broadened, inverted, discarded, revived. Close attention is paid to subtle shifts of vocal tone and emphasis. Homeless lines wander hopefully from verse to verse. A single ill-fitting word chokes progress for half an hour. Flood smokes sympathetically. Dan keeps careful notes. Shannon [Strong, assistant] and Robbie [Adams, assistant engineer] keep all the many logs up to date. Work continues in this way until several vocal tracks are recorded. The picture becomes more detailed.

Later, Dan and Flood work through the tracks, "comping" a line-by-line best-of from that evening's work and making a rough mix. Bono listens to and studies this comp over the next few days, changes a word or a line or a verse, rephrases and resings, and the process takes place again. In this way, he begins to home in on a performance, an attitude, a persona. He discovers who is singing the song and what kind of world that person inhabits. Who and where.

In the meantime, someone will come in with an old rough mix he's just rediscovered that for all its shortcomings *has something*. What is it? Can we get it back without abandoning everything that's happened since? Can we get the best of both of them? When it fails, the outcome is diluted, compromised, homogenized. When it succeeds and a hybrid comes into being, there is a synergy of feelings and nuances that nobody ever foresaw. If that happens, it's news. There's a lot of that kind of news on this record: "So Cruel" is epic and intimate, passionate and chill; "Zoo Station," perkily manic, industrially jovial; "Ultra Violet (Light My Way)" has a helicopter-ish melancholy; "Mysterious Ways" is heavy bottomed and lightheaded. To find a single adjective for any song proves difficult: It's an album of musical oxymorons, of feelings that shouldn't exist together but that are somehow credible.

And this is exactly what I've always liked about pop music: its ability to create crazy emotional landscapes and then invite you to come and dance in them.

ELYSA GARDNER

ACHTUNG BABY ALBUM REVIEW
★ ★ ★ ★ ½

Bring the Noise

HAVING SPENT MOST of the Eighties as one of the most iconic bands in the world, U2 hardly needs to resort to a cheekily absurd title to draw attention to its first album in three years. Then again, subtlety has never been one of the group's virtues. In its early days and in its basic musical approach—a guitar, a few chords and the truth, to paraphrase one of Bono's more garish assertions—U2 fell in with other young bands that cropped up in the wake of punk. But U2 immediately distinguished itself with its huge sound and an unabashed idealism rooted in spiritual aspiration. At their best, these Irishmen have proven—just as Springsteen and the Who did—that the same penchant for epic musical and verbal gestures that leads many artists to self-parody can, in more inspired hands, fuel the unforgettable fire that defines great rock & roll.

At their worst . . . well, the half-live double album *Rattle and Hum* (1988)—the product of U2's self-conscious infatuation with American roots music—had some nice moments, but it was misguided and bombastic enough to warrant concern. With *Achtung Baby,* U2 is once again trying to broaden its musical palette, but this time its ambitions are realized. Working with producers who have lent discipline and nuance to the group's previous albums—Daniel Lanois oversees the entire album, with Brian Eno and Steve Lillywhite assisting on a number of songs—U2 sets out to experiment rather than pay homage. In doing so, the band is able to draw confidently and consistently on its own native strengths.

Most conspicuous among the new elements that U2 incorporates on *Achtung* are hip-hop-derived electronic beats. The band uses these dance-music staples on about half of the album's twelve tracks, often layering them into guitar-heavy mixes the way that many young English bands like Happy Mondays and Jesus Jones have done in recent years. "Mysterious Ways" is a standout among these songs, sporting an ebullient hook and a guitar solo in which the Edge segues from one of his signature bursts of light into an insidious funk riff.

Elsewhere, as in the fit of distortion and feedback that opens "Who's Gonna Ride Your Wild Horses," Edge evokes the cacophony and electronic daring of noise bands like Sonic Youth. Indeed Edge's boldness on *Achtung* is key to the album's adventurous spirit. His plangent, minimalist guitar style—among the most distinctive and imitated in modern rock—has always made inspired use of devices like echo and reverb; his shimmering washes of color on "Until the End of the World" and soaring peals on "Even Better Than the Real Thing" and "Ultraviolet (Light My Way)" are instantly recognizable. But other tracks find the guitarist crafting harder textures and flashing a new arsenal of effects. On the first cut, "Zoo Station," he uses his guitar as a rhythm instrument, repeating a dark, buzzing phrase that drives the beat while his more lyrical playing on the chorus enhances the melody. Similarly, "The Fly" features grinding riffs that bounce off Adam Clayton's thick bass line and echo and embellish Larry Mullen Jr.'s drumming.

Bono's task, then, is to lend his sensuous tenor and melodramatic romanticism to expressions that match this sonic fervor. He announces on "Zoo Station" that he's "ready to let go / Of the steering wheel"; what follows are the most fearlessly introspective lyrics he's written. In the past, U2's frontman has turned out fiercely pointed social and political critiques but his more confessional and romantic songs, however felt, have at times seemed vague. On *Achtung,* though, Bono deals more directly with his private feelings—not to mention his hormones. "The hunter will sin . . . for your ivory skin," he sings on "Wild Horses," and boasts on "Even Better Than the Real Thing" that "I'm gonna make you sing / Give me half a chance / To ride on the waves that you bring."

Almost as surprising, and even more affecting, are Bono's reflections on being an artist. On "Acrobat," over an arrangement that recalls the apocalyptic frenzy of "Bullet the Blue Sky," he pleads for inspiration: "What are we going to do now it's all been said?" On "The Fly" self-doubt gives way to self-indictment: "Every artist is a cannibal," he sings in a whispered groan, "every poet is a thief." Squarely acknowledging his own potential for hypocrisy and inadequacy, and addressing basic human weaknesses rather than the failings of society at large, Bono sounds humbler and more vulnerable than in the past. "Desperation is a tender trap," he sings on "So Cruel." "It gets you every time."

That's not to say that U2 has forsaken its faith or that Bono has abandoned his quest to find what he's looking for. On the radiant ballad "One," the band invests an obvious message—"We're one / But we're not the same / We get to carry each other"—with such urgency that it sounds like a revelation. Few bands can marshal such sublime power, but it's just one of the many moments on *Achtung Baby* when we're reminded why, before these guys were the butt of cynical jokes, they were rock & roll heroes—as they still are.

Island Records is a little pissed off that another band is living off the Edge. "U2," a single by the group Negativland that features a parody of U2, was squashed like a grape by the supergroup's label before the band even heard of the controversy. "I understand these guys are sort of media guerrillas and it's basically a plot they initiated that's gone horribly wrong," says U2 manager Paul McGuinness. "I feel very sorry for them." But now that Negativland's label, SST, has shifted all financial responsibility onto the group and has initiated a "Kill Bono" ad campaign, which Negativland doesn't endorse, the band has parted ways with the indie label. "On one level, it's been fascinating," says Negativland's Mark Hosler. "Putting out that single was just the beginning of an entire art piece. And we're following it through to its conclusion. But we're beyond broke."

1992 MUSIC AWARDS

March 5, 1992

Only critics—with their advance copies of *Achtung Baby*—managed to hear the new U2 release in time to note it as one of 1991's best (it was issued near the end of the year and readers had to submit their picks by November). The readers would show their approval in 1992's survey.

CRITICS PICKS:
COMEBACK OF THE YEAR
Guns n' Roses
Bryan Adams
U2
Natalie Cole
Bob Seger

BEST ALBUM
Out of Time, R.E.M.
Achtung Baby, U2
Nevermind, Nirvana

Use Your Illusion I, Guns n' Roses
Everclear, American Music Club

BEST DRUMMER
Larry Mullen Jr.

COMEBACK OF THE YEAR
U2

ARTISTS PICKS:
THE EDGE
1. Neil Young, Weld
2. Nirvana, Nevermind
3. The Young Disciples, Road to Freedom
4. Insekt, Stress
5. Prince, Diamonds and Pearls
6. Massive Attack, Blue Lines
7. Pixies, Trompe le Monde
8. Sounds of Blackness, The Evolution of Gospel
9. Sharon Shannon, Sharon Shannon
10. R.E.M., Out of Time

PARKE PUTERBAUGH

PERFORMANCE REVIEW

Charlotte Coliseum, Charlotte, North Carolina,
March 3, 1992

"WELCOME TO THE VIBE," said a British-accented DJ operating from within a European automobile plopped smack-dab on the floor of the Charlotte Coliseum. "This is the vibe of tonight. It's very mysterious." A tape of the Beatles' *Magical Mystery Tour* followed this Woodstock-style pronouncement, helping to set a mood for U2's eventual arrival onstage.

U2's Zoo TV Tour is the Irish band's magical mystery tour for the Nineties: part postmodern happening, part pre-*Achtung Baby* crowd pleasers and total sensory overload. The staging expresses the band's radicalized reaction to life in the video age. Six more boxy German cars hung over the stage, headlights serving as spotlights. One was decorated with a sunflower; another, a Keith Haring figure. A bank of TV sets and video screens projected a blitzkrieg of words and images.

It became clear U2 did not come to pander. The group opened bravely and a little defiantly with eight consecutive songs from *Achtung Baby*. Simply seeing U2 onstage again was a charge in this otherwise grim concert season. Bono strode out swaddled in black leather and shades to the corrosive intro of "Zoo Station." He lurched across the lip of the stage with the exaggerated serpentine cool of Jim Morrison by way of Oliver Stone during such numbers as "Even Better Than the Real Thing" and "Mysterious Ways."

For all his occasional swagger, however, Bono was generally restrained, delivering no windy preachments (à la *Rattle and Hum*) and keeping mum between songs. Guitarist the Edge, bass player Adam Clayton and drummer Larry Mullen Jr. maintained a typically low profile, engrossed more in the music than the theater of live performing.

"The Fly" was a brilliant, full-frontal assault on sense and sensibility with screens flashing a dizzying array of verbiage—PANIC, EMERGENCY, BOOM, SEX, DEATH, DRUGS, NO ANSWERS, EVERYTHING YOU KNOW IS WRONG—while the band ripped into the song's cranky innards with feral relish. In this one cathartic number, U2 realized the potential of all its video hardware and refurbished new music; it was easily the show's pinnacle. For the most part, the live run-throughs of *Achtung Baby* material were competently duplicative but didn't expand on the studio originals. Thanks to the wonder of technology, "Zoo Station" sounded similar to the record; it would have been more interesting to hear the band develop a less-produced version for the stage. The relatively weak "Who's Gonna Ride Your Wild Horses" was a momentum stopper, yet "One" was beautifully sung by Bono, and "Tryin' to Throw Your Arms Around the World" possessed the shimmering, ethereal throb of classic U2.

It was intriguing to watch U2 (and especially Bono) wrestle with its stature as an object of adulation, aspects of which the band members variously embraced and repelled. A walkway extended from the stage, allowing the musicians to mingle with the audience up close and at eye level. Bono spent a good portion of the evening in the throng and was joined by the rest of the band for a brief but welcome acoustic interlude that included a shambling, folkish "Angel of Harlem."

The band members eventually reassumed their positions onstage for a rattling, humming finale that included four songs from *The Joshua Tree* and a set-closing "Pride (In the Name of Love)." A verse from "All I Want Is You" led into an electrifying "Bullet the Blue Sky." The spirit was willing but the vocal cords were weak on "Pride," and Bono, gesturing to his throat, let the crowd sing the chorus and its hard-to-hit high notes. For the encore, Bono reappeared in a spangly jacket with a full-length mirror, into which he preened with mock self-absorption.

Quite an enigma, that Bono: He enters in leather and leaves in glitter. The singer strikes a pose one moment, then knocks down the fourth wall between performer and audience the next. Half the show dares the audience to venture to U2's brave new postmodern world; the rest rewards its forbearance with familiar favorites. Certain performances ("The Fly," "Bullet the Blue Sky" and a hair-raising "I Still Haven't Found What I'm Looking For") were as exciting as one could possibly hope for; then again, U2 occasionally sounded underprepared ("By the time we get back here, we'll have rehearsed the endings, all right?" Bono joked after "With or Without You" meandered to an uncertain conclusion).

At its cutting-edge best, U2 remains—to quote a lyric from "Love Is Blindness"—"a dangerous idea that almost makes sense."

MICHAEL GOLDBERG

U2: THE ZOO TOUR MOVES OUTDOORS

U2 HAS DUBBED ITS NORTH AMERICAN summer stadium tour Zoo TV Outside Broadcast. The forty-date tour begins at Giants Stadium, in New Jersey, on August 11th and ends November 3rd in Vancouver, British Columbia. The group is revamping and expanding the indoor show it took on the road earlier this year. "The main thing is that it's a lot bigger," said U2 manager Paul McGuinness. "The set will be longer. The Zoo TV Tour was perfect for arenas. We've been dreaming up ways of amplifying it for stadiums."

U2 has hired Fisher Park, the company that worked on visuals for the Stones' *Steel Wheels* tour and Pink Floyd's *Wall* tour, to help make the stadium shows special. "These are men with a great sense of the absurd," said McGuinness, referring to Mark Fisher and Jonathan Park, the principals of Fisher Park.

Video will continue to be a major part of the presentation. "We've learned to play with the video organ," said McGuinness of the complex video system of onstage monitors that gave the indoor shows an eerie *1984* quality. "It's easier for us to feed different images more spontaneously."

About three weeks of production rehearsals were scheduled to begin in mid-July in Pennsylvania. McGuinness would not disclose the specifics of how the show is changing beyond noting that in addition to performing most of *Achtung Baby*, U2 will perform "God, Pt. II" from *Rattle and Hum* as well as a handful of other older songs. "But we're not turning this into a greatest-hits show," he cautioned. "Just assume it will be different and better. We couldn't do it unless it was going to be more fun. There will be surprises. Some things will even surprise me, because they haven't been thought up yet."

■ **RANDOM NOTES** (April 2, 1992)

The U2s tried to repeat the traffic-clogging success of their spontaneous, on-location-in-Los Angeles video of "Where the Streets Have No Name" by pulling a similar stunt in London. This time, however, not only did the street have a name (Carnaby), but the venue, a clothing store, had one too (Zoo). The boys, who picked the spot because the store shares a name with their upcoming world tour, managed to draw a crowd of about 200. It is impossible to determine, however, how many in the throng were fans and how many were simply slaves to fashion who saw the lights and were hoping for an after-hours clearance sale.

■ **RANDOM NOTES** (September 17, 1992)

What if the U2s played a week of shows and nobody came? Sort of. Rehearsing privately for its stadium tour in Hershey Stadium, in Pennsylvania, the band honored requests from the thousands who flocked to the parking lot. At week's end, the boys satisfied the horde—putting on a low-dough (fifteen dollars) charity concert on their last night in town.

DAVID FRICKE

U2 FINDS WHAT IT'S LOOKING FOR

"THIS IS DEFINITELY THE MOST surreal night of my life!" Bono exclaims halfway through the show, with all the sincerity a guy in pelvis–hugging black leather and space–pimp sunglasses can muster. Coming from someone decked out like a futuristic-sleazeball version of the Lizard King, it still sounds like a standard-issue rock-star snake-oil pitch. But in fact, it's a king–size understatement. Even on a tour remarkable for its giddy spirit of postmodern pranksterism, tonight's edition of U2's traveling Zoo TV party in Stockholm, Sweden, is prize-winning weird.

The competition has been stiff. There was the night in Detroit when Bono, using his special onstage phone hookup, called a local pizzeria and ordered a thousand pies to go. There was the night when Bono, merrily zapping his way through the satellite-TV menu with his remote control, unexpectedly treated the audience to a live broadcast of Paul Tsongas's announcing his withdrawal from the Democratic presidential race. And there were the nights—quite a few, actually—when during the encore, Bono picked up the phone and dialed the White House (202-456-1414, in case you're interested). Although he never got through to George Bush, he did get chummy with the puzzled White House operator. "Who are you?" she'd ask. "Why do you keep calling at night? Sounds like there are a lot of people with you."

At the Globe arena, in Stockholm, though, the techno-clowning of Zoo TV mutates into interactive Zoo theater. The usual show is a dizzying feast of video high jinks and high-definition irony (Bono kissing a mirror, pumping his crotch into the camera) set to most of *Achtung Baby* and the requisite hits from *The Joshua Tree* and *Rattle and Hum*. But tonight, Bono, guitarist the Edge, bassist Adam Clayton and drummer Larry Mullen Jr. are supplementing their regularly scheduled programming with a live TV feed to and from the home of John Harris of Nottinghamshire, England. Harris, an ardent U2 fan who works for the Pretty Polly lingerie company, won an MTV Europe contest, the prize being a private simulcast of the Stockholm gig, complete with an ample supply of champagne.

Except Harris isn't just watching the show; he's *in* it, popping up in the hyperactive Zoo video mix with big, boozy grins and exchanging quips with the host via satellite, like *Nightline* gone nutty.

"So, John, you work in a knickers factory?" Bono says with a mock snicker. "Well, we don't wear underwear in Sweden."

"Prove it!" Harris retorts, emboldened by drink. Bono actually goes for his zipper but punks out to an arenawide chorus of female Swedish groans. Those groans soon turn to cheers when, as a consolation prize, U2 brings out Swedish pop gods Björn Ulvaeus and Benny Andersson of the late, great ABBA for a genial romp through its 1977 hit "Dancing Queen."

Later, during the melancholy sway of "Tryin' to Throw Your Arms Around the World," from *Achtung Baby,* Harris and Bono are caught on adjacent video screens in a moment of sweet serendipity: Harris slow dancing with his girlfriend, Bono giving the Edge a loving choke hold during the latter's guitar solo. The most genuinely surreal moment of the show, however, comes at the end, when Harris and his inebriated pals in Nottinghamshire appear on the video screens doing the *Wayne's World* bow—"We are not worthy! We are not worthy!" The Swedes, already in hysterics, respond in kind, bowing and cheering in sync.

"You can't plan stuff like that," the Edge marvels later, stroking his thin, monkish beard. "Sometimes in amongst all the trash, these moments of incredible poignancy happen. In 'Even Better Than the Real Thing,' there were shots of the band and shots of the people in the house and all these TV ads superimposed over that. It was beautiful, this Nike ad with the big shoe coming down. And it was the perfect image and message for the song, sliding down the surface of things.

"That's the thing, I suppose," the Edge continues. "The jokes and the fun aspect, the props, the weird suits and all—they are making a joke of rock & roll stardom. But they *do* work."

"There is a lot of soul—I think it shines even brighter amidst the trash and the junk," Bono insists after the show. "Sam Shepard said, 'Right in the center of contradiction, that's the place to be.' And rock & roll has more contradictions than any art form. U2 spent the Eighties trying to resolve some of them. Now we've started the Nineties celebrating them.

"Rock & roll is ridiculous," Bono states emphatically. "It's absurd." He is, appropriately, still wearing his leathers and shades. "In the past, U2 was trying to duck that. Now we're wrapping our arms around it and giving it a great big kiss. It's like I say onstage—'Some of this bullshit is pretty cool.' I think it is the missing scene from *Spinal Tap*—four guys in a police escort, asking themselves, 'Should we be enjoying this?' The answer is, fucking right. It's a trip. It's part of the current of rock & roll that just drags you along—and you can feed off it.

"Mock the devil," Bono adds with a conspiratorial smile, "and he will flee from thee."

BACKSTAGE AT THE GLOBE, a couple hours before show time, B.P. Fallon is talking about the difference between U2's brand of rock spectacle and the way it really was in the good old Seventies—when excess was king and the stars talked about social and moral responsibility with a small *r*. It is a subject Fallon knows well. An elfin, animated Irishman billed in the Zoo TV Tour program as "guru, viber and disc jockey" (he spins records before U2's set and warms up the crowd with hippie chatter), Fallon has been a writer, radio personality and publicist since the Sixties and has worked for and with the likes of Jimi Hendrix, the Beatles, the Rolling Stones and Led Zeppelin.

"With Zeppelin, it was just more of everything—more drugs, more sex," he says with just a faint hint of nostalgia. "Now there's less drugs, less casualness about sex. And the recession is being felt the world over, not just in America. So there's more to worry about.

"But this is also a different U2 in a way, not knights in armor," Fallon continues. "It's warmer, funnier, more human. They go out there trying to give the audience something to take home with them—the idea that for all of the things that are wrong, you don't have to feel mortally wounded all the time. Here's a bandage, some hope and some fun. It's like if you walk around with an umbrella over your head all the time. Sure, you won't get rained on. But you won't get any sun, either. U2's out there saying: Fuck the umbrella. So what if you get a little wet?' "

Zoo TV and the triple-platinum *Achtung Baby* are the sight and sound of U2 leaving the hair shirts at home and singing in the rain. At a time when rock's established order has been upended, with skate-teen gods like Pearl Jam and the Red Hot Chili Peppers holding the Top Ten hostage while Bruce Springsteen is left knocking at the back door, U2 has regained critical and commercial favor by negotiating an inspired balance between rock's cheap thrills and its own sense of moral burden. The po-faced asceticism of its *Joshua Tree-Rattle and Hum* days is, for the most part, history. Gone is the spiritual-gladiator image immortalized by that shot of Bono in the video of "Sunday Bloody Sunday," waving the white flag against the hell's-caldron glow of the fires at Red Rocks Amphitheater.

The members of U2 have retooled themselves as wiseacres with heart and elephant bucks to burn on the hallucinatory video sport of Zoo TV (a wordplay on MTV and the loony Morning Zoo shows dominating American Top Forty radio). Created in part by Brian Eno and the production team responsible for the English avant-video show *Buzz,* Zoo TV's agitated splash of appropriated video images and glib buzz phrases triggers eye-popping juxtapositions of cliché and truth: EVERYTHING YOU KNOW IS WRONG; GUILT IS NEXT TO GOD; I WANT A JOB, PUSSY, SCHOOL; EVERYBODY IS A RACIST. (One befuddled interviewer recently asked the band members why they thought everybody was a "rapist.")

The Outside Broadcast version of Zoo TV now on the U.S. stadium circuit jacks up the mind-fuck quotient. George Bush calls the congregation to order in hilariously doctored footage, chanting Queen's "We will, we will rock you!" in that irritating read-my-lips whine. Two East German Trabant cars attached to huge mechanical arms and outfitted with spotlights scan the crowd like alien prison sentries while a patchwork video quilt of Gargantuan screens, multi-image Vidiwalls and TV monitors spews words and pictures with exhausting velocity—Rock & Roll Mission Control running on amphetamine fast forward. During "Even Better Than the Real Thing," Bono appears on the screens in his lizardy leathers in grossly magnified, jump-cut distortions of his real-time posing, looking like God-zilla gone MTV.

Offscreen, from the cheap seats, he looks more like a gnat. But Bono has undergone a striking onstage makeover as the Fly, a shotgun personality marriage of discount Jim Morrison shamanism and Jerry Lee Lewis narcis-sism greased with used-car-salesman smarm and resonant with comic mis-chief and healthy, if occasionally overheated, self-parody. In "Tryin' to Throw Your Arms Around the World," he slow grinds with a young woman plucked from the crowd and showers the fans with a phallic spray from his champagne bottle, a sweet 'n' silly mix of lemon squeezer/lover man charm. For "Desire," a song about the addictive properties of success, Bono serves his irony straight up, hitting the stage dressed in a silver-spangled preacher's suit and kissing a mirror. In a decade rife with cynicism and distrust for public figures, pop stars included, U2 has finally recognized that sometimes subversion and a less furrowed brow can be the better part of valor.

"We had this idea that irony was the enemy of soul," Bono says of the early days, winding down back in Stockholm with a postshow snack of white wine and Swedish hash in a café. "There was a decision to stare down the Eighties, to photograph ourselves in the desert, to take the Shaker-Quaker lyrics to a conclusion.

"The Nineties demand a very different response than the Eighties," he argues. "Comedians are the real rebels of the Nineties. They are the proph-ets. They can tell us where it's at and make us laugh at the same time. Our guard isn't up. Rock & roll now, if they see you coming with a placard, they duck. They close the doors and pull down the blinds, go back to watching a game show."

Bono pauses thoughtfully, toying with the sunglasses, which he has finally taken off. "We have to outsmart the ones without heart," he says firmly.

That might be because U2 got tired of taking it on the chin from old fans and once-friendly critics during the 1987–89 mega-hoopla over *The Joshua Tree* and the album-movie package *Rattle and Hum*. ROLLING STONE writers actually had the temerity to name the band Comeback of the Year in the magazine's 1991 music poll. Bono says he thought the accolade was funny; Larry Mullen hung the clipping in his house, right next to one from a British music weekly proclaiming, U2 IN SEMIHIP SHOCK! But it's closer to the truth than either of them might care to admit. *Achtung Baby,* says Adam Clayton, is an album "about what happens when you come back from being out in the world and how you pick up the pieces and how you deal with life."

Catapulted to worldwide success by *The Joshua Tree,* then savaged by the rock press for what they judged to be the stuffy, pseudo-field-trip air of their blues and gospel forays in *Rattle and Hum,* the members of U2 hit the sales jackpot but found themselves caught between their rock dreams and the hard truth of super-celebrity. They were cursed for their suffocating omnipresence on radio and MTV. Their evangelical seriousness was mocked in cover records like the Pet Shop Boys' sly electro-disco version of "Where the Streets Have No Name" and Negativland's notorious release *U2,* a sampling satire of "I Still Haven't Found What I'm Looking For." In an ironic twist, the latter precipitated a harsh copyright-infringement suit by U2's record and publishing companies against Negativland and its label, SST Records—which, in turn, triggered a press backlash against U2, former college-radio darling, for harassing an underground band. (Bono now claims that U2 tried to mediate a truce and that it objected not to the sampling—"We have no problem with people using our music"—but to the record's cover, which it felt was deceptive to U2 fans.)

Ultimately, everything U2 did, said and sang "became writ too large," in Bono's words, and the band couldn't help but squirm. "I remember being onstage and most of the time thinking, 'This is *not* quite where we should be,' " Bono recalls ruefully of the *Joshua* days. "Musically speaking, we were unprepared. We didn't want to be the band too stupid to enjoy its own success. At the same time, I wanted to push out the extremes. I didn't feel that on that tour we reached the extremes that we could."

"We were the biggest," Larry Mullen agrees, "but we weren't the best. That was an awful thing to feel—to go onstage in front of 17,000 people and go, 'Whoopee!' when we were feeling like shit, that it wasn't as good as it should be, that we really hadn't done our homework."

"Plus we were so stupid that we actually decided to put it on film," Clayton adds with a sour laugh, referring to *Rattle and Hum*. "Only an Irish band could do something like that."

Today, the general consensus within U2 about *Rattle and Hum* is that it was a good idea—a modest production documenting U2's American adventures on the road and in the studio, supplemented by a souvenir album of live tracks and new songs—that spun out of control. Bono admits the movie had flaws but defends the film's director, Phil Joanou, saying: "He was into the Big Music. He wanted to make a Big Picture. He gave the music the same weight that Scorsese gave the boxing ring in *Raging Bull*. You may not like it, but it was a strong point of view."

What bugged the Edge was the Big Push. He remembers going into the publicity office of Paramount Pictures and being taken aback by the eight-foot-high promotional posters of each U2 member, especially the one of him on which the studio had airbrushed his stubble. "I realized then that something was a bit wrong," he says grimly.

"Even I would have probably hated us then," Bono concedes. "What was scary to me was that people who were criticizing us weren't really listening to the records. The records were not propagating any kind of 'men of stone' thing. *The Joshua Tree* is a very uncertain record. 'Still Haven't Found What I'm Looking For' is an anthem of doubt more than faith.

"The media has rock & roll by the balls," he says, almost snarling. "They draw cartoons, and it's indelible ink. It's an attempt to reduce you, your humanity, your sense of humor. The only way to deal with it is to create a cartoon even bigger.

"Which," Bono adds, putting his Fly sunglasses back on, "is where this show comes in."

IRONICALLY, THE ONLY THING funny about *Achtung Baby* is the title, which U2 pinched from the Mel Brooks film *The Producers* via the band's sound engineer Joe O'Herlihy, who used it as a pet phrase during the recording sessions in Berlin. Oh, and there's the naked photo of Adam Clayton featured in the cover montage (his manliness has been censored by a painted X). At one point, there was actual talk of using *that* shot as the cover and calling the record *Adam*—"tipping the hat to *Boy* as being *Man*," Clayton claims, trying to put a serious spin on the idea. Bono is a little more truthful.

"You know, when you're kids, you sit around and think, 'Well, if we're gonna get in trouble, let's get in a lot of trouble,' " he says, smirking.

"You wake out of it the next day. But it was a good idea at the time."

Not really. The metallic blue and monochrome brown splatter effect of the montage, including shots of the band in drag, better suit *Achtung Baby*'s deceptively bittersweet, at times even harsh disposition. The impish corrosion of songs like "Zoo Station" and "The Fly" is boldly undercut by darker musings such as "Love Is Blindness" and "One," Bono's disenchanted take on the *nouveau* hippie revival: " 'One, man, one world, one love.' I liked the idea of taking that and saying, 'One, man, but not the same.' "

There are also strong currents of rebellious angst and defensive claustrophobia blowing through songs like "So Cruel" and "Acrobat" (with its bristling chorus line "Don't let the bastards grind you down"), reflecting not only the setting where the album was made—Berlin during the first anarchic flush of German reunification—but also personal circumstances like the Edge's recent, painful separation from his wife, Aislinn. The guitarist admits that Bono, who writes all of U2's lyrics, "was influenced by what I was going through." When asked which *Achtung* songs specifically bear that influence, he laughs sheepishly and says, "The whole album."

"It's a con, in a way," Bono says dourly. "We call it *Achtung Baby,* grinning up our sleeves in all the photography. But it's probably the heaviest record we've ever made. There is a lot of blood and guts on that record. It tells you a lot about packaging, because the press would have killed us if we'd called it anything else."

U2's musical turnaround from *The Joshua Tree*'s clarion twang and *Rattle and Hum*'s soul-blues-arena-rock pastiche to *Achtung Baby*'s Germanic clatter and hum was at least partly the result of the Edge's off-hours listening back at the hotel during the 1989 Lovetown Tour, in particular industrial art-funk bands like Nine Inch Nails, the Young Gods and KMFDM. "You could hear the end of the world coming out from under his door every night," quips Bono. Several genres away, Larry Mullen was getting deep into Blind Faith, Cream and Jimi Hendrix records, picking up tips from Ginger Baker and Mitch Mitchell on how to play *around* the beat. The latest rap and house records were also making the rounds.

Still, *Achtung Baby* was not an easy record to make. Several demo tapes recorded in Ireland were stolen early in the Berlin sessions—either from the studio or the band's hotel (no one is exactly sure)—and bootlegged within weeks. Also, the Edge confesses: "Berlin was difficult. I had quite a strong feel where I thought it should go. Bono was with me. Adam and Larry were a little unsure. It took time for them to see how they fit into this.

"I also think Danny [producer Daniel Lanois] didn't fully understand where we were headed, because we were working on more of the throwaway, trashy kinds of things," the Edge says. "The U2 that he loved was the U2 of *The Joshua Tree* and *The Unforgettable Fire,* the textural and emotional and cinematic U2. By the time we finished with the lyrics and the mixes, it came back a bit toward more usual U2 terrain. But for a while, I think Danny was at sea."

For Bono, Berlin was a dadaist escapade. The band members arrived in the city literally on the eve of reunification. As soon as they got off the plane, they hit the streets and joined the parade—the wrong one, though. "It was really, really dour-looking German people holding up big signs, looking very unhappy," Bono explains, laughing. "We're walking around, going, 'Wow, these Germans really don't know how to throw a party.' Then we discovered we were in the wrong parade. We were in a demonstration for people who wanted to put back up the wall, all these Stalinists and hard-core Communists. We could just see the headlines the next day: U2 ARRIVE TO PROTEST THE DESTRUCTION OF THE WALL."

Later that night, the band settled into its temporary quarters in the former East Berlin, a onetime guest house used by high Soviet officials, including Leonid Brezhnev. At about 7:00 A.M., a naked Bono went downstairs to get a drink of water and discovered a German family standing in the foyer: "I said, 'What are you doing in our house?' And the guy said: 'This is not *your* house. This is *my* house. This is my father's house.' And it became very clear that indeed the man had found the house that had been seized from his family, probably by the Nazis first and then the Communists. He'd found it after forty-five years."

The surreal effect of getting history in the making right in his face—not just in Berlin but in the barrage of body counts, "smart bomb" stats and Pentagon disinformation that he saw on TV during the gulf war—left its mark on Bono's lyric game, although not in a way he was happy about. "I realized I couldn't write songs about it," he says. "Everything we'd learned in the last ten years meant nothing in the face of this, that we could talk so coldly about flesh being burned off people's bodies. Humor was the only response. I knew we had to find different ways of saying the same thing. Writing and approaching this head-on just would not work."

Any fears that U2 had gone off the deep end with the *Sturm und Clang* of *Achtung Baby* were dispelled for Bono at the première of the Zoo TV Tour, in Florida last February. The show opened with no less than eight songs from the album, and "people went for it," Bono now says proudly. "The first show, you just didn't know. How is this going to go down? And they went for it. I think our audiences are smart and that they expect us to push and pull them a bit. They had to swallow blues on *Rattle and Hum,* for God's sakes! They can take it."

Not every fan, though. Bono explains that while U2 was recording *Achtung Baby* in Berlin, two German girls—"rings in their noses, the whole sepulchral look"—appeared on the studio doorstep to give the band an earful about *Rattle and Hum*. " 'So what was wrong with it?' we asked," says Bono. " 'Too many love songs! What is with the love songs? George Michael writes love songs. We don't want you to write love songs.' And we said, 'Your timing is excellent. We're making a new album.'

"We played Vienna the other week, and those two German girls were standing in front of the hotel waiting for us," he says. "And I said, 'Well, what did you think of the album?' And they said, 'It was shit!' " Bono shakes his head in amazement. "They waited all that time and stood in front of the hotel all night waiting for us, just so they could tell us we'd made a shit record!"

N̲O ONE IN THE ZOO TV TOUR entourage, almost 200 strong for the outdoor shows, is enjoying the show's spirit of subterfuge more than Bono himself. While the other members of the band make no concessions to rock-star fashion offstage—Larry Mullen is usually outfitted in basic biker apparel, and the Edge is never seen without his wool stevedore's cap— Bono revels in his alter ego, the Fly, whenever he gets the chance. He walks through hotel lobbies and crowded discos wearing his shiny black leather, and the lounge-lizard sunglasses are never far from his grasp when they're not already on his face.

"It's plastic, in the most enjoyable sense of the word," he says exultantly of his Fly shtick. "When I put on those glasses, anything goes. These are the paraphernalia of the rock star. I've had to stop 'not drinking.' I've had to smoke incessantly. I've learned to be insincere. I've learned to lie. I've never felt better!"

Bono doesn't quite have his insincere act down yet. In Stockholm, during an interview in a bar, he is approached by a doe-eyed Swedish girl who shyly begs him for a dance in the disco next door. Bono makes a series of lame excuses in a soft, polite voice—"I have some more work to do here," "I actually have a bad knee," "I'm a bit drunk, and I might fall down"—but the girl won't take even a gentle "no" for an answer.

Eventually, he caves in. "Okay," Bono says with a smile and takes her for a turn on the dance floor. He may like to play the role of the Posey Rock Star, but underneath that faux asshole exterior still beats the heart of a guy who finds it hard just to say, "Fuck off." Which is just as well, because as the Edge points out, "None of us will ever be allowed to become assholes, because three other guys in the band will just not let them get away with it."

The Fly is not Bono's first stab at role overhaul. In pre-U2 days, he was plain old Paul Hewson; he became Bono Vox when a member of his Dublin school gang nicknamed him after a local hearing-aid store. (Bono then did the honors for his friend Dave Evans, dubbing him the Edge.) But the Fly is more than just pop hubris incarnate, according to its creator.

"It's like Jerry Lee Lewis and Jimmy Swaggart, in my mind, are the same guy," Bono explains, noting that the song "The Fly" was written "like a phone call from hell, but the guy liked it there."

"It was this guy running away—'Hi, honey, it's hot, but I like it here,' " he says. "The character is just on the edge of lunacy. It's megalomania and paranoia."

" 'The Fly' is not just about irony," the Edge suggests. "There are these characters, certainly in Dublin and I'm sure everywhere else, who sit on these stools by the bar all day. And they know *everything*. They seem to have moles in the White House and seem to know exactly what's going on in Moscow. They're bar-stool philosophers, with all these great theories and notions. And they're on the edge of madness and genius. Some of the things they say can be incredibly smart. And yet they are probably mad. I think that's what Bono was playing with."

In that sense, the Fly is very much an offshoot of Bono's own outspoken, proselytizing nature and his willingness, ever since U2's earliest days, to go out on a long, thin limb to explain his and the band's sociospiritual agenda. The difference is, he agrees, in the Fly's comic exaggeration—the leathers, the shades, the posing in hotel lobbies.

"We came from punk," Bono says, "and that wasn't very funny. Johnny Rotten was very funny in interviews, but the Clash weren't funny. And the immediate aftermath of punk, Joy Division and that funereal, fuguelike music, that was the music we came out of. I suppose now I'm rediscovering the more irresponsible roots of our music, which is just for the *blast*."

In the end, though, Bono can't help agonizing over the "blast" either. When the subject turns to rock & roll itself—the oppressive weight of its Sixties and Seventies past, its immediate future and embattled relevance in an atrophied society—the bar-stool prophet takes over, in all seriousness. The sunglasses come off, and the heat goes up.

"We've gotta love things because they *are* great, not because they remind us of something great," Bono declares with his trademark urgency. "It's a very rare thing when a new mood arrives. You guys have to get excited every month, every week, about something new. But a lot of times it's not. It's just a feeling you've heard before, a resonance that you dig. I think groups are only as great as that ability to create something new, say something that hasn't been said before. Or if it has been said, it's never been said *quite* like this.

"Sex and music is all a lot of people got right now," he goes on at high, impassioned speed, "because organized religion is in demise, and I personally won't miss it. I don't think religion has anything to do with God anymore or very rarely has. It is also becoming clear that the material world is not enough for anybody. We had a century of being told by the intelligentsia that we're two-dimensional creatures, that if something can't be proved, it can't exist. That's over now. Transcendence is what everybody, in the end, is on their knees for, running at speed toward, scratching at, kicking at.

"That's why music is, for me, important. I've stopped answering the 'for you' questions and the 'for them' questions. But, yes, for me. Rock & roll music—the noisier the better—is still my alarm clock. It still keeps me awake. It's a hymn to the numbness, a reasonable response to the way we live.

"I saw a documentary on World War II, and somebody was saying that a nervous breakdown is the reasonable response of a sane man to an insane situation. I think rock & roll still has to be the sound of that nervous breakdown. Because that scream, from Howlin' Wolf to Nine Inch Nails, is part of it. The other part of it is Marvin Gaye, Smokey Robinson, music that makes the light brighter.

"But I like both; I *want* both for my band." Bono raves, pounding his hand dramatically on the table and nearly smashing his Fly glasses, which are lying nearby. "I want heaven *and* hell. We've always been given this choice, to choose between the flesh and the spirit. I don't know anyone who isn't both."

March U2 opened its glitzy Zoo TV Tour in Lakeland, Florida, unveiling a louder, brasher sound and a trailerful of goofy threads. The thirty-one-city tour was the group's first stateside trip since 1987. Bono and the boys played the bulk of *Achtung Baby,* as well as hits and near misses from *The Joshua Tree, Rattle and Hum* and *The Unforgettable Fire.* All the while, they carried out a multimedia assault replete with giant video screens, frenzied electronic phrase-making and a bunch of phone calls to the White House. Their message? Thou shalt not worship false idols, but who else is there?

August Now playing center field: U2. The leather-clad minstrels became only the second rock act to play New York's Yankee Stadium when they plugged their Zoo TV Tour into the house that Ruth built. The show's success, however, failed to spur the Bronx Bombers, who not only tied for fourth place but received word of George Steinbrenner's return.

On the Road U2 learned how to lighten up this summer, touring with a goofy, glittering multimedia fest the band dubbed its Zoo TV Tour. "Rock & roll is ridiculous," Bono said of his black leather and bug-eyed shades. "It's absurd. In the past, U2 was trying to duck that. Now we're wrapping our arms around it and giving it a great big kiss. It's like I say onstage, 'Some of this bullshit is pretty cool.' I think it is the missing scene from *Spinal Tap*—four guys in a police escort, asking themselves, 'Should we be enjoying this?' The answer is 'Fucking right.' "

1993 MUSIC AWARDS

March 4, 1993

READERS POLL:

BEST SINGLE
"One," U2
"November Rain," Guns
 n' Roses
"Under the Bridge," Red Hot
 Chili Peppers
"Drive," R.E.M.
"Tears in Heaven," Eric
 Clapton

BEST BAND
U2
Pearl Jam
R.E.M.
Guns n' Roses
Black Crowes

BEST MALE SINGER
Bono
Eddie Vedder
Michael Stipe
Axl Rose
Eric Clapton

ARTIST OF THE YEAR
U2
Pearl Jam
Red Hot Chili Peppers
R.E.M.
Bruce Springsteen

BEST ALBUM
Achtung Baby, U2
Ten, Pearl Jam
Automatic for the People,
 R.E.M.
Blood Sugar Sex Magik,
 Red Hot Chili Peppers
The Southern Harmony and
 Musical Companion, the
 Black Crowes

BEST PRODUCER
Daniel Lanois
Rick Rubin
Scott Litt
Brian Eno
Rick Parashar

BEST SONGWRITER
Bono
Axl Rose
Elton John
Chris Cornell of Soundgarden
Prince

BEST ALBUM COVER
Achtung Baby, U2
Nevermind, Nirvana
Blood Sugar Sex Magik,
 Red Hot Chili Peppers
Automatic for the People,
 R.E.M.
Angel Dust, Faith No More

SEXIEST MALE ARTIST
Bono
Eddie Vedder
Anthony Kiedis
 of Red Hot Chili Peppers
Axl Rose
Michael Bolton

BEST GUITARIST
Eric Clapton
Edge
Slash of Guns n' Roses
Eddie Van Halen
Nuno Bettencourt of Extreme

BEST TOUR
Zoo TV, U2
Lollapalooza II
Guns n' Roses-Metallica

Bruce Springsteen
Garth Brooks

BEST KEYBOARDIST
Elton John
Dizzy Reed of Guns n' Roses
Bruce Hornsby
Edge
Tony Banks of Genesis

BEST BASSIST
Flea of Red Hot Chili Peppers
Adam Clayton
Duff McKagan of Guns n'
 Roses
Jason Newsted of Metallica
Geddy Lee of Rush

BEST DRUMMER
Larry Mullen Jr.
Lars Ulrich of Metallica
Neil Peart of Rush
Alex Van Halen
Bill Berry of R.E.M.

COMEBACK OF THE YEAR
U2
Bruce Springsteen
Queen
Def Leppard
Bon Jovi

CRITICS POLL:

WORST TOUR
Zoo TV, U2
Too Legit, Hammer (tie)

BEST BAND
R.E.M.
U2 (tie)

BEST TOUR
Zoo TV, U2

ALAN LIGHT

BEHIND THE FLY

Bono: The ROLLING STONE Interview

I T DOESN'T TAKE LONG TO FIGURE out which car in this little Dublin parking lot belongs to the rock star. There it stands, a tribute to all that's garish and excessive: a canary yellow 1973 Cortina with leopard-print interior and, of course, fuzzy dice hanging from the rearview mirror.

Bono grins sheepishly as the parking-lot attendant cruises over with the Cortina. "I suspect there was some drink involved when I chose this one," he says. "Now I have to live with the consequences."

Not long ago, this car would have seemed a shocking accouterment for U2's singer, an indulgence completely out of keeping with the band's status as benefit headliner, champion of famine relief and Amnesty International, crusader for all that's good and righteous. But with U2's bestselling package deal—the stunning album *Achtung Baby* and the extravagant multimedia roadshow Zoo TV—the past year has seen Bono, guitarist Dave Evans a.k.a. the Edge, bassist Adam Clayton and drummer Larry Mullen Jr. dive headfirst into the glitz and glamour of rock & roll.

Bono has led the charge, wrapping himself in an alter ego he's dubbed the Fly (complete with a skintight leather suit and bug-eyed sunglasses) and seldom breaking character throughout the Zoo TV tour. He's been strutting through hotel lobbies and dispensing attitude onstage and off like a lifelong master of hype, holding the pose through a year that included a U2 summit with Bill Clinton in a Chicago hotel room and carrying barrels of radioactive waste onto a British beach to protest the Sellafield nuclear power plant.

At first, it was hard to know how U2's impassioned fans would react to the visual transformation or to the churning rhythms and tense sexuality of *Achtung Baby*. But the band's virtual sweep of the 1992 ROLLING STONE Readers Poll—like its domination of the polls in 1987 and 1988—reconfirms its status as the world's biggest rock band.

Back home in Dublin, though, preparing to take Zoo TV into European stadiums later this spring, Bono seems just a touch ashamed of the Cortina and all it represents; he's just too close to real life here for such shenanigans. The parking lot is in Temple Bar, the city's bohemian district, a short block away from the tiny club where the band played its first shows, in 1978. As Bono drives through these familiar streets, telling stories of his encounters with Bob Dylan and Johnny Cash, he sheds his rock-star skin and settles back into the much less demanding role of a rock fan.

He still won't go more than a few minutes, though, without talking about plans for U2. He and the Edge are finishing two songs for the soul legend Al Green. The group is working on a half-dozen new U2 songs as well, with plans to release them as an EP in the next few months. For all his new-found fondness for glittery decadence, the character acting has also given Bono a new discipline, a genuine rock & roll work ethic.

"We've never worried before about what key a song is in," Bono explains later that evening over his third or fourth pint of Guinness in a pub down the street from the U2 business office. "I've never really worked on my singing. We're just starting to figure out what to do with Edge's guitar."

"We've been playing to our weaknesses for too long," he declares finally. "It's time to start playing to our strengths."

Y*OU'VE PLAYED THIS WHOLE TOUR in character, but our readers still voted you Sexiest Male Artist. Does that mean people aren't getting the joke?*
Even better—they're *believing* the joke. I don't know. I've said it before, but there were reports of egomania, and I just decided to become everything they said I was. Might as well. The truth is that you are many people at the same time, and you don't have to choose. It's like Edge describes me—as a nice bunch of guys.

You say that this role-playing is all about embracing the stupidity, the ridiculousness of rock & roll. But is it really fun when it's so choreographed?
That's what it's designed for. It's a language of scale, of surface—the Fly needs to feel mega to feel normal.

One of the lines that didn't make it into the song "The Fly," one of the clichés that we developed, was that "taste is the enemy of art." There's a point where you find yourself tiptoeing as an artist, and then you know that you're in the wrong place. It's like you have a rule book, but you don't remember where you got it.

And along with that being true of the music, it can become true in a wider sense. I felt like I didn't recognize the person I was supposed to be, as far as what you saw in the media. There's some kind of rape that happens when you are in the spotlight, and you go along with it.

The media version of you determines how you see yourself.
I used to think that if you just had enough time you could get it right. You could just say, "Well, this isn't true, no, no, that isn't so." But this

machine is so hungry that you can't. You can just feed it. So what we're doing is like misinformation.

The contrast with 'Rattle and Hum' is striking. For better or worse, the point of that project seemed to be its spontaneity, but it was the one time when the image, the perception of a U2 album, got very far away from you.

Maybe we just weren't paying attention. The whole thing was just throwaway to us, in the best sense of the word—not the movie, but the record. That showed us just how powerful the media is. We genuinely believed that it was a record about being fans of rock & roll. And we put a bit of Johnny Cash there and a song about Billie Holiday here to kind of show we were just fans. It was so obvious to us. Maybe we didn't understand how successful we were and that it looked like we were hanging out with these guys so, by association, that we were one of the greats. We never saw it that way.

How much of the hyper imaging of 'Achtung Baby' and Zoo TV was in reaction to that?

I think that we just knew it wasn't fun the other way. This trying to explain yourself—which is what I'm doing right now—wasn't fun.

It's all about imagination, nothing else. Nothing else is important. It's not about scale—big, small, independent, alternative, anything. Whether you earn a million dollars or lose a million dollars. None of it really matters. What matters is the work and the imagination of the work.

We used to have this thing about our image: "What image? We don't have an image. We're *playing* with images, like the desert or whatever, and we dress in a way that is sympathetic with the music, but it's not an image." And finally, I just said, "Fuck it, maybe it is." In fact, if it is, let's play with it, and let's distort it and manipulate it and lose ourselves in the process of it. But let's write about losing ourselves in the process of it, 'cause that's what's happening to everybody else on a smaller scale anyway.

Do you have more respect for somebody like Madonna?

Oh, yeah.

Is that something you would have seen before?

No. No, it wasn't where we were at anyway, it just wasn't for us. But Madonna—I'm interested in anything she does. The music is a little off the shelf for me, but it's almost like the lack of personality in the music heightens the personality in her voice.

Does having a rock & roll fan like Bill Clinton as president of the United States defang rock & roll? Can there still be any sense of the rock & roll rebellion you're playing ?

We obviously need to find a new word. Saying Clinton likes rock &

roll is like saying Clinton likes books. It's the stuff written in the books that's important. Did you see the inauguration? I watched it all.

What did you think?

There was a sense of people wanting it to work. More than I had ever seen before. It strikes me that people just so want it to work. There's almost a last-chance feeling about it.

Larry and Adam went over there. They ended up doing a version of "One" with the guys from R.E.M.—with Mike Mills and Michael Stipe. The song always deserved a good singer, as far as I'm concerned. Stipe's just a great singer. He's kind of like a Bing Crosby of the Nineties, though, isn't he? He's a crooner.

Tell me about U2's meeting with Bill Clinton.

We were on tour, and we got into the Ritz-Carlton in Chicago at about midnight, one o'clock, and I had this really over-the-top Cecil B. DeMille suite. So it was the room for the meetings and the parties, and there was a party in my room—and there was drink involved—and we'd heard he had arrived earlier in the evening, and we said, "Get Bill around, he'd like a slice of pizza." This is like three o'clock in the morning, but some-body thought we were serious and went out to wake him up and was met with twenty-five Secret Service guys who said, "You know, I'm not sure, it's late, he's gone to bed, had a hard day." But the next morning he got the message and said, "I'd love to have seen them, where are they now?" and he came round to my room. We were all looking fairly rock & roll after the night before, and he just laughed out loud. He was very relaxed with it.

Larry asked him, "Why would you want to be president?" and he said: "Well, you know, I don't know if the president of the United States can be the one person to turn it all around, but I know one thing: No one else can." What's interesting about him is that he seems very accessible and wants new ideas and wants to be challenged. We told him that we weren't going to endorse him, that wasn't what we did. And if he got in, that we'd be on his back for the next four years anyway, 'cause there is an uneasy relationship between us and politicians. But he knew that. He got that. That's when I realized he's pretty cool.

I always thought it was dumb and dangerous to write off all politicians as corrupt. It's just too easy.

Is there any other moment like that you'll take away from this tour?

I'm getting on with my father better than I ever have.

Is that something new?

My mother died when I was, like, thirteen or fourteen, and it was just three men in the house. And one of them, you know, was pretty obnoxious [*laughs*]. My father tried very hard to keep it together. He managed, he did keep it together, but he had to become a kind of general to do so. I mean, he kept the house together, but I suppose at that point it wasn't really a home. And I often wonder if that's the reason I feel so rootless sometimes, if that's what attracted me to the wanderlust aspect of rock & roll. I would sleep on Edge's floor, turn up at people's houses at meal times. I can still sleep anywhere. I can sleep on the street. It must have something to do with that.

And now you have enough distance from that time?

Yeah, to get on. I met somebody recently who told me that my father was incredibly smart at school and when he was taken out, the Christian brothers went around to his mother and said, "Don't take him out of school, he's really great, and he should be able to go on to college and probably be a lecturer." But he did leave, and he went on with his life very practically. He actually taught me not to dream. His idea was, don't get into that, it'll only make trouble.

He was never one to dish out a compliment, that's not his way. I remember I brought him over to the U.S. to see us play, I think it was Miami or Atlanta on the *Joshua Tree* tour, and I told one of the spotlight operators to get ready. I just introduced this guy—"It's his first time in America, here's my father, he's come here to see us play"—and 20,000 people turned around, and he just stands up and gives me the finger. Like "Don't you do this to me." I just laughed. He's very cool like that.

But afterwards backstage, I remember hearing footsteps behind me as I left the stage, and I looked round, and here's my father, and he put his hand out. I looked at him, and I thought, "Wow, he's really gonna say something really big here," and he just looked at me and said: "You know something? You're very professional" [*laughs*]. And of course, that was a high compliment from where he was. The fact that professionalism has nothing to do with . . . for me, that's like the last thing I'm interested in. It was very funny.

I don't generally talk about my family, but another thing he did, he taught me chess. That's something I've never admitted to because it was always so uncool to be a chess player. It's the most un-rock & roll thing you could do, so I never ever talked about it, but that was actually my obsession before rock & roll. When I was a kid, I played in adult tournaments and played internationally when I was ten or eleven. Things like that were important moments for me. I really, really enjoy opera now, 'cause he used to listen to it all the time. He'd just kind of throw you something like that.

Has he come around to your work?

Yeah, I think he almost likes the music now. In fact, he'll say, "I like that one, I don't like this one." He's full of opinions. He plays at being a crank. It's traditional in our family to have a row at Christmas. We always have a fight at breakfast at Christmas—it's like the polite thing to do where we come from. And I only recently figured out that he was doing it with a wink. I'd spot it in the schoolyard, I'd spot it from anyone else. I just didn't think that's where he was coming from. And he's just one of those, a stirrer. But I'm really enjoying my father at the moment. I put him in the "One" video.

You mentioned R.E.M. earlier, and it seems like U2 and R.E.M. are among the few bands to strive for a mass audience while maintaining a respected position in the alternative-rock camp. What do you think of the resistance to mainstream success that seems prevalent in the alternative scene?

It hasn't happened before in America, but it's been like that in the U.K. for a long time, so we're used to it. And a bit bored by it, having been there. "We'll never play theaters, we'll stay in the clubs!" Oh, all right, okay. Then a year later, these groups say, "Oh, we'll only play theaters, we'll never play arenas." Then it's "We'll play arenas, we'll never play stadiums." AAAAGHH! Let me out! To hear it all happening again is just incredible to me. And it's all middle-class kids that are saying it. You never hear working-class people saying those things, you never hear blacks saying it. It's such a bourgeois phenomenon. It almost identifies you as bourgeois.

From where U2 started, do you understand the impulse?

Yes, especially in the American culture, I do understand it. I don't think it's very rigorous, though, I don't think it's well thought out. I can see why somebody would just retch on the lowest common denominator that has dominated rock & roll from radio play and sales pitch. There is a sense in which you say, "Well, whatever that's a part of, I'm out of there." I can understand that. But you gotta think it through, and in my experience in England, what they call independent is a bogus term. With independent record companies, a lot of times you have smaller corporations bullying you.

By the way, I think it's good that Sonic Youth and Nirvana are on Geffen Records. I don't think they should be embarrassed by it. I think Kurt Cobain is a fine singer. I know the "R.E.M. with a fuzz box" argument, but I actually think they are an important group and they've got vitality and they should just do anything they want to do. The fact that they sell as many records as Madonna is great. You see, we've been there. There is kind of a Catholic guilt that can go with success, but I just hope some of these groups don't start tiptoeing.

I always felt it was our responsibility to abuse our position. That was one of the ways we went into the sessions for *Achtung Baby*. Because we had been spoiled by success financially, we had what Groucho Marx called "fuck-off money." If you waste that, you're just a wanker, you don't deserve anything. At this point in U2, we've made more money outside U2 than we ever did inside U2, so there's only one reason for walking into a recording studio, and there's only one reason for going out on tour, and that is to do exactly what we want to do.

Is there any concern that in playing the showbiz stuff to the hilt, you risk tarnishing your protest image? To stage a dawn raid on the Sellafield nuclear plant in full Fly gear—can people sort that out?

Well, I always thought of the Fly as a meltdown kind of a guy. I don't want to put too much emphasis on this character, but you gotta find new ways of saying the same things, you really do. I don't think it's a contradiction to find yourself on the beach at a nuclear power plant wearing those sunglasses. I think it is very surreal, and it was amusing to us even then. We were aware of how ridiculous it was.

What did you think of last year's pope-shredding incident by Sinéad O'Connor?

Maybe you have to be Irish to understand her bitterness toward the pope. You could argue that the pope is sincere, but to deny people contraception at this moment in time is a very irresponsible act. It's more than an irresponsible act. You can't buy condoms in this country—not easily—and so when Sinéad talks about him being the enemy, I imagine that's what she's talking about.

I don't want to be her apologist, and she doesn't need one. I felt very close to her in the early days, and I still feel strongly about her. We fell out with her, with her manager actually, who was her boyfriend, and as a result we were the devil for a few weeks. But now that she's the devil [*laughs*], I think we're getting on a lot better. To live off your emotions is a necessary evil if you're a singer, but it doesn't make for an easy life.

What's the band's history with David Wojnarowicz [a controversial American artist who died of AIDS last year]? You used his images in the "One" video. Did you collect his work before?

Adam is the man who turned me on to Wojnarowicz's work. Whatever you do now, you are in the post-AIDS age. It's there, and you've got to walk through it or around it. And if a record deals with any kind of erotic subject matter, the specter of AIDS is even all the more close.

You know, if Freud was even half-right, if sex is even close to the center of our lives, how is it that we leave it to pornographers and dum-dum guys? We leave the subject to them, and it's reduced to titillation in the cinema, to these kind of half-baked plots. Wojnarowicz dealt with the subject seriously, he took it on. I can't believe how people can just walk around it, you know? I'm sympathetic to Madonna in that respect, too. Whatever you think about her work, she's actually just trying to say: "Look, here I am, and I have these feelings and ideas, and I know you do, but you're not owning up. I will."

Releasing multiple videos for "One" and "Even Better Than the Real Thing," all the remixes—it seems like you're approaching this album as something mutable, more like a performance-art piece than a fixed statement.

Rock & roll is mutating into something else at the moment. The video-game business is bigger than the music business. Images are everything, and we want to be there when the sort of audiovisual-microchip-interactive music is born.

The exciting thing about what's about to happen is we're working with Sega on a Zoo TV interactive CD. You're going to be able to mix your own videos to our songs. There will be a color box, if you like, of images. I'm really excited about that. And you're going to be able to remix our music for yourself, which scares me a little. You have to swallow hard before agreeing to something like that.

'Rattle and Hum,' and even 'The Joshua Tree' in its way, seemed to be about stripping down, getting into the more elemental part of rock & roll.

Yeah, but even from our earliest days we were always best when we were in new territory. And technology is there to get to that. To me, the technology is there to abuse—like Jimi Hendrix's fuzz box. With Edge onstage now, my stage left, well, it's like Cape Canaveral. It's a technocratic side that helps him get to other places and sounds you've never heard before. This is one thing that I don't quite get—did you say that I won singer, Best Male Singer? Did Edge win?

The Edge was the runner-up for Best Guitarist.

You see, people are getting it the wrong way around. I'm a *good* singer, he is a *great* guitar player. He is so far ahead of the posse. It's embarrassing for me to have to say this, but it's kind of indisputable, 'cause everybody else is still painting the same colors. While everyone is imitating, he's creative.

To abuse technology, to find new tones, new moods, that's what U2's about, and I was trying to put words onto those new moods. And sometimes those moods are not specific. I just try to put into words what the others are doing with the music. Occasionally, it is idea driven, but usually, that's what I'm doing.

That's hardly the same thing as "All I need is a red guitar, three chords and the truth."

Um . . . am I blushing? [*Laughs*] Well, anyway, the point of that whole thing was to say, to quote the Clash. "We're a garage band, we come from garage land." It's just that idea that all you need is three chords and something to say. It's what rappers say as well. Instead of three chords, replace three chords with a beat—you need a beat and a line, and that's it.

'Achtung Baby' is a very European-influenced record. What stayed with you from all your explorations of American music, from working with people like Roy Orbison and B.B. King?

One word: Rhythm. Which is the sex of music. You learn a lot watching somebody like B.B. King and going back to those early R&B records. That was the thing we needed, I think. That's what was missing in the puzzle for U2. It's a different place that was necessary for us to go in light of the new subject matter. You can't write songs about sex if you don't have it in the music.

What prompted the darker sexuality of 'Achtung Baby'?

I'd often found the sort of neon-light aspect of sex very funny, the leather and lace aspect. It wasn't a sexuality that I particularly related to, but it does seem a dominant sexuality. It's the one used to sell products, and it's the one on every corner, and so I got into it [*laughs*], and it's great! It's just something I'm trying to understand, and I understand it a lot better having dressed up as a con man for the past year.

But there are moments—say, the line in "So Cruel" where you sing, "I'm only hanging on to watch you go down"—that are almost nasty. You've said a lot of that comes from Edge's divorce.

Oh, there's lots of stories in there, by no means only his. In fact, it's the story of just about everybody I know. People are desperately trying to hold on to each other in a time when it's very hard to do that. And the bittersweet love song is something I think we do very well. It's in a tradition, and Roy Orbison was probably the greatest in that tradition.

Some of these songs, though, are much more bitter than sweet, much angrier and edgier than Roy Orbison ever was.

I think the opposite of love is not hate. It's apathy. You only get angry about things you really care about. So that kind of anger can emphasize the positive by allowing it to come out, to be bitter, to bring up all that stuff.

The Fly character has become the dominant image of this phase of U2. How do you get out of it? How do you get the glasses off when the tour ends?

[*Long pause*] We're right in the middle of it now, but the music . . . the music tells you what to do, and in the end that's what you gotta do. The music tells you what clothes to wear, it tells you what kind of stage you should be standing on, it tells you who should be photographing you, it tells you who should be your agent. You might see the glasses as a mask, but Oscar Wilde said something like "The mask tells you more about the man." Something like that.

But it's always the music that tells you what to do. And so if I want to take the glasses off. I just gotta change my tune.

DAVID FRICKE

ACHTUNG, BABIES! A NEW U2 ALBUM!

JUST WHEN YOU THOUGHT IT was almost time for U2 to fold up its Zoo TV roadshow and go into hibernation, the band kicks into even higher gear with a brand-new, ten-song studio album, *Zooropa,* to be released on July 6th.

Recorded in Dublin from March to May of this year during a work-intensive break between legs of the ongoing, worldwide Zoo TV Tour, the album was produced by mixer-engineer Flood, Brian Eno and U2's guitarist the Edge and takes the futurist-pop sound of the group's last LP, 1991's *Achtung Baby,* to new extremes. It also arrives quite abruptly—a little over a year and a half after *Achtung Baby.* In fact, Bono freely admits that the project took the entire band by surprise.

"There's a kind of freak energy that follows you home from a tour," he says excitedly, just forty-eight hours after the final mixing session. "Most times, you just slowly try to come down from it. Whereas after the Zoo TV shows last year, we thought: 'We have all this energy. Why not use it? Why not go into the studio and see what happens?'"

What happened was enough writing and recording to fill *two* albums. "There were a few ideas that had been left over from the *Achtung Baby* sessions," Bono explains. "But the more interesting stuff came out of improvisation, which was a call of Eno's. His vibe on this record was 'Stop songwriting. If you're playing so well, approach it in a different manner.' We thought it would be a very abstract record at first, but a lot of the things we decided to put on the record actually turned into songs." According to Bono, the material from the sessions for *Zooropa* that didn't make the album may turn up on still another record further down the line.

Musically, the two big curveballs on the record are "Numb," a spooky, industrial groove thing with a bizarre sing-speak vocal by the Edge, and "Daddy's Gonna Pay for Your Crashed Car," a highly studio-processed piece of metallic dance rock grounded by a corrosive backward-bass loop. "We messed with the reverb on my voice," Bono says of the song, "so it's very dry on one word and very wet on another. It's quite strung out."

Other surprises include "Some Days Are Better Than Others," which is punctuated by thick, reptilian fuzz-guitar outbursts by the Edge, and "Dirty Day," a grim, eerie mantralike song dedicated to the hard-boiled writer, poet and barfly Charles Bukowski. And in the album's closer, "The Wanderer," a U2 original that Bono suggests is a kind of metaphysical takeoff on Dion's 1962 hit of the same name, guest lead vocalist Johnny Cash brings a haunting, bedrock quality to the track that rivals Adam Clayton's bass line for shuddering, low-end resonance.

"We had talked before about writing together," Bono says of Cash, "and we had started this song called 'Ellis Island,' which is more in *his* tradition. Then I had the idea for this song, which we provisionally called 'Wandering.' And I didn't feel like I could really sing the words. Johnny was coming into town that day, so I said, 'I'll write it for Johnny.' I wrote it for him, and he finished it that day." Bono, by the way, doesn't appear on the track at all.

U2 expects to work material from *Zooropa* into the Zoo TV show sometime in midsummer, but Bono—claiming that the band will really need a break by tour's end—says there will be no further American shows. "Which is a shame," he concedes, "because in many ways the show will be more coherent with these new songs. Zoo TV is a great thing to play with, and *Zooropa* has come out of that."

That also means American audiences will be denied the chance to see MacPhisto, Bono's latest stage manifestation, in action. Born shortly before the European tour, MacPhisto replaces the mirror-suit cowboy-preacher in the show's encore and is a hellishly kitschy sight—gold lamé suit, platform shoes, white-face makeup and little red devil's horns. "I just didn't feel like doing the mirror-ball man in Europe," Bono explains. "Like, who is the mirror-ball man anyway? Well, he is the devil.

"So I thought, great, put on a pair of horns," Bono says, laughing. "Might as well spell it out."

ANTHONY DeCURTIS

ZOOROPA ALBUM REVIEW

★ ★ ★ ★

Zooropa, Mon Amour

BOSNIA AND HERZEGOVINA. The resurgence of Nazism in Germany. Mafia terrorism in Italy. Escalating unemployment throughout the former Western Bloc. *Zooropa,* indeed.

None of those issues is explicitly addressed on U2's startling new album, of course. But the chilling emotional atmosphere of *Zooropa*—one of grim, determined fun, a fever-dream last waltz on the deck of the *Titanic*—is well suited to contemporary times in the Old World. "I feel like I'm slowly, slowly, slowly slipping under," Bono wails amid the dizzying disco rhythms of "Lemon." "I feel like I'm holding onto nothing." From that vantage of desperate spiritual dislocation, the vanished certainties of Cold War Europe look comforting.

Principally recorded earlier this year, *Zooropa* began as a toss-off EP to crank some juice into the European leg of U2's worldwide Zoo TV tour. Deeper inspiration struck, however, and with Brian Eno, the Edge and Flood producing, this fifty-minute, ten-track album emerged.

Historically, U2 have always attempted to follow up breakthrough albums with less ostensibly ambitious efforts. Live EPs came hard on the heels of both *War* (1983) and *The Unforgettable Fire* (1984), and for the most part, they effectively eased the pressure on the band and left U2 free to explore whatever new aesthetic directions they pleased.

Unfortunately, the strategy backfired the last time U2 attempted a "spontaneous" one-off. In 1988, to get some distance on the prodigious success of *The Joshua Tree,* U2 perpetrated *Rattle and Hum,* an album-book-movie media blitz so self-conscious and contrived that it seemed about as unplanned as the invasion of Normandy.

With *Zooropa* the results are far more satisfying: The album is a daring, imaginative coda to *Achtung Baby* (1991), U2's first unqualified masterpiece. *Zooropa* defuses the daunting commercial expectations set by that album while closing off none of the band's artistic options. It is varied and vigorously experimental, but its charged mood of giddy anarchy suffused with barely suppressed dread provides a compelling, unifying thread.

The title track sets the tone from the very start. As the song opens, a stately piano figure, beautiful and foreboding, underlies indecipherable, static-stricken signals from the information-age inferno of Zoo TV. That alluring sonic chaos ultimately yields to the wah-wah blast of the Edge's guitar and the insistent groove of Adam Clayton's bass and Larry Mullen Jr.'s drums. Bono enters like a Mephistophelean seducer, offering jaded pleasures, nurturing dissatisfaction and stoking desire, crooning the pander's eternal appeal, "What do you want?"

The exuberant paranoia of Bob Dylan's "Subterranean Homesick Blues" gets a postmodern twist on "Numb." Above a hypnotic rhythm track and a repetitive, industrial guitar screech, the Edge blankly intones a long string of disconnected injunctions, postapocalyptic advice for stunned survivors: "Don't move / Don't talk out of time / Don't think / Don't worry everything's just fine/Just fine." Meanwhile, Bono coos in a woozy falsetto, "I feel numb / Too much is not enough."

For "The Wanderer," *Zooropa*'s concluding statement, U2 usher in Johnny Cash to handle the lead vocal. It's a wildly audacious move that could so easily have proved a pathetic embarrassment—U2 overreaching for significance yet again—but it works brilliantly. Speak-singing with all the authority of an Old Testament prophet, Cash movingly serves as a link to a lost world of moral surety ("I went out walking with a bible and a gun / The word of God lay heavy on my heart / I was sure I was the one / Now Jesus, don't you wait up / Jesus, I'll be home soon"), literally replacing the various corrupted and confused personas Bono (and, on "Numb," the Edge) had occupied in the course of the album.

Cash's "Wanderer" is no less lost than the album's other dead souls, but his yearning to be found and redeemed sets him apart. *Zooropa* never resolves whether that yearning is merely nostalgic—a wish for a resurrection that has long ago been canceled—or a genuine intimation of hope. No matter: The album's true strength lies in capturing the sound of verities shattering, of things falling apart, that moment when exhilaration and fear are indistinguishable as the slide into the abyss begins.

■ **RANDOM NOTES** (August 19, 1993)
Bono, Bono, Bono. Take off the Kabuki makeup, lose the lamé, and let's just get ahold of ourselves, shall we? Bono's manager, Paul McGuinness, bid £10,000 in a London auction for a chance to play world chess champ Gary Kasparov in September, which he bestowed upon the U2 frontman. Bono then said: "It's a dream come true to take on one of the grandmasters. I reckon I stand a good chance of winning."

THE 100 TOP MUSIC VIDEOS

ROLLING STONE editors chose the 100 best rock videos of all time for a special issue (which, coincidentally, featured Edge on the cover and an in-depth look at U2's Zooropa tour in Europe). U2 reached Number 76 with the "Mysterious Ways" video and Number 99 with "One."

#76 Mysterious Ways, 1991

When French director Stephane Sednaoui was chosen to work on the video for "Mysterious Ways," off U2's 1991 album, *Achtung Baby,* his concept was, he says, "something very basic and very abstract—water, earth, space, sky, maybe fire." The band members wanted to tie Sednaoui's naturalistic approach to a more specific theme. "It was just after the war with Iraq," the director says, "and they felt Europeans were closing their minds to the Arabic world. They wanted to convey the message that sometimes we don't understand the mysterious ways of other parts of the world." Shot in Morocco, the video's often distorted images create a mosaic of radiant humanity, from the creased face of an old man to the sinuous moves of a belly dancer, the most alarming images of which may be the Edge's face bloating and expanding and Bono rippling uncontrollably.

—Elysa Gardner

#99 One, 1992

Director Mark Pellington's video for "One"—the first of three versions made for the single—may not have gotten as much attention as the other two, but his slow-motion, out-of-focus footage of running buffalo is a quietly eloquent tour de force. Its power lies in its simplicity: The piece includes no band shots and was intended as a meditative video background for U2's live performance of the song, which deals with AIDS and intolerance toward gays. "We had done a cut of it, which we used in rehearsals," says bassist Adam Clayton. "When the need for a video came up, we went back to it." Built around the closing image of the beasts being herded off a cliff (a photograph by artist David Wojnarowicz, who died of AIDS in

1992), the video was played on MTV until, according to the band, the network determined it wasn't right for heavy rotation, and it was replaced by the other two more MTV-friendly clips, one by director Phil Joanou, the other by photographer Anton Corbijn.

—Dulcy Israel

ANTHONY DeCURTIS

ZOO WORLD ORDER

With a lot of help from the Edge,
U2 are reborn with a case of the giggles—
and a new sense of mission

"Uncertainty . . . can be a guiding light."
—*From* "ZOOROPA," *the title track of U2's latest album*

SITTING IN THE FERRYMAN, a dockside Dublin pub, U2's guitarist, the Edge, speaks about the political crisis in Europe: "The single most powerful feeling we have is of the uncertainty of the situation here. "Nothing really can be taken for granted anymore," he goes on, a Guinness close at hand, as strains of traditional Irish music float in from the bar's main room. "The old ideologies have fallen away. Capitalism won out. You can't even say it was democracy, because ultimately the ground upon which the battle was fought was economics—it was about money. And the West's economy won, and communism is pretty much over."

"Money, money, money / Always sunny / In the rich man's world"
—*From* "Money, Money, Money," *one of the many ABBA songs played over the PA on the Zoo Plane, U2's private tour jet*

"But rather than the sense that 'Well, that's over—now we can move forward with certainty,' the opposite has happened," the Edge continues. "People are perplexed. Maybe the stability that the Cold War created was the foundation of the West's movement forward, and now that that's gone and we have the resurgence of radical nationalism, people in Europe don't know who they are trying to be. Not only do they not know who they are, they don't know who they want to be. They don't know whether they want to be Europeans, part of the European community, or whether they should be fighting to protect their national and ethnic identities.

"Even national boundaries don't mean much anymore. You've got the movement in Italy to partition the country into two or three autonomous states. There's the Basque-separatist movement that's alive and kicking. Northern Ireland is still no closer to a real solution. And Yugoslavia is the most obvious example of where things are starting to dissolve. Sarajevo has been a symbol of this."

"We would like to hear the music, too, but we hear only the screams of wounded and tortured people and raped women."
—*A Bosnian woman speaking live by satellite from Sarajevo to 35,000 people at the U2 concert in Glasgow, Scotland, Aug. 8*

To THE INATTENTIVE EYE of the Irish regulars and German tourists sucking up beer and whiskey at the Ferryman a few feet to his left, the Edge might have seemed like just another bar-stool philosopher gassing about the issues of the day before heading home to pass out in front of the telly. True, he and his three comrades in U2—Bono, Adam Clayton and Larry Mullen Jr.—have spent plenty of time in front of televisions lately.

For the band, however—and in particular the Edge, whose increased musical and conceptual input earned him a co-production credit on the new *Zooropa* album (he also sang lead on the first single, "Numb")—the pangs of European politics have been anything but remote. In retooling the Zoo TV stadium extravaganza that blitzed the United States in the summer of '92 for European audiences, U2 charged straight into the belly of the beast. The show's opening visual assault on gigantic vidiwalls and banks of televisions now included dramatic footage from *Triumph of the Will,* Leni Riefenstahl's Nazi propaganda film from the 1930s. Huge flaming swastikas and burning crosses appeared on the vidiwalls during "Bullet the Blue Sky." Meanwhile, *Zooropa,* the *Achtung Baby* follow-up the group released in July, chillingly evoked the exhilaration and fear of Europe in the throes of the new world disorder.

During the Zooropa '93 tour, U2's frequent live-satellite transmissions from Sarajevo—in which residents of the besieged city spoke uncensored to stunned stadium crowds—triggered a heated media debate abroad about the ethics of mixing up rock & roll special effects with heart-ravaging disasters.

At one of the Wembley shows in London, Salman Rushdie—who has been in hiding since the late Ayatollah Khomeini sentenced him to death three years ago for blasphemies against Islam in his novel *The Satanic Verses*—joined U2 onstage in front of 72,000 people. And as if to assume the role in which many commentators were casting the band, Bono replaced his glitzy Mirror-Ball Man persona, the preening narcissist who closed the Zoo TV shows in the U.S., with Mister MacPhisto, an aging, world-weary theatrical devil, complete with horns.

"Ranking with the major megagigs of the 1970s and '80s, Zoo TV is the best live-music act in yonks. But again, it's like watching and rewatching atrocity footage such as, say, the Zapruder film, and trying to force the reality of it into your head. To paraphrase Bowie: In this context, whether it's Nazi Germany or Sarajevo onscreen, 'this ain't genocide, this is rock 'n' roll!!!' "
—*Mic Moroney, "Irish Times," Aug. 24*

★

"What's the difference between Sarajevo and Auschwitz?"
"What?"
"In Auschwitz they always had gas."
—*Popular joke in Sarajevo, where gas supplies have been cut off*

Bono is stretched out on the Zoo Plane, his legs resting on the seat opposite his own, as the band flies from London to Dublin. It is the evening after the fourth Wembley show—a truly spectacular performance in which Bono and the lads seemed only to gain inspiration from the steady rainfall—and he is tired and hoarse.

He is also hungover. After the show the previous night, the band threw a bash at the Regent Hotel, and given that it was closing night in London and one of the band's management crew was celebrating a birthday, the partying was especially intent. At about 3:30 A.M., Bono switched from beer to whiskey. I left at about 5:30; Bono was still going strong. He's suffering now. The couple of glasses of wine earlier in the day evidently didn't help. "Does anyone feel sick besides me?" he asks no one in particular.

Adding insult to injury, seated next to him is drummer Mullen, official U2 hunk, who always looks fit, groomed and at the peak of health, regardless of the hour, location or extent of alcohol intake.

MULLEN: The essence of good rock & roll—it's about confusion on every level. That's what makes Zoo TV so odd. On one hand, you can have Sarajevo, which is real, and then you have to continue on with the show. I mean, even for us, after the Sarajevo linkups we did, carrying on the show was incredibly difficult. People took it in different ways. People took it as "How can you have irony and then be serious?" But that is the point.

BONO: That's TV!

MULLEN: That *is* TV. You can switch the fuckin' channel any time you want. So I think a lot of people missed the point. I understand and accept the criticism, but it's not meant to be easy. It's not like going to a theater show, where you've got a beginning, middle and end. It's a different journey. This is coming to a rock & roll show and watching TV and changing channels.

BONO: It's about contradictions. It's about all those instincts—we have all of them.

> "Serious shit—fan letters and murder in the same sentence. I don't like it."
> —Bono, switching Zoo TV channels at Wembley, Aug. 21, after a news report about a woman who shot an abortion doctor in Kansas. She had sent fan mail to a Florida man who is charged with murder in the death of a doctor outside an abortion clinic.

BASSIST ADAM CLAYTON is standing in a gazebo on the estate of Chris Blackwell, the founder and CEO of U2's label, Island Records. It's not a gazebo in the sense that you may have come to understand gazebos. It's shaped like a gazebo, but it's really more like a study, enclosed by glass on all sides, comfortably furnished and perched, surrounded by trees, on the edge of a large pond. In a silent way, the scene is breathtaking.

The U2 gang has driven some forty miles south from London to spend this gray, cool Sunday afternoon enjoying Blackwell's tasteful hospitality and the secluded beauty of his home and grounds. Strangely, in this serene atmosphere, everyone seems a bit shellshocked.

Clayton, smoking, sporting his dyed semi-mohawk haircut and decked out in purple pants, black hiking boots and black vest, takes in the enormous drooping willows, the people pushing small boats out onto the pond, the calm inside this room. He shakes his head.

"I haven't been programmed for an experience like this of late," he says with a laugh. "I feel quite vulnerable. I mean, there's not a TV in sight."

How did you hook up Salman Rushdie with your man MacPhisto?

BONO: In his isolation, I guess he gets to listen to a lot of music [*laughs*], so he's pretty tuned in. He turned up at our Earls Court show in London last year. We've kept in contact with him here and there. The issue of freedom of speech should be very close to rock & roll. At one stage we talked about sending him a satellite dish, and we would speak to him. We knew he was coming down to the show—which is very rare for him—and so we thought, "Well, look, if you're up for it . . . you *did* write *The Satanic Verses*."

"I also owe U2 a debt of gratitude for the gesture of solidarity and friendship they made by inviting me to join them onstage at Wembley. Not many novelists ever experience what it's like to face an audience of over 70,000 people—and, fortunately for everyone, I didn't even have to sing.

"Afterward I suggested that perhaps we could rename the band

U2 + 1? ME2?—but I don't think they were for it. Still, one can always hope."

—*Salman Rushdie, "Irish Times," Aug. 24*

★

"ROCK & ROLL—it's the new religion, rock & roll. I have a great interest in religion. Some of my best friends are religious leaders. The ayatollah, the pope, even the Archbishop of Canterbury—I think he's fabulous. They're doing my work for me. . . . Nobody's going to church anymore. Shall I give the archbishop a call?"

—*Bono as Macphisto, while dialing the Zoo telephone onstage, Wembley Stadium, Aug. 20*

★

"We're not scared of dying, but you can't get used to seeing wounded people everywhere. . . . Something has to be done to help us."

—*A Bosnian woman speaking live by satellite from Sarajevo at the U2 concert in Glasgow, Aug. 9*

THE EDGE: One of our Sarajevo connections had three women. One was a Serb, one was a Croat, one was a Muslim—all Bosnians. All in Sarajevo, all with their own story to tell. One of the girls said the thing that we'd always hoped no one would say—but she did. She said: "I wonder, what are you going to do for us in Sarajevo? I think the truth is you're not going to do anything."

It was so hard to carry on after that. It killed the gig stone dead. It was so heavy. I don't know how Bono managed to carry on singing. It was such a crushing statement.

"If you're watching TV and something serious comes on, you can just change the channel."

—*Bono, while channel surfing onstage at Wembley, Aug. 20*

BILL CARTER, A STARTLINGLY fresh-faced twenty-seven-year-old filmmaker and relief worker in Sarajevo, sits in the bar at the Conrad Hotel in Dublin and describes how, after he'd traveled from Sarajevo to Verona, Italy, to interview Bono for thirteen minutes, the plan for the live-satellite hookup was hatched.

"I had a real serious conversation with Bono and Edge about what was going on," Carter says. "They said, 'Well, what can we do?' That hit me with a huge trip—the largest rock band in the world is asking me what can they do. They wanted to play—Bono and Edge, all of them, really— wanted to come play in the disco in Sarajevo. But it was a difficult time then: a lot of shelling. I went back to Sarajevo and thought about it.

"A few days later, someone in their office called me and said, 'They really want to come—bad.' I wrote a long fax explaining why that shouldn't happen, but what about linking up to the show? They said, 'Let's do it.'

"We'd talk to 70,000 people and hit them with reality on their rock & roll fantasy. That's a huge medium. . . . In Sweden we got the fiancee of a guy in Sarajevo—she lives in Sweden, his family, too—to come to the stadium. He talked very powerfully about what was happening, and then he spoke to her. She hadn't seen him in seventeen months. There she is, a refugee in Sweden, being feted backstage, and then looking up at him on the video. That was a heavy thing.

"We were offering a true human reality. This is one fact that is really important: No one in seventeen months had allowed Bosnians—besides the politicians—to speak live to the world. When I first went back to Sarajevo with this idea, ABC News and all the rest, they were like 'Are you nuts? You're going to let someone from here speak live?'

"The trust from U2 to me was tremendous, to say, 'Okay, go ahead—you're in a war zone, speak live to us.' They didn't know me. They knew me for one evening."

THE EDGE: The Sarajevo connection was so different from what you were seeing on the news. It underscored for me the difference between the reality of people telling their stories and the editorialized sound-bite style of most TV news programs, where everything is packaged and contextualized through some sort of journalistic narration. This was raw, unedited, live and at times almost unbearable. It suddenly dawned on me—actually it's something that I've probably known for a long time—that the TV news is now entertainment."

ART IS MANIPULATION

REBELLION IS PACKAGED

ROCK AND ROLL IS ENTERTAINMENT

—*Mottoes flashed on the video screens during U2's Zoo TV shows*

CLAYTON: It's taken a long time for television to be thought of as rock & roll.

U2'S LAST SHOW AT Wembley was attended by, among 72,000 others, Eric Clapton, Robbie Robertson and French singer and film star Charles Aznavour. Aznavour, 68, was asked if he wanted to leave the stadium early in the show when rain began to pour, but he refused, insisting on staying till the end. Among his other current projects, Aznavour is recording a duet with Frank Sinatra for his upcoming album of duets. So is Bono.

Bono wanted to do a version of Nancy Sinatra's "These Boots Are Made for Walkin'." "That could have been good," he says, preposterously. Sinatra, displaying his characteristically impeccable taste, refused, suggesting Cole Porter's "I've Got You Under My Skin" instead. Understandably, Bono is concerned.

"I don't know what I can do with that," he says. "I'm not going to croon it next to him. I might talk. I want to spook it up, because those Cole Porter songs are spooky. I don't know if you heard that 'Night and Day' thing we did [on the album *Red Hot + Blue*]—that's where we connect with Cole Porter. They're spooky, fucked-up songs of obsession. Some people perform them so fruity—[*belts in lounge-lizard fashion*] 'Night and day/You are the one'—it's like *whoa!* These are really dark pieces of work.

"I listen to Sinatra a lot," Bono continues. "Miles Davis was a great appreciator of Sinatra's phrasing. That turned me on to him, listening to him in a different way. I've seen him about five times. We met him in Vegas—we went backstage, and we were hanging out with him. It was like Rent-a-Celebrity, and we were like gyppos, just knackers. Larry was talking to him about Buddy Rich, who'd just died, and he didn't want to talk about anything else. He came alive. You got the feeling that maybe not a lot of people talk to him about music, and maybe that's what he's most interested in. There were people knocking at the door, big names, and he wouldn't go out. He wouldn't leave the dressing room.

"Then there was a very amusing incident in Dublin. We all went to see him in this big stadium. He was with Sammy Davis Jr. and Liza Minnelli—that tour. We didn't go backstage; we didn't think he'd remember us. But the lord mayor went back to see him, to have his photograph taken with him. When the lord mayor came back to his seat—and this is very Dublin—he kind of leaned over a few rows and said, 'Oh, Bono, Frank was asking for you all.' *That* might have been the moment!"

DID YOUR ROLE IN *the band shift during the making of "Zooropa"?*
        THE EDGE: Quite why on this record I've taken a production credit and not on other records is hard to explain. I don't think my role has changed that much. But we're in an age where it's very hard to be clear about people's roles in the making of records.

I suppose I took on a level of responsibility that I haven't on previous records. That meant sitting in with Bono on lyric-writing sessions—just being the foil, the devil's advocate, bouncing couplets around—down to completely demoing some pieces, establishing their original incarnations, which then served as the blueprint when we began to formally record them. And then, generally, just worrying more than everyone else.

We're at a point where production has gotten so slick that people don't trust it anymore. This is something that we were really feeling over the last two records. We were starting to lose trust in the conventional sound of rock & roll—the conventional sound of guitar, in particular—and, you know, those big reverb-laden drum sounds of the '80s or those big, beautiful, pristine vocal sounds with all this lush ambience and reverb. So we found ourselves searching for other sounds that had more life and more freshness.

That's something we were talking to Wim Wenders about. He's finding that—because of the way certain images have been stolen by advertising or bad movie makers—that it's increasingly difficult to use imagery to tell his stories. He's now resorting much more to music and dialogue. He said that on his first movie he spent all his time editing and ten percent of the time working with music and dialogue. Now it's the reverse. He spends very little time editing—he gets it so that he's happy with the overall series of images, but then he spends all his time working on music and getting the dialogue the way he wants it.

It's really bizarre how things are melting into one another: We're now using imagery to underscore our songs.

Tell me, what was the Edge's role in the making of 'Zooropa'?

BONO: When we start records, Edge is a slow starter. He's not quick to be enthused about a project. But at the end, when everybody else is fading, he's the guy who's up all night for weeks. I mean, I'm allergic to the studio after a few weeks. We wanted to acknowledge the baby-sitting that Edge does.

Brian Eno was coming and going, Flood went to the end when there were mixes to do. I mean, we're all a part of it—we always have been. But Edge is the guy with the screwdriver.

MULLEN: And the patience of a saint.

BONO: One of the things that worked about this record is that it was so quick. Edge is so good with the screwdriver, but we didn't give him much time to use it—which was great. He had more of an overall picture because he wasn't so taken up with the details.

There was a lot of publicity around the time 'Achtung Baby' was released about your separating from your wife, Aislinn. How are things going for you personally?

THE EDGE [*long silence*]: It's a learning experience, Anthony [*laughs*]. I'm really no closer to bringing my private life to a conclusion than I was a year ago. I'm getting on really well with my wife, actually. I don't know, I'm feeling very positive about life in general, and that includes my private life. Whatever way it pans out, it's going to be Okay. That's another thing that being off for nine months will help to clarify.

When you get off the road, you've got to reintroduce yourself to all your friends and family. We're lucky—we have a lot of very good friends and very patient families. But there is a limit [*laughs*]. And I think we passed that limit a long time ago.

So when are you and Naomi Campbell getting married?

CLAYTON: I really don't know. I would say it would be some time next year. We'll take January to have a clear break away from everything. I think in that time we'll decide what's best and how we want to do it. It's kind of a scheduling thing [*laughs*].

You're taking a rehearsal break, then playing Japan and Australia for five weeks. That will take you till the end of the year. What then?

BONO: One of us has to die in a car accident. One of us has to book into the Betty Ford clinic. One of us should get married. And one of us has to become a monk. We'll have nine months off.

MULLEN: It'll be time to do things that we haven't had the opportunity to do—and I'm not necessarily talking about solo projects—so that we'll come back with new ideas and start up again. That's the idea. It's not nine months' holiday.

BONO [*incredulous*]: Jesus!

MULLEN: Bono thought he was going to have his holidays [*laughs*]. I really noticed while we were making *Zooropa*—because we were all in the studio at the same time—that there were things I wanted to say on a musical basis that I couldn't articulate. I could only say what I felt, and it took so much time to explain. What I'd really like to do is . . .

BONO: Learn how to speak.

MULLEN: What's your problem [*laughs*]? I'd like to learn how to talk in basic musical terms. The great thing about U2 is that there are no rules: Everyone has the chance to contribute as much or as little as they wish. After ten years of being on the road, it's time now to advance a bit musically. I really want to learn how to explain myself in musical terms, the basics of music theory.

"The catatonic note-repetitions of the voice part in 'Numb' add up to a clear effect. The use of different texts simultaneously in 'Lemon' works well. It is

a technique that seems to have been out of favour since the medieval motet. A lively song this, with its repeated-note accompaniment."
—*Dr. Seorise Bodley, composer and associate professor of music, "Irish Times," Aug. 24*

THE U2 MANAGEMENT crew, friends and hangers-on pile on a bus that will travel from Wembley to the Regent Hotel in London, about a half-hour trip. It's about 1:30 A.M., the third Wembley show ended a few hours ago, only three shows remain until the end of the European leg of Zooropa '93. It feels like the last week of school.

Bottles of wine are being passed around and someone shouts for music. Someone else pops a cassette in the deck. Over the speakers comes the fanfare that begins "Daddy's Gonna Pay for Your Crashed Car," on *Zooropa.* An instant collective drunken groan: "Oh, nooooo!"

The Zoo TV show, which starts out so explosively, fades out on a far more ambiguous, introspective note. A desperately searching "Ultraviolet (Light My Way)" is followed by an equally desperate, equally searching "Love Is Blindness." Then comes Bono's eerie, falsetto rendering of Elvis Presley's "Can't Help Falling in Love." "Elvis is still in the building," Bono says softly, as U2 exits the building and Elvis' own version of the song comes up on the PA. Through all this Bono is dressed as the devil.

What's the meaning of all that Elvis business at the end of the show?
THE EDGE: Well, we wanted to move away from the well-established and longstanding tradition of ending on "40" [*laughs*]. It seemed like the only way to make sure we didn't have to.

Really, who else but Elvis could have made that possible? You have to call in the big guns, it always comes down to that.
I think at this stage, yeah. People still start singing "40" at the end of the set. I guess it'll be a while before we can lay that one to rest. People come to the shows who have seen U2 before, and you're constantly having to deal with their expectations as opposed to what you're trying to do. I know there are a lot of people who come away disappointed from the Zooropa show because we didn't play "Sunday Bloody Sunday" or whatever other old song they wanted to hear.

But you close the set proper with "Pride." How does a song as emotionally direct as that fit in with all the irony and media chicanery in the rest of the show?
At the beginning we weren't sure if that was going to work. I think it does work. It may be a bit of a jump to go from something as ironic as Bono as MacPhisto or the Fly and yet pull off "Pride," complete with Martin Luther King on the video screen. But it comes at a part of the concert where

to make a connection like that is important. Amid the uncertainty there are
certain ideas that are so powerful and so right that you can hold onto them
no matter how screwed up everything else is.

> "Everybody wants a long life. Longevity has its place. But I don't care about
> that now. I may not get there with you, but I want you to know tonight that
> we as a people will get to the promised land!"
> —*Passage spoken by Martin Luther King on the vidiwall during U2's*
> *version of "Pride"*

There's a really theatrical element to that MacPhisto character.

BONO: The cabaret aspect . . . I was called by a tabloid photographer,
who said, "You know, the fellow you do in the fin-ah-lay" [*laughs*]. I
thought, "Oh, wow."

It's great, your singing an Elvis song in the fin-ah-lay, too.

For me, MacPhisto is sort of sad, bad, not so funny but might be. It's
like taking the rock jerk that the Fly is and—if you're going to play
him—take him to his logical conclusion, which is when he's fat and playing
Las Vegas. It's a bookend to the funky and fucked-up swagger of the Fly.

It's rather poignant. Also, whoever he is now—Jesus or whoever—Elvis once
was the devil.

The "devil's music"—that was the thing, wasn't it? The beat. The
sadness of that last song, though, that child's voice, that falsetto as the song
ends, is the most poignant moment of the show, because, in among all those
fucked-up qualities, there's just that little childlike voice. That voice to me
is the cover of *Boy.* If you study those films of Elvis—and I have—there
were some very powerful moments as he was in decline. Maybe more
powerful than when he was the svelte pop hero.

What's your feeling about the future of U2?

THE EDGE: I think with *Zooropa* we were reminded in a very nice way
of how special the chemistry is between the musicians in the band. That was
an unanticipated surprise, to rediscover how unique this collection of individuals is. I'm feeling very positive about our collaboration—there's a lot
more there.

When things get really hairy, you start to think, "Well, maybe I should
just excuse myself and wander off into something a little less hectic." Then
I start to think, "Well, what would I like to do?" Well, I'd like to play guitar
still. And I'm really not into working alone, so I'd like to get a group of
people to work with. "And what sort of people would I like to work with?"

Well, there are these other three guys that I've been getting on with really well for a while . . . [*laughs*]. You end up redesigning the band—again.

What would you like to see happen now as far as U2 and the situation in Bosnia is concerned?

BILL CARTER: The ultimate connection would be for whoever in the group wants to to come to Sarajevo. But it's critically important that it not be a circus and that nobody know about it. The connection is not for the media, the connection is for the people in Sarajevo. The point is not to announce, "We're going to Sarajevo"—that's pure bullshit. That's useless. They should go in a way that's very personal, to solidify the connection. It would be very powerful.

What would it mean for the people there?

It means a great deal. They have no faith in politics anymore at all. But it's a very cultured city. The Olympics were there ten years ago. It's like Vienna—it's a beautiful city. U2 are huge cultural heroes, so the connection is important spiritually. They know that U2 speak to a lot of people, especially young people. And if they care, then that means people will remember Sarajevo for at least that little while. Because they're afraid that people are forgetting that they're there.

CLAYTON: Although it's a confusing time, I think it is genuinely exciting. I think the world is filled with possibilities at the moment.

Any final thoughts as we land?

BONO: How is my hair?

DISCOGRAPHY

ALBUMS

BOY
Release date: October 1980
Produced by: Steve Lillywhite
Singles: A Day Without Me, I Will Follow
Additional tracks: Twilight, An Cat Dubh, Into the Heart, Out of Control, Stories for Boys, The Ocean, Another Time, Another Place, The Electric Co., Shadows and Tall Trees

OCTOBER
Release date: October 1981
Produced by: Steve Lillywhite
Singles: Fire, Gloria
Additional tracks: I Fall Down, I Threw a Brick Through a Window, Rejoice, Tomorrow, October, With a Shout (Jerusalem), Stranger in a Strange Land, Scarlet, Is That All?

WAR
Release date: March 1983
Produced by: Steve Lillywhite
Singles: New Year's Day, Two Hearts Beat as One
Additional tracks: Sunday Bloody Sunday, Seconds, Like a Song . . . , Drowning Man, The Refugee, Red Light, Surrender, 40

UNDER A BLOOD RED SKY
Release date: November 1983
Produced by: Jimmy Iovine
Tracks: Gloria, 11 O'Clock Tick Tock, I Will Follow, Party Girl, Sunday Bloody Sunday, The Electric Co., New Year's Day, 40

THE UNFORGETTABLE FIRE
Release date: October 1984
Produced by: Brian Eno and Daniel Lanois
Singles: Pride (In the Name of Love), The Unforgettable Fire
Additional tracks: A Sort of Homecoming, Wire, Promenade, 4th of July, Bad, Indian Summer Sky, Elvis Presley and America, MLK

WIDE AWAKE IN AMERICA

Release date: May 1985
Produced by: U2, Brian Eno, Daniel Lanois and Tony Visconti .
Tracks: Bad, A Sort of Homecoming, The Three Sunrises, Love Comes Tumbling

THE JOSHUA TREE

Release date: March 1987
Produced by: Brian Eno and Daniel Lanois
Singles: With or Without You, I Still Haven't Found What I'm Looking For, Where the Streets Have No Name
Additional tracks: Bullet the Blue Sky, Running to Stand Still, Red Hill Mining Town, In God's Country, Trip Through Your Wires, One Tree Hill, Exit, Mothers of the Disappeared

RATTLE AND HUM

Release date: October 1988
Produced by: Jimmy Iovine
Singles: Desire, Angel of Harlem, When Love Comes to Town, All I Want Is You
Additional tracks: Helter Skelter, Van Diemen's Land, Hawkmoon 269, All Along the Watchtower, I Still Haven't Found What I'm Looking For, Freedom for My People, Silver and Gold, Pride, Love Rescue Me, Heartland, God Part II, The Star Spangled Banner, Bullet the Blue Sky

ACHTUNG BABY

Release date: November 1991
Produced by: Daniel Lanois with Brian Eno
Singles: The Fly, Mysterious Way, One, Even Better than the Real Thing, Wild Horses
Additional tracks: Zoo Station, Until the End of the World, So Cruel, Tryin' to Throw Your Arms Around the World, Ultra Violet (Light My Way), Acrobat, Love Is Blindness

ZOOROPA

Release date: July 1993
Produced by: Flood, Brian Eno and the Edge
Singles: Numb, Lemon
Tracks: Zooropa, Babyface, Stay (Faraway, So Close!), Daddy's Gonna Pay for Your Crashed Car, Some Days Are Better than Others, The First Time, Dirty Day, The Wanderer

VIDEOGRAPHY

SINGLE-SONG VIDEOS

"Gloria"
Date: October 1981
Director: Meiert Avis
Location: Dublin

"A Celebration"
Date: April 1982
Director: Meiert Avis
Location: Kilmainham Jail, Dublin

"New Year's Day"
Date: December 1982
Director: Meiert Avis
Location: Sweden

"Two Hearts Beat as One"
Date: March 1983
Director: Meiert Avis
Location: Montmartre, Paris

"Sunday Bloody Sunday"
Date: June 1983
Director: Gavin Taylor
Location: Red Rocks, Denver, Colorado

"Pride" (#1)
Date: August 1984
Director: Donald Cammell
Location: St. Francis Xavier Hall, Dublin

"Pride" (#2)
Date: July 1984
Director: Barry Devlin
Location: Slane Castle, Dublin

"Pride" (#3)
Date: August 1984
Director: Anton Corbijn
Location: London

"A Sort of Homecoming"
Date: October/November 1984
Director: Barry Devlin
Location: Paris, Brussels, Rotterdam, London, Glasgow

"Bad"
Date: October/November 1984
Director: Barry Devlin
Location: Paris, Brussels, Rotterdam, London, Glasgow

"The Unforgettable Fire"
Date: January 1985
Director: Meiert Avis
Location: Sweden

"With or Without You"
Date: February 1987
Director: Meiert Avis
Location: Dublin

"Red Hill Mining Town"
Date: February 1987
Director: Neil Jordan
Location: London

"Where the Streets Have No Name"
Date: March 1987
Director: Meiert Avis
Location: Los Angeles

"In God's Country"
Date: April 1987
Director: Barry Devlin
Location: Arizona

"I Still Haven't Found What I'm Looking For"
Date: April 1987
Director: Barry Devlin
Location: Las Vegas

"Desire"
Date: September 1988
Director: Richard Lowenstein
Location: Los Angeles

"Angel of Harlem"
Date: November 1988
Director: Richard Lowenstein
Location: New York City

"When Love Comes to Town"
Date: March 1989
Director: Phil Joanou
Location: Various

"All I Want Is You"
Date: April 1989
Director: Meiert Avis
Location: Rome

"Night and Day"
Date: November 1990
Director: Wim Wenders
Location: Berlin

"The Fly"
Date: September 1991
Director: Ritchie Smith and Jon Klein
Location: Dublin

"Mysterious Ways"
Date: October 1991
Director: Stephane Sednaoui
Location: Morocco

"One" (#1)
Date: February 1992
Director: Anton Corbijn
Location: Berlin

"One" (#2)
Date: February 1992
Director: Mark Pellington
Location: New York City

"One" (#3)
Date: March 1992
Director: Phil Joanou
Location: New York City

"Even Better Than the Real Thing"
Date: February 1992
Director: Kevin Godley
Location: London

"Wild Horses"
Date: September 1992
Director: Phil Joanou
Location: Chicago

"Numb"
Date: July 1993
Director: Kevin Godley
Location: Berlin

"Lemon"
Date: September 1993
Director: Mark Neale
Location: London

"Stay"
Date: October 1993
Director: Wim Wenders
Location: Berlin

ABOUT THE CONTRIBUTORS

David Breskin is a ROLLING STONE contributing editor. He has produced records for Vernon Reid, Bill Frisell, Ronald Shannon Jackson, and John Zorn, and he is the author of a novel, *The Real Life Diary of a Boomtown Girl,* and *Inner Views,* a compilation of his ROLLING STONE interviews with film directors.

Debra Rae Cohen's reviews have appeared in ROLLING STONE, the *Village Voice,* the *New York Times,* and numerous other publications. A former editor of the *Voice,* she teaches English at the University of Mississippi.

Christopher Connelly, a former editor at ROLLING STONE, is an executive editor of *Premiere* magazine and the host of MTV's "The Big Picture."

J.D. Considine has been writing about music since 1977. In addition to his duties as pop music critic at the *Baltimore Sun* and *Evening Sun,* he is a contributing editor at *Musician* and writes regularly for ROLLING STONE; his work has also appeared in a variety of other publications, including *Playboy,* the *Village Voice,* the *Washington Post,* and *Request.* He also contributed to *The* ROLLING STONE *Illustrated History of Rock & Roll,* third edition, and *The* ROLLING STONE *Album Guide.*

Toby Creswell is the former editor of ROLLING STONE Australia.

Anthony DeCurtis is a writer and editor at ROLLING STONE, where he oversees the record review section. He is the editor of *Present Tense: Rock & Roll and Culture* and co-editor of *The* ROLLING STONE *Illustrated History of Rock & Roll* and *The* ROLLING STONE *Album Guide.* He won a Grammy for his liner notes for the Eric Clapton retrospective *Crossroads* and has twice won ASCAP Deems Taylor Awards for excellence in writing about music. He holds a Ph.D. in American literature from Indiana University and lectures frequently on cultural matters.

Non-musician, producer, video artist, perfume maker, cultural theorist, lecturer, **Brian Eno** has made a career out of giving dilettante-ism a good name. Over the last twenty-five years, his stubborn refusal to be categorized has led to his becoming one of the most influential figures of his generation. Musically, through his groundbreaking solo work and his collaboration on albums by, among others, Bowie, Talking Heads, and, of course, U2, Eno is now widely sought after for his ideas and innovative approach. He has continuously refused to accept limitations, particularly those of the technology he has used. Be it tape recorders, sequencers, or photocopiers, Eno has always challenged the designer's intentions, using them in ways that were never envisioned. This flagrant disregard for instruction manuals has now been officially recognized, with an Honorary Doctorate of Technology from the University of Plymouth.

David Fricke is the Music Editor of ROLLING STONE. He joined the magazine in 1985 as a senior writer. He is also the American correspondent for the English weekly *Melody Maker* and has written about music for *Musician, People,* and the *New York Times.* He is the author of *Animal Instinct,* a biography of Def Leppard, and wrote the liner notes for the box set *The Byrds,* released in 1990.

Elysa Gardner is a regular contributor to ROLLING STONE, and has also written for *Musician, Spin, Request,* and *Harper's Bazaar,* among other publications. In addition to her freelance work, she currently covers pop music each week for the "Night Life" column in *The New Yorker.*

Michael Goldberg is a contributing editor at ROLLING STONE. He has also written about rock & roll, the music business, and new technology for *Esquire, Wired, Mirabella, Musician,* and other publications.

Jimmy Guterman is the author of five books, among them *12 Days on the Road* and *Rockin' My Life Away,* and was the editor of *CD Review.* He produces and compiles reissue records, writes books, and lives in Massachusetts.

James Henke was on the editorial staff of ROLLING STONE from 1977 to 1992. During that time, he held a variety of positions, including managing editor, music editor, and Los Angeles bureau chief. His 1980 article on U2 was the first profile of the band to appear in a major U.S. publication. Co-editor of *The ROLLING STONE Illustrated History of Rock & Roll,* third edition, and *The ROLLING STONE Album Guide,* he is now chief curator of the Rock & Roll Hall of Fame and Museum.

Steve Hochman writes about pop music for the *Los Angeles Times* and is a regular contributor to ROLLING STONE. His work has also appeared in *Pulse, Request, Musician, Guitar Player,* and *Us*.

Alan Light is the music editor at *Vibe* magazine and a former senior writer at ROLLING STONE. His writing appears in *The ROLLING STONE Illustrated History of Rock & Roll* and in *Present Tense: Rock & Roll Culture*. He has also contributed to *Vogue,* the *South Atlantic Quarterly,* the *World Book Encyclopedia,* and various other publications.

Kurt Loder was an editor at ROLLING STONE from 1979 to 1988 and is still a contributing editor. He is the author of *I, Tina,* a best-selling biography of Tina Turner. He is currently an anchor of *MTV News*.

Jon Pareles was an associate editor at ROLLING STONE in 1979. He has worked at the *Village Voice* and *Crawdaddy*. Currently, he is the chief pop music critic at the *New York Times*.

Steve Pond is a ROLLING STONE contributing editor. His work also appears in the *New York Times, Premiere, Playboy, GQ,* and the *Washington Post*.

Parke Puterbaugh is a contributing editor to ROLLING STONE and *Stereo Review*. His writings on music, travel, and the environment have appeared in many other newspapers and magazines as well. He is co-author of a series of travel books published by McGraw-Hill. He lives in Greensboro, North Carolina.

Jeffrey Ressner covers the entertainment business for *Time* magazine, and has also written for ROLLING STONE, *Spy,* and the *New York Times*. He first met the members of U2 in 1983.